TRAPPINGS OF
POWER

TRAPPINGS OF
POWER

*Ballistic Missiles in
the Third World*

JANNE E. NOLAN

THE BROOKINGS INSTITUTION
Washington, D.C.

Library of Congress Cataloging-in-Publication Data

Nolan, Janne E.
   Trappings of power : ballistic missiles in the Third
World / Janne E. Nolan.
     p.   cm.
   Includes bibliographical references and index.
   ISBN 0-8157-6096-5 (alk. paper)
   ISBN 0-8157-6095-7 (pbk.)
   1. Ballistic missiles—Developing countries.
2. Developing countries—Defenses. 3. Munitions—
Developing countries. 4. Arms control. I. Title.
UG1312.B34N65 1991
358.1'75'091724—dc20   90-28751
                                       CIP

9 8 7 6 5 4 3 2 1

₿ THE BROOKINGS INSTITUTION

The Brookings Institution is an independent organization devoted to nonpartisan research, education, and publication in economics, government, foreign policy, and the social sciences generally. Its principal purposes are to aid in the development of sound public policies and to promote public understanding of issues of national importance.

The Institution was founded on December 8, 1927, to merge the activities of the Institute for Government Research, founded in 1916, the Institute of Economics, founded in 1922, and the Robert Brookings Graduate School of Economics and Government, founded in 1924.

The Board of Trustees is responsible for the general administration of the Institution, while the immediate direction of the policies, program, and staff is vested in the President, assisted by an advisory committee of the officers and staff. The by-laws of the Institution state: "It is the function of the Trustees to make possible the conduct of scientific research, and publication, under the most favorable conditions, and to safeguard the independence of the research staff in the pursuit of their studies and in the publication of the results of such studies. It is not a part of their function to determine, control, or influence the conduct of particular investigations or the conclusions reached."

The President bears final responsibility for the decision to publish a manuscript as a Brookings book. In reaching his judgment on the competence, accuracy, and objectivity of each study, the President is advised by the director of the appropriate research program and weighs the views of a panel of expert outside readers who report to him in confidence on the quality of the work. Publication of a work signifies that it is deemed a competent treatment worthy of public consideration but does not imply endorsement of conclusions or recommendations.

The Institution maintains its position of neutrality on issues of public policy in order to safeguard the intellectual freedom of the staff. Hence interpretations or conclusions in Brookings publications should be understood to be solely those of the authors and should not be attributed to the Institution, to its trustees, officers, or other staff members, or to the organizations that support its research.

Foreword

SINCE the beginning of the crisis precipitated by Iraq's invasion of Kuwait in August 1990, the threat posed by Iraq's arsenal of ballistic missiles has been the focus of international attention. In the opening days of the U.S.-led military counteroffensive beginning on January 16, 1991, Iraq launched ballistic missiles against population centers in Israel and military bases in Saudi Arabia. The attacks intensified the terror of the war and prompted renewed efforts by the multinational force to destroy Saddam Hussein's military machine.

The countries aligned against Iraq were prepared for attacks by chemically armed missiles, but Iraq's missile force proved to be of little military consequence. The missiles that survived the opening hours of Operation Desert Storm were conventionally armed, inaccurate, and unreliable. Most of those that were actually launched either were intercepted by American antimissile defenses or failed to hit vital targets.

But the political impact of the missiles was inestimable. The strikes symbolized Iraq's determination to prosecute the war no matter what the cost. By threatening to involve Israel, they created severe tensions and posed the risk that the multinational military coalition would be dissolved, and they underscored the potential vulnerability of all the states in the region to Iraqi aggression.

In this book, Janne E. Nolan argues that the use of missiles is a harbinger of the altered international security environment confronting the United States and its allies in the late twentieth century. Long believed to be a distant prospect, the adaptation of technological resources to missile development is already occurring in over a dozen developing countries, many of them long-standing regional antagonists. These capabilities present complicated challenges to American interests and foreign policy, challenges that have only begun to be explored as a result of the Iraqi crisis.

The author examines the evolution of the international technology market, surveys third world missile programs, and analyzes the military significance of ballistic missiles in potential third world combat. She also discusses the way in which domestic and international policy decisions are made to promote or restrain the export of military technology, and assesses the strengths and weaknesses of current policy. Finally, she emphasizes the need for institutional reforms to balance the requirements of protecting the technological edge on which the United States relies for its own security against the growing pressures of international militarization.

The author wishes to thank John D. Steinbruner, director of the Foreign Policy Studies program, for his counsel on this project. Other colleagues who shared their support and expertise include Barry Blechman, Charlotte Brady, W. Seth Carus, James Fluhr, Lise Hartman, Geoffrey Kemp, Brett Lambert, Thomas Mankhen, Joseph Smaldone, Leonard Spector, Richard Speier, and Albert Wheelon. Andrew Portocarrero, Shelley Stahl, and Marian Sullivan provided research assistance. James Schneider edited the manuscript and Vernon Kelley and Michael B. Levin verified its factual content. Louise Skillings incorporated revisions, Susan Woollen prepared the manuscript for typesetting, and Margaret Lynch prepared the index.

This project was made possible by funds from the John D. and Catherine T. MacArthur Foundation and the Carnegie Corporation of New York. Brookings gratefully acknowledges their support.

The views expressed in this book are those of the author and should not be ascribed to the persons acknowledged, to the MacArthur Foundation, or to the trustees, officers, or other staff members of the Brookings Institution.

BRUCE K. MAC LAURY
President

January 1991
Washington, D.C.

Contents

Tables

Figures

CHAPTER ONE

The Challenges of Technology Diffusion

ON MAY 22, 1989, at a launch site on the Bay of Bengal, India successfully tested its first medium-range ballistic missile. Designated the Agni, the two-stage rocket was said to have a potential range of 1,500 miles, making it capable of reaching targets throughout Pakistan and in some parts of China.[1] In startled tones, Western commentators announced that India, one of the poorest nations of the world, had joined a technological elite: a demonstrated ability to produce and launch a ballistic missile had previously been the domain of only the United States, the Soviet Union, France, Britain, Israel, and China.[2]

The Agni test prompted instantaneous criticism from the Bush administration and Congress. Beginning in late 1988, American officials had tried to persuade New Delhi to cancel the Agni test, decrying the program as "a highly destabilizing development in the region."[3] Twenty-two senators were more strident in their criticism, denouncing India's actions in a letter to President Bush as being "in direct contradiction of U.S. and Soviet efforts to lessen global tensions by reducing ballistic missiles."[4] But from the standpoint of the Indian government and the hundreds of technicians and engineers who had worked for decades to modernize India's military-industrial capacity, the success of the Agni test was "a milestone in the progress of Indian science and technology in general and defense research and development in particular."[5] After a patently cosmetic portrayal of the test as a scientific venture aimed at enhancing expertise in satellite technology, these officials made it clear that they considered U.S. efforts to interfere with India's obvious military aspirations impertinent and patronizing.[6]

Ironically, the Agni program owed its genesis to India's adaptation of

1

the civilian space technology and technical assistance that the Soviet Union, the United States, France, and Germany had provided since 1962. And the test took place just one week before meetings scheduled between American and Indian officials to discuss ways the United States could expedite sales of advanced American technology to assist India's space program.[7] Indeed, one of the issues to be discussed was a pending request from New Delhi for an export license for technology pertinent to missile testing—the Combined Acceleration Vibration Climatic Test System (CAVCTS)—whose sale had been approved by the U.S. Commerce Department before the approval encountered opposition from the Department of Defense and the Central Intelligence Agency.[8] Despite its rhetorical outrage, then, the Bush administration rebuffed suggestions that the meetings should be cancelled or that the deepening American involvement in India's space modernization efforts be reconsidered.[9]

The stated policy of the United States is to prevent countries from importing technology needed to design and manufacture ballistic missiles, especially countries with incipient nuclear programs. On the surface, this principle is unassailable, supported as it is both domestically and by U.S. allies. But, as many previous efforts to impose security-related export controls have demonstrated, actual enforcement of measures to restrain the diffusion of technology is a far more complicated and politically challenging matter.[10]

Coincident with the uproar over the Agni, a U.S.-Japanese agreement to cooperate in developing an advanced fighter aircraft—the so-called Fighter Support–Experimental, or FS-X—was provoking protracted political controversy within Congress and among agencies in the executive branch. Originally heralded as a model of technological cooperation between close security partners, the FS-X contract now prompted vitriolic attacks from domestic critics of Japanese trading practices, who seized upon it as a symbol of the decline of American technological superiority. Given Japan's huge trade surplus with the United States, its relatively modest defense expenditures, and its continued success in dominating the international market in advanced technologies vital to U.S. commercial and security interests, opponents now believed an agreement to provide sensitive U.S. military technology would constitute a virtual surrender to an economic competitor.[11] Less in deference to the importance of the U.S.-Japanese security relationship than as a reluctant concession that even a bad deal was better than ceding the contract to European firms, the Senate approved a modified version of the FS-X agreement by a narrow margin in mid-1989.[12]

Seemingly unrelated, the events surrounding the Agni test and the FS-X agreement actually shared important characteristics. Both highlighted the deteriorating ability of the United States to dictate or even to influence significantly the industrial and security policies of emerging regional powers. Faced with a growing number of competing foreign sources of advanced scientific and technical capabilities and with a weakening domestic economy, America is finding it can no longer rely on its technological preeminence to dominate the terms of its overseas relationships. The maturation of the international economy, a development Washington has aggressively fostered since World War II, has pushed the United States into a position of genuine interdependence as it enters the last decade of the twentieth century.

Technology Diffusion and U.S. Interests

The challenges posed by the Agni and the FS-X are microcosms of the more general kinds of challenges confronting U.S. policy as it adapts to the new international environment. Although Japan's technology is far more sophisticated than India's and the two countries represent quite disparate problems for U.S. policymakers, the experiences with both illustrate the need for America to redefine its role in a world in which technological and military accommodation with other sovereign nations is becoming less a matter of choice than of necessity and self-preservation. America's diminishing technological superiority in an environment of intensified economic and military competition suggests that its security and foreign policy will be linked with industrial and economic policy to an extent historically unprecedented.[13]

Believing that the United States somehow has been stripped unfairly of its technological dominance, growing numbers of politicians and analysts have been pressing for protectionist trade measures to try to regain the lost power. Trade barriers and punitive sanctions have figured prominently in debates about policy toward both Japan and India, albeit for different ends. The central, if unspoken, premise is that the United States can still command international change by threatening retrenchment and blocking access to advanced technology.

The crucial questions addressed in this study are whether such a premise can serve as an effective basis for policy as the United States faces the global diffusion of military production capabilities; and if not, what alternative or additional instruments might be appropriate. The analysis in this book focuses in particular on the production of ballistic missiles in countries commonly classified as part of the third world.[14] Although America's technological rivalry with other advanced industrial nations has dominated most of the concern about waning U.S. power, the proliferation of high-technology goods and expertise in the third world is potentially as vital a factor in contributing to the change in America's global stature.

The underlying concern is how the United States will balance the imperatives for cooperation with allied and other nations against the enduring requirement to protect the technological edge on which its security has traditionally relied. This is, of course, a conundrum that has been part of U.S. policy throughout the postwar period. It is the leitmotif of the chronic controversies over how best to implement strategic trade controls against military adversaries without unduly penalizing economic interests. A preoccupation with preventing the diffusion of technology to the Soviet Union and Eastern Europe, however, has long overshadowed the problems posed by its diffusion to newly industrialized and industrializing countries. The export of U.S. military goods to the third world in the past forty years has been guided by the assumption that industrialized states would retain sufficient technological superiority to stay ahead of and to counter threats posed by the growing military capabilities of developing nations. Even as the size and quality of third world military forces increased, the assumption of technological stratification supported an implicit concept of stability.[15] Indeed, providing conventional armaments has traditionally been a principal means of dissuading states from pursuing nuclear ambitions and, as such, has itself been an instrument to ensure a continued military demarcation between states with nuclear weapons and those without them.

Structural changes in the international technology market, however, are testing the pertinence of these traditional policies. In the 1950s and early 1960s, U.S. military exports consisted of obsolescent weapons and materiel transferred to close allies. In the late 1960s and early 1970s, America provided more sophisticated weapon systems to nations outside NATO and began cooperative weapon production ventures with them. By the end of the 1970s the United States and other Western industrial countries had begun to sell the third world the same types of weapons that they fielded with their own forces and to compete for contracts in which offering to share production processes was an essential quid pro quo for capturing third world markets.[16]

The ability of advanced countries to control the proliferation of technology so as to influence policies of third world countries has been eroded by their own domestic economic imperatives. The high cost of innovations critical to security has sometimes required them to engage in technology-sharing arrangements with other countries simply to produce weapons more cheaply. In addition, their dependence on foreign revenues has driven them to export military technologies to the third world. Finally, the progressive constriction of individual shares of the international arms market, spurred by the growing number of arms suppliers, has intensified pressures for industrialized countries to export more advanced equipment and more sophisticated technology-sharing arrangements to retain a foothold in needed markets.[17]

On their part, third world countries, perhaps more than thirty of them, have become determined to develop independent defense industries. Despite apparent diseconomies and dubious security advantages, they consider the ability to manufacture weapons a sine qua non of national sovereignty and a means of capturing technological resources to achieve overall modernization and international status. Notwithstanding their continued dependence on the advanced countries for the most sophisticated technologies, many developing nations have themselves become arms suppliers and are helping still other countries elude any strictures on military ambitions that the great powers may seek to impose.[18] And with the the progressive integration of Eastern Europe into the international economy, the number of industrialized countries seeking revenues from arms exports can be expected to rise even higher.

As the medium of exchange between industrial and industrializing countries has increasingly become technology rather than finished weapon systems, the importance of traditional instruments to control proliferation has progressively diminished. The ready availability of commercial technologies that have potential military applications, along with maturing third world defense industries capable of exploiting these applications, has made distinguishing between civilian and military exports more difficult. This is especially true for exports of space technology, which traditionally have not been subject to the same kind of political scrutiny as arms exports, despite their importance to indigenous missile programs in some developing nations.

Emerging defense technologies may make differentiating among military and civilian exports more difficult still. Technologies that are at the cutting edge of Western military modernization, including advanced information processing, composite materials, directed energy systems, and biotechnologies, are to varying degrees equally vital to civilian modernization. Advances in biotechnology for superlethal pathogens usable in biological warfare, for instance, can also be used to develop more cost-effective and efficient agricultural techniques and medicines. Although access to biotechnologies could destabilize regional military balances, the technologies could also improve stability in countries where poverty and disease are important determinants of social unrest.[19]

Even more pointedly for ballistic missile development, the advanced satellite reconnaissance capabilities that are so useful for weather prediction and crop surveys are also likely to be in high demand for military operations. In addition to improving targeting and accuracy, satellite intelligence can assure countries in range of an adversary's missile forces that they are not under attack or can give them warning of such an attack. Third world countries may increasingly perceive access to such intelligence and other modalities for command and control as necessary to mitigate unstable military conditions brought about by the growth of missile arsenals among regional rivals.[20]

The endurance of the international nuclear nonproliferation regime also may be strained by the global redistribution of high technology. Aside from their efforts to divert resources from civilian nuclear energy programs to military applications, states such as Taiwan and South Korea, whose nuclear programs were slowed by international intervention, have received compensation in the form of advanced conventional technologies. Many can now produce a variety of delivery systems that may be useful for carrying nuclear or other nonconventional munitions. In particular, the development of missiles by countries with the potential for producing nuclear weapons could very well accelerate nuclear deployments.[21]

Trends toward a more open international trading system may mean that the market for military technology could become more resistant to intervention by the governments of advanced industrial nations. Aside from complications posed by pressures of international competition, the effectiveness of trade barriers will be compromised by the declining share of technology that is under government control. Fiber optics, advanced composite materials, and other key components and processes vital to modern military capability are increasingly based on technological innovations driven by and directed toward the commercial market.[22] As Ashton Carter has argued, "the overall trend is for defense to make up an ever smaller part of the global technological enterprise, and . . . the Department of Defense will have far less leverage over the nature of this enterprise."[23] Governments' influence over industry could further diminish as companies meld their commercial and defense sectors and join together as multinational enterprises.

The effects of technology dissemination for U.S. and international security will depend on the technology and country in question. To continue to exert influence in the third world, retain a competitive share of the global technology market, and protect its own security interests, the United States will have to devise policies that can capture the benefits of trade while retaining some control over technologies with military applications. This may require a new framework for international trade policy that can better balance the goals sought from military and dual-use exports with the necessity to control technologies whose international diffusion is deemed inimical to U.S. security interests. The transformation of East-West relations since 1985 has already prompted major alterations in the practices and institutions guiding trade with Eastern Europe. The implications of these changes for technology diffusion in the developing world, however, have yet to be reflected in new policy.

The premise that the West will inevitably retain power based on enduring technological stratification may thus be tested more severely in coming years. If current trends continue, the pace of diffusion may eventually vitiate the reliance of industrial countries on technological superiority to influence international events. The rapid transformation of technology from state-of-the-art to obsolescence may make the quest for advantage ever more elusive. And the possibility of any edge in quality may disappear if equipment widely available internationally begins to approximate the capabilities of recent innovations, or can at least interfere with the performance of such innovations. In other words, there may be a point of exhaustion in which an increment in technological superiority yields diminishing military returns.

The idea that the West can continue to subsidize its own military preparedness by helping smaller states prepare for war may hasten the point at which technological superiority ceases to be a decisive determinant of national influence. As developing countries' military forces improve, any remaining international hierarchy may disappear. Thus, in the same way that the transfer of Western technology was thought to help the Soviet Union achieve military parity with the West, a more even distribution of military power will also result from the spread of technology from North to South. The consequences for international stability and U.S. interests will depend on the technology and its destination, but it is important to recognize that military powers that may not share common values with the West are emerging throughout the world.

The Case of Ballistic Missiles

The development of ballistic missiles by third world countries has been mistakenly portrayed by many observers as a distinctly new dimension of international politics.[24] But missile programs have been evident in some countries for many years, albeit on a limited scale. Attention is higher now because of Iraq's arsenal of ballistic missiles, which it used against Israel and Saudi Arabia during Operation Desert Storm in January 1991, Iran's and Iraq's use of ballistic missiles against population centers in the 1988 "War of the Cities," the emergence of the People's Republic of China as a missile supplier, evidence of missile production programs in South Africa, Iraq, and Libya, and Israel's flight test of a missile potentially capable of reaching targets in the Soviet Union.[25] Sixteen third world nations currently possess ballistic missiles, twelve of them developing or producing the systems domestically.[26] Even as the great powers embark on ambitious arms and force reductions, the quest for modern armaments in the developing world continues unabated.

The spread of missile technology to unstable regions of the world poses serious dilemmas for policymakers. The technical characteristics of ballistic missiles, including the speed with which they can reach targets, their invulnerability to defenses, their adaptability for delivering warheads of mass destruction, and their particular utility for preemptive military operations, make them inherently destabilizing in regions where combat is likely to occur.[27] Not coincidentally, most of the significant new missile producers are in the Middle East, the Persian Gulf, and South and Northeast Asia, all regions of chronic tension. (Argentina and Brazil are special cases because they are developing missiles largely for export.)

In addition to increasing regional tensions, proliferation may increase the lethality and frequency of conflicts. Because of the close proximity of many potential combatants, even short-range systems could reach significant targets. Armed with chemical warheads or other nonconventional munitions, they could terrorize populations and, even with their limited accuracy, could have some effect against military targets such as airfields. Moreover, a latent or tested ballistic missile capability can spur adversaries to develop similar systems or acquire the means to destroy the rival's arsenal before it is used.

With the spread of longer-range ballistic missiles, local or regional military conflicts could have wider international consequences. Armed with nuclear, chemical, or even advanced conventional munitions, these systems could expand the scope of conflict well beyond the spheres of the combatant states. India, Israel, and Saudi Arabia, for example, already possess missiles that can reach targets in the Soviet Union.

Such systems in the possession of bellicose countries could also affect advanced countries' conduct of military operations, a possibility presaged by such incidents as Argentina's use of French-made air-to-surface missiles to attack British naval forces in the Falklands and Iran's missile attacks against U.S.-flagged Kuwaiti tankers in the Persian Gulf. As is clear from the ongoing crisis in Iraq, the growing sophistication of missile arsenals in countries that may be willing to risk attacking U.S. forces can complicate decisions about whether and when to intervene in regional conflicts. The arsenals have already prompted concern about the safety of Western military installations and forces overseas.[28] At a minimum, the United States and its allies might have to incur heavy costs to protect military assets—including hardening command centers, sheltering aircraft, building additional runways and launch pads, and adding to intelligence-gathering capabilities. In addition, the increasing range and capabilities of new missiles may pose the risk of attacks on U.S. territory by terrorists or lawless states, an argument used to promote the domestic deployment of U.S. defenses.

Perceptions of the dangers of ballistic missiles are also linked to concerns about their possible contribution to the proliferation of chemical and nuclear weapons. Iraq's breaking of the decades-long taboo on the use of chemical weapons in 1984, along with evidence of acquisition of chemical weapons by more than a dozen other countries in the third world, has fueled alarm that combining these weapons with missile delivery has gained particular status as a valued instrument in military operations.[29] And many of the states that are developing ballistic missiles are also pursuing nuclear programs. Thus the effort to prevent countries from acquiring nuclear weapons—previously focused on impeding their ability to test nuclear devices—has now become an effort to stem the spread of delivery vehicles as well.

Even where the acquisition of missiles is not associated with the near-term development of nuclear or chemical weapons, the high cost of missiles relative to their utility as conventional weapons has suggested that they inevitably contribute to such ambitions. As one commentator noted, for instance, Saudi Arabia's pledge never to arm its Chinese-made CSS-2 ballistic missiles with nonconventional munitions is unconvincing: "Saudi Arabia is believed to have paid more than $50 million each for its CSS-2s. Using them merely to dump a little high explosive somewhere near their targets is like buying a Ferrari to collect groceries."[30]

Many of the dire prognostications about the risks of missile proliferation have fortunately yet to be borne out. The ability to build ballistic missiles need not signify an intent to pursue aggressive military policies. Current limitations on the accuracy and range of most systems produced in the third world, as well as the financial burden involved in developing sophisticated missiles, precludes a rapid transformation of combat environments very soon. Moreover, it is difficult to generalize about the military significance of missile forces. Regional realities vary starkly in the third world and are marked by shifting alliances, disputed borders, and intractable patterns of enmity, often based on ethnic or religious antagonisms of centuries' duration. The consequences of missile proliferation will depend on the particular conditions of these local and regional hostilities, the countries' overall military capabilities, and their political alignments, and they must be assessed with these differences in mind.

For now, missile programs may be far more significant politically than militarily. The limited foundations for common understandings among rival states about what constitutes stability or how to design force postures that avoid signaling provocative intent suggest that their transition into the missile age will be marked by uncertainty. Still, the question is no longer whether industrializing countries will develop and deploy advanced missiles but when. India, Israel, Argentina, and Brazil have demonstrated steady progress toward indigenous manufacture of such systems despite immense technical and political impediments; North Korea, Syria, Egypt, Iran, Iraq, and Libya will try to follow suit as soon as it is financially and technologically feasible.

The development programs provide a tangible example of the effort by developing countries to prosecute local and regional ambitions without having to observe the dictates of the great powers. With China, Israel, and even North Korea already serving as significant sources of technical assistance to other third world producers, this trend appears to have become a matter of intra–third world diplomacy, potentially circumscribing the ability of the industrial powers to impose meaningful trade controls or exert decisive political influence. Aside from causing economic losses, the decline of great powers' influence over their clients' force structures may impinge on efforts to reach political accommodations, including attempts to resolve regional tensions, stem the proliferation of nuclear and chemical weapons, and avoid direct involvement in conflicts beyond their control.

The proliferation of ballistic missiles can be seen as a harbinger of alterations in international power alignments, whether or not it poses the dire security threats that some recent rhetoric has portrayed. The diffusion of missile technology can serve as a prism through which to examine the implications of the global redistribution of military and technological power and, arguably, the decreasing utility of protectionist instruments to influence military developments.

Some industrializing countries apparently do not share the developed world's concerns about the importance of or means for limiting the proliferation of missiles. They consider efforts to discourage their military ambitions, especially by denying them access to high technology, discriminatory. Western denunciations of the legitimacy of ballistic missiles (and chemical and nuclear weapons) can provoke jaundiced accusations of hypocrisy from countries whose fledgling military arsenals are so obviously dwarfed by those of the five major nuclear powers. As two Indian analysts commented in late 1989, "It is fashionable among industrialized nations to deplore acquisition of high-technology weapons by developing nations, but this moralistic stand is akin to drug pushers shedding tears about the weaknesses of drug addicts."[31]

Not all developing countries have a vested interest in acquiring missile systems or in encouraging their proliferation. And even incipient missile powers have a strong stake in stemming destabilizing military developments in their regions. As evidenced in efforts by industrial countries to promote nuclear nonproliferation, however, initiatives that appear to be wholly inspired by the concerns and objectives of the "first world" are resisted for political reasons: they suggest unwarranted and insensitive intrusion into the sovereign interests of developing nations.

Export controls on advanced technologies represent efforts by the great powers to assert prerogatives in a world in which the foundations for such prerogatives are eroding quickly. However desirable in the short term, controls on missile exports on the part of a few industrial countries probably cannot endure without support from more countries. Policies that developing countries consider discriminatory will eventually be circumvented by those determined to evade them. Indeed, the proliferation of ballistic missiles is probably already sufficiently advanced that it cannot be reversed or eliminated, even if some of its most troublesome aspects can probably be contained.

A more careful focus on the proliferation of ballistic missiles in the third world could certainly address some problems, however. More effective domestic and international institutions could be developed to confront the challenges of technology proliferation, coordinate the competing strands of industrial countries' policies toward the third world, and find new ways to combine controls with desirable forms of technology dissemination. Efforts should be made to encourage accommodations among combatant states and to contain the incidence and scope of regional conflicts. Countries must also clearly identify technologies whose significance to national security warrant efforts to protect them from being sold on the free market.

If industrialized and industrializing countries consider how to develop institutions and procedures to regulate proliferation, they may be able to anticipate the problems posed by technology diffusion in routine force planning, assessments of long-term threat, and overall trade and economic policy. A challenge more important than controlling missiles may be to develop means for anticipating technological changes that could have even more adverse effects on the technological and military stature of the United States and could heighten global tensions. Equally important, an international policy infrastructure with the flexibility to manage the consequences of such changes in constructive ways, must be developed. If it is too late to halt the spread of ballistic missiles, it may still be possible to temper the diffusion of new generations of weapons.

Significant reforms of U.S. domestic institutions may be necessary to achieve a coherent foundation for these kinds of innovations. As the controversies over the Agni and the FS-X have shown, the usefulness of existing arrangements, which pit jurisdictional interests against one another amidst the chaos of conflicting interpretations of U.S. policy objectives, is already in question.

The proliferation of ballistic missiles may not be the most urgent or significant development generating the diffusion of global economic and military power, but missiles symbolize the kinds of alterations in global security arrangements that industrial countries must confront. Concerns about the diffusion of military power have long been preoccupied with nuclear weapons and with ways to keep advanced technology out of the hands of Communist adversaries. In the coming years, however, the continuing development by smaller states of advanced weapons may have to be accorded a more important role in international politics.

CHAPTER TWO

The Context of Third World Defense Investment

LIBERAL THEORISTS have often portrayed the third world as an environment ripe for the pursuit of enlightened policies, from promoting disarmament to protecting the environment to achieving social equity. Implicit is the idea that developing countries somehow can be spared the Faustian bargains that industrial states made in their own struggles for modernity. The third world, the theorists argue, should be guided toward achieving the industrial world's unfulfilled aspirations for a more rational international system.[1]

In practice, of course, the third world has emulated industrial countries' modernization strategies, however inappropriate these theorists may consider them, with the complicity of the advanced nations. The transfer of manufacturing processes from industrial to developing countries, for instance, has not been based on careful considerations of the recipient countries' most pressing development needs. Patterns of trade have tended to follow market forces, with industrialized countries seeking out the advantages of the lower wage rates and less restrictive laws on environmental protection, labor safety, and product quality typically found in developing economies.[2] In the effort to capture the benefits of industrialization, third world countries thus have acquiesced to the social stratification, ecological destruction, and unbalanced patterns of economic growth that theorists vilify.

The disjuncture between lofty principles and calculated practices is particularly pronounced in developing countries' military policies. International forums and academic critics of military expenditures routinely denounce burgeoning third world arsenals, but even the most sweeping proposals for global disarmament, such as those adopted

14

unanimously by the United Nations in the 1977 Special Session on Disarmament, have had no measurable impact on the steady expansion of the number of participants in the arms market. Indeed, many former colonial states that were initially seized with the rhetoric of disarmament have since heralded their arrival into the industrial age with their own arms industries.[3]

The industrial countries' long history of investment in military arsenals notwithstanding, many analysts consider third world arms production programs an aberration. Efforts to achieve independence in defense production, they argue, lead to diseconomies that divert scarce resources from far more vital modernizations, particularly improvements in social welfare. Arms programs are thus risky ventures impelled by transitory impulses to achieve prestige rather than programs based on rational calculations of economic development needs or even military requirements. Industrialization for arms manufacture, the critics assert, is not legitimate until a certain unspecified level of overall development has been reached.[4]

Few people, of course, believe that military expenditures are the best way to sustain competitive industrial growth. The United States is beginning to appreciate the adverse effects on its technological competitiveness that have resulted from its prolonged reliance on military spending to fund technological innovation.[5] And so is the Soviet Union, where decades of disproportionate emphasis on military priorities has helped bring the economy to the verge of collapse. But third world countries' desire to achieve an independent capacity to develop weapons, especially such complicated and expensive systems as ballistic missiles, is not restrained by any traditional logic of economic or military efficiency. Some are investing significant resources in efforts to produce components that are manufactured far more efficiently in industrialized countries. The burden they assume in trying to develop missile guidance systems, for example, a burden already exacerbated by industrial countries' restrictions on exports of guidance technologies, is compounded by the reduced reliability of systems they manufacture indigenously. As such, some states have found themselves condemned to expending scarce resources not only to reinvent the wheel, but to do so less effectively and at a higher cost.[6]

The idea, however, that third world countries can be persuaded to succeed where the industrial countries have failed, that they will subject their military investments to strict calculations of efficiency and comparative advantage, is unrealistic. As it has been in most of the developed countries, investment in defense industries has been a primary focus of economic and industrial strategy in many developing countries. In Israel, Argentina, and South Korea, among others, defense industries have been accorded unique importance as symbols of modernization, and they exert a dominating influence in setting overall scientific and technical priorities.[7] Again as in the industrial world, considerations of national independence, security, economic and technological advancement, and diplomatic leverage drive investment. Although the relative importance of these considerations varies from country to country, the principal rationale for producing weapons is to demonstrate sovereignty.

Given an international system in which military prowess has been a leading determinant of national stature, the efforts of third world nations to acquire the most advanced weapons available in the international market should come as no surprise. In both developed and developing countries, ballistic missiles in particular have long been perceived as according enhanced military status because they seem the supreme offensive delivery system, especially for nuclear weapons. As General Thomas Powers, former commander-in-chief of the Strategic Air Command noted in 1960 in reference to the impending development of missiles by the Soviet Union, "Because of their tremendous speed . . . ballistic missiles offer a unique advantage to an aggressor who plans a surprise attack."[8]

Possessing ballistic missiles does not, of course, automatically characterize a state as having offensive military ambitions nor endow it with the ability to prosecute such ambitions. Generalizations about military incentives driving nations toward missile acquisitions are not very revealing because they ignore the wide variations among countries. Some may want missiles strictly to dissuade an adversary from attacking; others clearly do have offensive objectives in mind. And still others are developing missiles largely for export. The contribution of a missile force to a state's military posture or policies depends on a number of considerations unrelated to the weapons' technical characteristics, and must be assessed case by case.

Another motivation for pursuing the ability to design and manufacture sophisticated weapons is to develop a national technological infrastructure. Weapon production or licensing ventures may contribute to industrialization simply by exposing a country to modern manufacturing and management techniques and providing experience in the use of computers, electronic systems, and other advanced technologies.[9] Some developing countries especially value investment in space research for its potential contribution to weather forecasting, agricultural surveys, and other vital nonmilitary applications.[10] And even relatively simple products that are produced indigenously can be a source of export revenues useful for overall economic development.

In becoming more independent in weapon production, developing countries also seek political advantages. The increasing competitiveness of the sellers in the international market in defense technology, along with the maturation of defense industrial sectors, has allowed purchasing states to acquire technology from multiple sources and thus mitigate the effects of restrictions imposed by some suppliers. Even when countries have been denied access to advanced technologies by industrialized powers, efforts to build weapons, including ballistic missiles, have proceeded with technology and assistance provided through an expanding international system of private entrepreneurs. Figure 2-1 illustrates the complex patterns of supply and demand for missile technology that have emerged in the Middle East, where missile proliferation has been particularly pronounced.

The increase in developing countries' dependency on imported equipment, components, and other goods in the past three decades has helped hasten the pace of technology diffusion and given emerging producers more stature in the international technology market. The commercial availability of guidance and telemetry equipment, satellites, computer technology, and other components and systems with both military and civilian applications has contributed to the capacity of many third world countries for independent or quasi-independent weapon production programs, which in turn has provided them with export strength.[11] "Today's advanced military technology is tomorrow's intermediate-level weapon system," one analyst has commented, "and through a network of licenses, offsets and joint ventures, today's buyer is often tomorrow's producer."[12]

In some cases, initiating a missile production program has accorded a state greater access to imports and coproduction agreements from advanced countries in return for slowing or abandoning the program. As in dealing with developing countries that have continuing nuclear programs, industrialized nations' preferred (or perhaps only) instrument of dissuasion has been to supply advanced conventional technologies that are considered less destabilizing. In the 1970s, for instance, the

Figure 2-1. *Transfers of Missiles and Related Technical Assistance from Industrialized Countries to the Middle East, 1960–89*

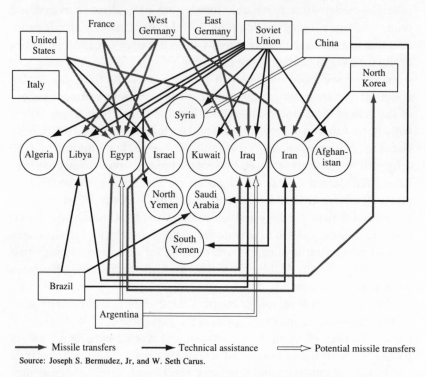

Missile transfers ➡   Technical assistance ➤   Potential missile transfers ⇨

Source: Joseph S. Bermudez, Jr, and W. Seth Carus.

United States accompanied its efforts to stop South Korea's development of a long-range surface-to-surface missile with compensatory transfers of advanced military equipment and more liberal agreements to allow Korean participation in the production of American weapon systems, including the F-5 fighter. The equipment, infrastructure, and expertise gained from such transactions may not only increase a state's overall defense industrial capacity but also its latent capability to resume missile programs at a later time.[13]

The technical and financial challenges involved in building advanced missiles are sufficiently daunting that most third world countries with missile programs are still far from having achieved full independence from industrialized powers. With the arguable exception of Israel and China, in fact, no country outside the industrial world could be considered independent in missile design and production. And because defense technology is subject to frequent design changes and improvements, significant progress in the production of high-performance weapons will continue to require third world producers to rely on imported technologies and specialized assistance.

Spurred in part by an interest in circumventing interference by industrialized nations, however, third world countries have begun to form partnerships for weapons development. In the mid-1980s, Iraq, Egypt, and Argentina established a consortium to develop the Condor II ballistic missile, and North Korea assisted Iran in modifying Soviet-origin Scud missiles.[14] Israel purportedly helped Taiwan, South Africa, and China develop various weapons, while China has offered to develop missile prototypes for Middle Eastern countries willing to underwrite the costs of production.[15] Brazil and China have formed a joint venture to develop space-launch vehicles, including a four-stage, solid-propellant system that may be marketed for export as a ballistic missile. And Libya has made demarches to several countries, including Brazil and Pakistan, to acquire missile technology.[16]

Some trade among developing countries is fueled by illegal or quasi-legal transactions made through commercial firms or renegade governments. American and Egyptian nationals attempted to export missile warhead material to the Argentinian-Iraqi-Egyptian Condor program; and an effort by two Iraqis to smuggle fusing devices from the United Kingdom, apparently for use in an Iraqi nuclear and missile program, was disrupted by an international sting operation involving the governments of several industrialized countries. As one analyst has argued, "a series of structural changes in the arms trade has led to the great increase in illegal commerce during the 1980s."[17] These changes have included a growth in demand for arms to sustain regional conflicts such as the Iran-Iraq war, restrictions by industrial countries on the legal supply of coveted technologies, and the increasingly diffuse character of the arms trade, marked by an ever larger and more diverse set of arms suppliers who are willing and able to evade national or international laws.

Cooperation among third world countries to develop weapons is likely to become far more important in international politics as emerging defense production bases become more sophisticated. Apart from gaining independence from industrial countries, these countries consider cooperative weapon programs a way to get the most from scarce technological resources, broaden their technological and scientific sectors, and create diplomatic relationships. And the necessity for cooperation brought about by the export restraints of industrial suppliers may also strengthen technological and political bonds within a wider network of developing states.[18]

Although third world defense industrial investment does not yield to strict measurements of comparative economic or military advantage, these countries' perceptions of less tangible benefits, including enhanced political status and greater independence from outside suppliers, over-shadow considerations of efficiency. For many countries, civilian and defense industrial capabilities are inseparable elements of overall development strategy. According to former Indian defense minister, Krishna C. Pant, "defence and development are two sides of the coin of nation building. Long ago, Jawaharlal Nehru defined the equation of defence as defence forces plus the industrial and technological background plus the economy. . . . This equation holds good even today."[19]

As has been the case in industrial countries, moreover, third world countries' investments in the military-industrial sector are sometimes undertaken without benefit of carefully defined missions. As one analyst described ongoing European cooperation for space development, for example,

The great programmes of European space cooperation . . . are arising from symbolic, political, and industrial stakes held in the European presence in space in the 21st century. The programmes are originating in a vision of the future whose practical applications are still uncertain, and in a long-term strategy where the engagement of states' political will and of symbolic evocation play a preponderant role. By definition, these programmes must be planned a long time in advance, when the rationale for their need in terms of the concrete uses to which they will be put can only be imperfectly outlined and defined.[20]

The similarities with the missile programs in developing countries are clear. Despite the substantial financial burden of missile development and the limited military utility of most of the first models produced, these efforts represent countries' long-term aspirations for sovereign technological status, however elusive a goal this may prove in the short term.

Industrialized Countries as Suppliers

The ability to build missiles has traditionally depended on external technical assistance. Immediately after World War II the United States and the Soviet Union used German missile technology and scientists to develop their nuclear arsenals. France and Britain continue to rely on cooperation with the United States to refine their nuclear missile forces.[21] In the 1960s, U.S. refusals to transfer missile technology to France, including denials of requests for large solid-fueled ballistic missiles and advanced computers, are thought to have slowed the pace of the French missile program.[22] But the refusals may have spurred France's aspirations for an independent missile capability and contributed to its export ambitions and relative antipathy toward policies for international export restraint.[23]

The diffusion of missile technology to the third world began in the 1950s, when Egypt attempted and failed to build missiles using technology and technical assistance provided by France and Germany. Since then, and particularly in the 1970s and 1980s, more than twelve third world countries have devoted resources to missile programs, with widely varying degrees of success. The list of producers and their relative capabilities is eclectic. Israel can make a variety of ballistic missiles almost entirely without external assistance. Iraq and Libya, however, are trying to enhance the range and capabilities of older imported missile systems, especially the Soviet-origin Scud-B.

The spread of missile technology to the third world has partly been unintended consequence of the great powers' pursuit of other policy objectives. The U.S. commitment to help rebuild the European defense industries in the 1950s, for instance, led to highly competitive European defense firms that rely on exports to the third world to sustain their commercial viability. European assistance for third world production programs has been significant, and includes French technical participation in the development of the Israeli Jericho I missile, German contributions to the Indian and Pakistani nuclear and missile programs, and contributions of German engineers to a variety of Middle Eastern missile programs going back as far as 1962.[24] Despite their recent political rhetoric, many European countries continue to consider missile-related exports vital for both their commercial and diplomatic objectives.[25]

Similarly, the U.S. pledge to help developing countries acquire the means for self-defense, stated in the Nixon doctrine in the early 1970s, encouraged allies in the third world to build their own defense industries, largely through weapon coproduction contracts. Providing weapon production technology has been a crucial element of U.S. policy toward Israel, Taiwan, South Korea, and, more recently, the People's Republic of China, among others. Although U.S. missile exports per se have been subject to strict controls, coproduction of other systems has helped develop the industrial capacity and technical know-how needed for missile production.[26]

For its part, the Soviet Union, though long eschewing weapon coproduction outside the Warsaw Pact, has increasingly fulfilled its own needs for hard currency through arms exports, including the widespread transfer of Scud and Frog missiles to the Middle East and North Korea and the transfer of the more advanced SS-21 to Syria in 1983.[27] With assistance from various sources, including private entrepreneurs, some clients have been able to exploit Soviet technology for indigenous production efforts. With or without Soviet sanction, Scud-Bs have been sold in large quantities by third parties. As one analyst commented, "A ubiquitous symbol in Middle Eastern military parades, the Scud has become so plentiful that a lively second-hand market emerged in the mid-1980s, with purchases made by Iran, Iraq, and Western intelligence agencies."[28]

The Soviet government also has sought commercial and political advantages by assisting India with its space program, an important, if unintended, catalyst for India's current missile-building capability. These cooperative space ventures have expanded Soviet influence, particularly since the United States, concerned about its commercial competitiveness, began to discourage international space cooperation in the early 1970s.[29]

The role of the Soviet Union in high-technology trade may grow as it modernizes its industrial base. Ambitious Soviet internal economic reforms are likely to require increased hard-currency export revenues. In 1985, arms sales accounted for more than 10 percent of the USSR's total hard currency earnings, a significant portion for a country that, partly for political reasons, had previously engaged only in grants of military aid.[30] Having long relied on strict controls over the disposition of weapons and weapon technology among its allies and clients, the Soviet Union may find it particularly challenging to try to balance the need for revenues against its traditional reluctance to share sensitive technology.[31]

Although Japanese policy prohibits arms exports, any change in this policy in the coming years could add a whole new dimension to the defense technology market. Given the formidable capacity of Japan's industry, more aggressive marketing of defense-related products could well spur the kind of frictions in international arms trade that have sorely tested its relations in commercial trade. To date, U.S. policy has assumed that Japan can be induced to be more forthcoming with expenditures for its own defense while somehow remaining inactive or compliant in its defense trade policy. This assumption may not long endure.[32]

The pattern of defense industrial investment in the third world has been said to exemplify the product life-cycle theory in international trade that was developed by Raymond Vernon. According to this model, as industrial products mature, they begin to be disseminated more widely in the international market. Those goods that once represented high technology become traditional products, and industrialized nations move their manufacturing processes to countries where low production costs make the goods most competitive. As is the case in commercial trade, defense production processes have been distributed internationally in a pattern described by Aaron Karp as "the migration of proven technology." Developing countries' use of proven space technology for missile development, for instance, has been a logical step in the evolutionary process that has "enabled third world manufacturers to assume huge shares of the world's output of steel, ships, textiles and consumer electronics."[33]

There is, however, an important difficulty to be recognized in applying the life-cycle theory to defense products. Industrial countries rarely promote defense coproduction or licensing ventures so that they can purchase the goods made or coassembled by developing countries. With few exceptions, such as a recent agreement between General Dynamics and the Arab Organization of Industrialization to manufacture components for the F-16 fighter aircraft, joint defense ventures are not intended primarily to reduce the production costs of advanced countries.[34] Instead, industrial powers use the ventures to achieve political objectives or because they want to capture markets for their own weapon exports, which increasingly requires sharing production as the price of making sales.

Developing countries thus have had to find market outlets for their defense products largely within the third world. And the small size of the demand within most third world arms-producing countries requires that these countries also export to sustain the viability of their manufacturing bases. Arms exports by these emerging producers have already altered the composition of the international market: in the early 1970s they accounted for about 2 percent of all arms sales; in the 1980s they accounted for more than 15 percent.[35] According to one estimate, the value of armaments manufactured by third world states grew from

$2 million in 1950 to $980 million in 1980 to $1.1 billion in 1984 in an overall market valued at $52 billion.[36]

In the effort to sustain their arms industries, South Korea, the People's Republic of China, Argentina, Brazil, Israel, and other producers have provided military equipment and assistance to U.S. adversaries and to combatant states whose conflicts the United States was trying to mediate. In many instances, such as China's sale of the CSS-2 missile to Saudi Arabia in 1988, U.S. attempts to stem exports it deemed undesirable proved futile.[37]

These efforts have, as a corollary, added a new dimension to North-South political frictions. Unauthorized exports have been a point of dispute between superpowers and their clients, notably between the United States and South Korea since the early 1980s and between the Soviet Union and Libya after Khaddafi's transfer of Scud-B missiles to Iran in 1985. Pressures by recipients to be allowed to export equipment that has been either coproduced or imported are likely to become increasingly prominent in U.S.–third world relations as the recipients assert more independent foreign policies and use their defense industries to advance these policies. The consequences will depend on the nature and destination of exports, but the availability of alternative suppliers who can circumvent advanced countries' export strictures poses interesting questions for any future efforts to limit the power and sophistication of armaments in a combat region.

The continued growth of defense industries in the third world also poses economic dilemmas for the West. The United States and other industrialized countries are losing or have lost sales of arms, both as a result of import substitution by new producing countries and because of these countries' own exports. As such, advanced countries may be contributing directly to their own future financial losses. For now, most third world exports are not technologically very sophisticated and must be directed at parts of the market that are already glutted. Advanced countries' apprehensions about economic losses resulting from the transfer of manufacturing processes are usually still outweighed by the greater losses they anticipate if they deny a recipient's request. In the future, however, the competitiveness of industrial countries may be more seriously compromised as developing states acquire the means to produce and export more advanced weapons.

Developing countries' efforts to build missiles symbolize their achievement of industrial sophistication, itself a by-product of an international economy no longer dominated by a few great powers. Despite new suppliers' current dependence on industrial powers for highly advanced technologies and components, they can be expected to continue to pursue their national ambitions without reference to the wishes of these powers. The realignment in North-South relations that brought far greater economic interdependence among developed and developing countries in the 1980s has affected the arms trade as well. The trade in defense technology has become a buyers' market in which recipients can play one supplier off against another. A supplier's refusal to agree to a recipient's terms can easily lose it contracts, which will promptly be filled by a competitor. This is not a climate in which supplier cartels or other trade restrictions are likely to prove easy to implement or sustain.

Controlling Arms Flows

Especially since World War II, the United States and its allies have used a variety of formal and tacit arrangements to keep conventional military technologies from diffusing to regions or countries they consider hostile. Typically, the United States has been the most aggressive supporter of these efforts. In 1948 it imposed a unilateral policy of export controls against Soviet bloc nations. Since then a network of multilateral institutions aimed at restricting the dissemination of advanced technology to Eastern Europe and the Soviet Union has evolved, including one of the most enduring mechanisms, the Coordinating Committee for Multilateral Export Controls (COCOM), established in 1949. U.S. legislation, such as the Export Control Act of 1949 and the Mutual Defense Assistance Control Act of 1951, reinforced the concept of international controls on technologies deemed essential to the defense of the free world.[38]

More recent legislation and international agreements to control other aspects of military trade have included the international nuclear nonproliferation regime, with its system of safeguards conducted by the International Atomic Energy Agency, established in 1957, and the 1968 Treaty on the Non-Proliferation of Nuclear Weapons. There have also been efforts to ban the production and use of chemical and biological weapons, the 1976 Arms Export Control Act guiding worldwide military exports, and periodic embargos against countries subject to international opprobrium, such as the UN prohibition on arms exports to South Africa.

The industrialized countries have struggled for decades to find ways to manage the challenges posed by the military ambitions of hostile or unstable countries while continuing to seek political and commercial advantages from arms sales. Even in the early days of the cold war, the U.S. effort to restrict technology exports to the Soviet Union was often opposed by Western Europe and Japan, whose commercial interests were disingenuously presented as principled opposition to a policy of economic warfare against the East.[39] Despite the appearance of a durable consensus among Western countries, actually restricting East-West military trade has been plagued by chronic controversies.

But however contentious in practice, East-West strategic trade controls have at least had the benefit of being directed at a coherent geographic area and a definable political philosophy, as well as the benefit of relatively straightforward objectives. In contrast, efforts to manage the North-South military trade with developing nations have been impeded by the geopolitical complexity of the third world and by the absence of any common agreement about the objectives of technology controls.

Identifying the challenges posed by the proliferation of conventional weapon technology is complicated by fundamental differences of opinion on even the most basic issues, such as whether and how the global diffusion of advanced military technology undercuts U.S. and international security, the extent to which the United States and the other great powers have legitimate and effective ways of influencing the pace of that diffusion, and how best to manage the potential threats associated with the expansion of arsenals in volatile countries.

Thus despite mounting evidence of the hazards to global security posed by the continued diffusion of conventional military technology to unstable regions, there is no solid national or international consensus in favor of restraining arms transfers. Formal efforts to control the arms trade have never succeeded in translating either ethical or pragmatic concerns into durable policy. International initiatives, such as the proposals put forward at the 1977 UN Special Session on Disarmament, or the Carter administration's demarches to the Soviet Union to limit sales of sophisticated weapons, had no lasting impact, and few efforts at regional restraint among developing countries have survived.[40]

The only instance in which an international embargo can be said to have succeeded was the Tripartite Declaration of 1950 by the United

States, Britain, and France, which imposed limits on arms exports to the Middle East. Vitiated five years later by Soviet weapon sales to Egypt and the withdrawal of British troops from Suez, the Tripartite Agreement nevertheless made effective use of a supplier cartel on behalf of great-power military objectives in the third world.[41] The conditions that made such a regime possible in 1950, including the limited ability of recipient countries to afford or use advanced armaments, the small number of arms suppliers, and the clarity of purpose among the Western industrial states bent on containing conflict in a vital region, have long since disappeared. Now experience with efforts to control the proliferation of conventional technology does not appear to be a promising guide for developing the kinds of international norms that would inhibit trade in nuclear, chemical, or biological weapons.

Still, missiles traditionally have been singled out for more stringent export control than is applied to other weapon systems, including high-performance aircraft and naval platforms, in part because of a perceived linkage between the diffusion of advanced missile delivery capabilities and nuclear proliferation. Surface-to-surface missiles were discussed as possible candidates for bilateral export restraints in the U.S.-Soviet conventional arms transfer negotiations during the Carter administration, for example, and both nations observed tacit restraints in transferring long-range missiles to allies in Korea and the Middle East throughout the 1960s and 1970s.[42]

Other than sales to Japan or NATO countries, U.S. policy has been particularly stringent with regard to sales of surface-to-surface missiles potentially capable of carrying nuclear warheads. Although Israel received the short-range Lance missile, for example, its request to purchase the Pershing I-A intermediate-range missile in the early 1970s was denied. The United States denied sales of the Lance to Saudi Arabia in the mid-1980s.[43] And Washington had discouraged Indian efforts to acquire the Scout space-launch vehicle for its civilian space program in 1965, recognizing that the missile could have military applications.[44] It did, however, permit the sale of the Nike-Hercules surface-to-air missile to Taiwan and South Korea, which led to South Korea's successful conversion of this system to a surface-to-surface configuration despite strict end-use assurances from Seoul.

The Soviet Union has provided perhaps ten countries outside the Warsaw Pact with missiles since the 1960s. It has transferred hundreds of Frog-7 and Scud-B missiles to its clients in the third world and has sold the more advanced SS-21 to Syria. Reflecting growing concerns about missile proliferation, however, Moscow denied Syrian requests for the SS-23 intermediate-range system in 1987 and has been unwilling to provide the SS-12 Scaleboard system to Libya and Iraq.[45] The Soviet Union has also traditionally controlled access to military manufacturing technology.[46]

Western European suppliers have been more permissive. French assistance helped Israel build the Jericho I missile in the 1960s, and numerous European programs have helped states develop and manufacture space-launch vehicles: France has provided the Mammoth propulsion system for production by Pakistan and India and French and German companies have been extensively involved in providing technical information with military applications and assistance to a wide variety of clients.[47] Not always legally, European commercial ventures have also recently been vital to missile programs in India, Brazil, Israel, Argentina, Iraq, and even Libya.[48]

In the final year of the Carter administration, officials in the Arms Control and Disarmament Agency and the Department of Defense began to point to a pattern of unwitting diffusion of U.S. missile technology through dual-use or commercial channels. Civilian inertial guidance technology and other components pertinent to missile design and production apparently were being sought by potential missile-producing states. As one official described the process, "attempts were being made to purchase U.S.-origin missile components on a part-by-part basis." To rectify this apparent policy weakness, President Reagan signed National Security Decision Directive 70 in November 1982, calling for the investigation of ways to control missile proliferation. After four years of negotiations, an agreement was reached among Canada, France, Germany, Italy, Japan, the United Kingdom, and the United States to establish restraint guidelines for missile-related exports. It was formalized in April 1987 as the Missile Technology Control Regime.[49] In deference to the political sensitivity of more formal arrangements, the regime was not designed as a treaty but as a consensual agreement, asking states to incorporate its guidelines into their national export codes and abide by them as sovereign countries.

The MTCR covers missiles and unmanned airborne vehicles with payloads in excess of 500 kilograms and a range of 300 kilometers or more (figure 2-2). It established a two-tiered system of review. One tier

Figure 2-2. *Range-Payload Trade-Offs for a Simple Single-Stage Ballistic Missile*[a]

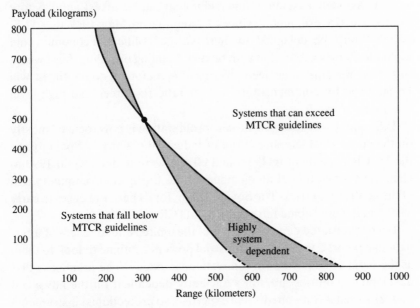

Payload (kilograms)

Systems that can exceed
MTCR guidelines

Systems that fall below
MTCR guidelines

Highly
system
dependent

Range (kilometers)

Source: Department of Defense.
a. Missiles that lie in the shaded region may exceed MTCR thresholds, depending on their design.

scrutinizes and restricts missile-related exports, including technologies subject to "a strong presumption of denial," such as complete ballistic missiles, space-launch vehicles, and sounding rockets. The second tier reviews requests for such dual-use components as rocket casings and staging mechanisms to determine that they are not intended for use in missile programs. Although initially focused on ballistic missiles, the regime now monitors the proliferation of cruise missiles as well.[50]

Both the Reagan and Bush administrations discussed the problem of missile proliferation in demarches to the Soviet Union and considered discussions with regional security partners as well. Restraining the spread of missiles has gradually become a more routine part of the broader diplomatic agenda that includes supporting the international nuclear nonproliferation regime, efforts to control chemical weapons, and discussions with key nations about ways to contain regional military tensions.[51]

Bush administration officials have suggested that efforts to constrain the international market in missile technology are a critical priority. For instance, Reginald Bartholomew, under secretary of state for security assistance, science, and technology, stated in testimony before the Senate Governmental Affairs Committee in May 1989 that U.S. policy "must be designed to increase the political, economic, and diplomatic costs associated with buying, building or selling these weapons."[52] It remains to be seen whether this rhetorical commitment will be matched by commensurate bureaucratic resources and high-level attention.

U.S. policy for stemming missile proliferation is now focused mostly on the consensual supplier cartel of industrial countries. Spain joined the MTCR agreement in 1989, and efforts were under way in 1990 to elicit the cooperation of all members of the European Community and of the neutral countries. The Soviet Union, for its part, indicated in early 1990 that it would abide informally by MTCR guidelines.[53]

Despite repeated demonstrations of the limited effectiveness of international export controls, the industrial powers continue to look to them as the point of departure for innovations in policy. The premise is that developing countries are still sufficiently dependent on the advanced powers for vital components and expertise, so protectionist instruments can be at least partially effective in slowing the pace of missile programs.

In the future, any policies that address the problems posed by missile proliferation will have to recognize the extent to which proliferation is already deeply rooted in international politics. As such, it may not be seriously limited by selective supplier controls. And the very few examples of deliberate military restraint among developing countries, including regional agreements such as the Treaty for the Prohibition of Nuclear Weapons in Latin America, do not inspire great optimism that regimes to control proliferation would receive the support of potential recipients. No such system of international controls has ever been fully articulated or been deemed a sufficient international priority to warrant concerted negotiations among governments.

Realism need not be a pretext for fatalism, however. If the proliferation of ballistic missiles cannot be reversed or eliminated, some of its most troublesome aspects probably can be contained. As has been demonstrated in nuclear nonproliferation matters and in efforts to ensure the security of Western technology, even an imperfect regime is preferable to one in which the trade in dangerous technologies is left to market forces. Although export controls may not be the best basis for policy in the long term, they can serve as a first step toward identifying other instruments for international cooperation, including measures for building regional confidence and ensuring security and, perhaps, for resolving the disputes that are encouraging the third world to acquire missiles. The outlines of a possible regime are discussed in chapter 6.

CHAPTER THREE

The Producers

ACHIEVING even modest independence in missile production is a slow, evolutionary process that requires significant investment of technological resources and expertise. Even rudimentary production requires some experience in missile design, manufacturing, testing, and systems integration. Actually assembling a missile requires personnel skilled in advanced materials development, microelectronics, computer engineering and software design, and rocket design.[1] Missile deployment and use require further infrastructure for basing, command and control, and other necessary logistical support.

Necessary Components and Technologies

Four components are vital to the success of a ballistic missile development program. In descending order of their degree of technical complexity, they are the guidance system, the reentry vehicle, the propulsion system, and the warhead.[2] The missiles that result can be single or multistaged and can vary widely in performance, depending on the synergism among such variables as range, accuracy, type and size of payload, and reliability.[3]

Guidance Systems

Guidance technology, the most vital and most complex aspect of ballistic missile design and production, has been described by one analyst as the "brain and central nervous system" of a missile, without which it could not be targeted or controlled in flight.[4] Guidance capabilities determine a missile's accuracy, the key measurement of its ability to reach and destroy a target. Because ballistic missiles are powered through only the earliest stages of their flight (usually 10 to 20 percent of total flight time), they must be guided toward their targets at exactly the right velocity well before reaching a destination: "this requires a sophisticated, computer driven guidance and control system adequate to position the missile as desired, exact knowledge of the coordinates of the launch site and target, and the ability to program a computer to achieve the desired flight path."[5]

Of the three kinds of guidance used in missiles—external command systems, flight programmers, and inertial guidance—the inertial system accords the greatest accuracy and reliability but is the most challenging to produce.[6] Manufacturing advanced inertial guidance systems requires precision machining, the ability to fabricate advanced materials, and access to computers used by the accelerometers, gyroscopes, and associated subcomponents needed for accurate warhead delivery.[7] "The complexity of materials development, and the precision of design, fabrication, and assembly required for even modest accuracy makes the manufacture of actual systems as much an art as a science. . . . The capability of most [third world countries] . . . to bring together the skilled personnel and necessary resources needed to develop or manufacture (or even assemble) inertial guidance systems is limited."[8] Sophisticated guidance systems designed specifically for advanced ballistic missiles are extremely complex and must be able to withstand high acceleration and a wide range of temperatures. These systems, of which there are relatively few, are subject to strict export controls.[9]

Inertial guidance systems can be acquired by developing the kinds of advanced systems used in intercontinental-range missiles or by purchasing far less complicated (and less accurate) systems available in the civilian or dual-use market, which can be used for shorter-range missiles. Not all missiles require advanced guidance to have some, albeit limited, military utility. Short-range missiles, such as the unmodified Soviet-designed Scud-B found in the inventories of many third world nations, can have accuracy errors of several hundred meters and yet be capable of doing considerable damage to targets in unprotected areas and population centers. Accuracy limitations can also be compensated for with the use of chemical or nuclear munitions. But to contribute more directly to modern military needs, such as the ability to attack military targets with high confidence using conventional warheads, greater accuracy is required.[10]

Highly accurate guidance systems present a formidable technological barrier for most developing countries. For this reason, almost all developing country that produce missiles have acquired guidance systems by importing them directly or diverting guidance packages designed for other systems, including aircraft. Acquiring aircraft navigation systems and other components useful for missile guidance has, in the past, been relatively easy.[11] France, China, the Soviet Union, the United States, and Britain used this method in developing their own missile programs.[12] Concern about the commercial availability of such dual-use guidance systems led Washington to impose controls on exports of inertial navigation and associated technologies under the Missile Technology Control Regime.

Successful conversion of dual-use guidance systems, however, is by no means a fait accompli for emerging countries. The demands placed on the inertial navigation systems (INS) used in aircraft only approximate those of missiles. Missile accelerometers, for example, "must be an order of magnitude more accurate than navigation accelerometers because missiles accelerate at a very high rate for a short period."[13] And adapting commercial INS for use in ballistic missiles requires advanced engineering expertise that for now is beyond the capacity of most developing states. Inertial navigation systems usable on manned aircraft can, however, be converted for use in cruise missiles. In the future, developing countries may be able to use commercially available navigational data from satellites, such as the U.S. Global Positioning system or the Soviet GLONASS system, to navigate cruise missiles with higher rates of accuracy.[14]

Although production of advanced inertial guidance is still the Achilles heel of incipient missile development programs, significant advances by India, Israel, and others suggest that countries determined to acquire the requisite technologies may be able to achieve some production capabilities by the turn of the century, given continued technical assistance from more advanced powers. Indeed, some analysts believe that accuracies of 100 meters or less could be achievable on some short-range third world missiles within this decade.[15]

Reentry Vehicles

The second most technically challenging element of missile development is the reentry vehicle, the container that helps a ballistic missile warhead withstand physical stress and heat when it reenters the earth's atmosphere. This means that technologies for designing, producing, and testing reentry vehicles must ensure they have "a structure and materials that will survive the physical stresses of reentry, minimize weight, accommodate the size and shape of the payload, and not appreciably degrade accuracy."[16] For missiles up to medium range, developing the systems for a durable reentry vehicle is not as challenging as it is for longer-range systems because shorter-range missiles are subject to less reentry stress and heat, and their briefer flight times distort accuracy less. (Some short-range missiles, of course, do not leave the atmosphere during flight and thus do not need reentry vehicles.)

Because most technologies required by reentry vehicles have no other uses, their identification as systems to be controlled under the Missile Technology Control Regime was relatively straightforward. Components usable for warhead safing, fusing, and firing mechanisms are subject to outright export prohibition, even if ostensibly requested for use in a civilian space program.[17]

Propulsion Systems

Gaining expertise in propulsion techniques is less difficult than acquiring guidance systems or designing reentry vehicles. Ballistic missiles can use either liquid or solid propellants. Liquid-propellant missiles carry fuel and oxidizers separately in the missile airframe, then pump them into the engine to burn and create thrust. In solid-propellant missiles the fuel and oxidizer are premixed. Solid propellants are easier to store and handle than liquid propellants and require engines with fewer moving parts. Liquid-propulsion systems are less simple to operate but can deliver greater payloads to longer distances and are easier to control in flight.[18] However, liquid systems may require an hour or more to launch; solid-propulsion systems allow a missile to be fired more rapidly. The trade-off, then, is the solid-fuel system's operational simplicity for the liquid-fuel system's superior performance.

Even the simpler solid-fuel systems, however, require a significant investment of technical resources: "The mixing, casting, curing, machining, and finishing of a solid propellant and the lining and preparation of the motor case is a volatile process which necessitates precise and careful handling of the materials. Cracks, contaminants, and inhomogeneities in the propellant can have major effects on performance and can lead to the failure of the engine.''[19] Such expertise is scarce in the third world, and although many countries have made progress in dealing with solid-fuel systems in recent years, most still require assistance.

An important means of acquiring expertise in propulsion techniques has been to import solid-fuel systems associated with space research. This has sometimes been easy: in the 1960s, for instance, the United States pursued bilateral agreements with Argentina, Brazil, India, and Pakistan for cooperative experiments with sounding rockets under the auspices of NASA. And over the years other suppliers of rocket and associated technologies have included France, Germany, Japan, and Italy.[20] Although sounding rockets are too small to carry military payloads, their propulsion technologies can be converted for use in ballistic missiles.[21] In principle, any solid-propellant rocket can be turned into a two-stage ballistic missile; stacking additional stages poses significant technological challenges and degrades performance, but some countries have overcome these problems.[22]

In the pursuit of cooperative civilian space ventures, India and Brazil, among others, have found that single-stage rocket systems could be modified to produce multistage ballistic missile systems. Multistage systems have also been imported directly and converted to a surface-to-surface mode, as South Korea did with the Nike-Hercules surface-to-air missile provided by the United States in the early 1970s. Still, the ability to extend the ranges of missiles is not in itself necessarily significant. Longer-range systems also need more elaborate guidance to ensure desired levels of accuracy, more powerful engines, and heat shielding to protect warheads during reentry.

Warheads

Depending on its type, designing and manufacturing a warhead arguably involves the least complicated of the processes required to produce a missile. Most states can manufacture high explosives for conventional munitions, and some are developing the means to build chemical weapons. The relative ease with which countries can adapt petrochemical, pharmaceutical, and pesticide manufacturing operations to make simple chemical agents has prompted intense international negotiations to reach agreement on a global prohibition of chemical weapons.[23] In addition, Western observers, including William H. Webster, director of the Central Intelligence Agency, have charged that

Egypt, Iran, Iraq, Israel, Libya, North Korea, Syria, and Taiwan, all of them missile-possessing states, are attempting to develop biological weapons.[24]

Developing nuclear weapons is an aspiration of some of the more successful missile-producing states, including India and Pakistan, but their nuclear programs pose special technical and political problems. Although Israel almost certainly possesses nuclear warheads for its missile force, this prospect is still fairly distant for other states. Even for those that have the capability of testing nuclear devices, the move from testing a device to producing reliable warheads that are light enough to be carried by missiles is not easy.[25] Still, India and Pakistan, among others, may well have such capabilities within the next few years.[26]

In the future, countries may acquire or produce advanced conventional munitions, which, married to missile systems of sufficient accuracy, could enable them to destroy adversaries' military strength without resorting to nuclear or chemical warheads. India, for instance, aspires to develop a range of conventional warheads for its more advanced missile systems, including so-called smart submunitions and fuel-air explosives.[27]

Other Constraints

Assessing the comparative difficulty of developing various missile components ultimately depends on the uses to which the systems are to be put. In principle, rocket engines can perform equally well in space-launch vehicles, sounding rockets, or ballistic missiles; but the performance of a guidance or propulsion system will vary widely according to its mission.[28] Possessing particular components for missile production is thus a necessary but not sufficient condition for launching a successful missile program. Missiles contain thousands of elements, all of which must be designed, manufactured, and tested carefully if a country is to be confident that they will operate reliably under the stress of combat.[29]

In theory, third world countries could shorten the time and lower the costs for producing ballistic missiles by benefiting from the experience of developed countries. Aside from receiving direct technical assistance, potential producers can learn about the phenomenology of missiles from the extensive literature, academic exchanges, and commercial expertise available internationally. However, the scarcity of technological resources, domestic political upheavals or international realignments, changing military threats and priorities, chronic fiscal constraints, and interference by the great powers have resulted in frequent interruptions in third world technological ventures, including slowed or abandoned programs and outright failures.

Still, a number of countries have made fairly significant progress in achieving access to subsystems and technical assistance made available by an increasingly competitive technology market. Largely because of its strong security relations with the United States, Israel has managed to avoid most technological reversals and to break through the barriers endemic in other developing countries. Even such a fairly underdeveloped state as Iraq has been able to produce a highly modified Scud-B ballistic missile in just over five years.

Finally, however, the most significant constraint on emerging missile-owning states may be the relative fragility of their technological infrastructures. Developing countries' claims to self-sufficiency notwithstanding, many vital components, including accurate accelerometers and gyroscopes for inertial guidance and advanced composites for reentry vehicles, remain in the hands of only a few industrialized nations. As such, continued cooperation with advanced countries remains an important determinant of the pace of third world missile programs.

Patterns of Missile Program Development

In most advanced countries, achieving the wholly indigenous ability to design, produce, test, and operate intermediate-range missiles took perhaps twenty years. To develop the requisite technical and managerial infrastructure, they tended to invest in several classes of missiles, increasing the number and sophistication of the classes as technological expertise grew. A typical progression might move from artillery rockets to air-launched unguided rockets, to pilotless vehicles, to air-to-air missiles, to air-to-surface and surface-to-air missiles, and finally to surface-to-surface missiles. This was the pattern followed by the United States, France, the United Kingdom, Italy, and Sweden.[30]

The most common strategy of third world development has been to concentrate on one fairly modest missile program in which the first test vehicles resemble the weapons that are finally deployed. These earliest models have then often served as the foundation for follow-on systems. More advanced capabilities are achieved by adding new missile stages to the original design, as in the Brazilian Sonda series, which has evolved from a single-stage system to the most recent design, the four-stage Sonda IV.[31]

Developing countries have used three major strategies for missile programs: modifying space-launch vehicles to create ballistic missiles, producing missile prototypes and systems in national defense industries, and acquiring foreign components, expertise, and resources to modify imported missile systems. These strategies may overlap, and some nations, such as Brazil and India, have both space programs and defense industries. Countries also vary in the relative emphasis they give to alternative technology sources and techniques for missile development.

These various strategies reflect the countries' political and military priorities, their level of industrialization, and the kinds of imports and outside assistance available to them. It is difficult to gauge which variable has been most influential. To the extent that the choice of a strategy is influenced by the necessity to consider competing modernization priorities, investment in space exploration may have an economic rationale. For a country such as India, with its vast territory and diverse population, satellites could contribute immediately to economic advancement and political integration by providing better communications, meteorological information, and resource development, quite apart from any military applications. A country like South Korea, by contrast, would have more difficulty justifying the expense of space exploration to promote the development of civilian industry in the early stages of its industrialization. Instead, South Korea's missile program grew from its defense needs and its emphasis on intensive investment in electronics, shipbuilding, aircraft assembly, and other sectors pertinent to indigenous defense production.

Considerations of domestic development aside, the nature of missile programs seems most directly influenced by how much access to advanced technology outside powers allow a given country. Until fairly recently, only a few countries had access to the manufacturing technology and assistance needed to develop defense industries. And even in the third world states that had defense firms, ballistic missile programs required considerable domestic investment and relatively high technical sophistication to elude restrictions on such activities by advanced powers.

Some countries with limited access to military manufacturing technologies found they could attract advanced technology more readily under the seemingly benign auspices of space cooperation agreements. India, for example, found space research an expedient way to circumvent tight controls on the high-technology components it produced under Soviet license and to diversify its sources of supply. Space cooperation ventures also helped attract foreign investment and expertise and provided a peaceful cast to India's technological ambitions, an important political benefit domestically and internationally. Though long recognized by the advanced countries to have military applications, exports of space technology have never prompted the international attention or opprobrium attracted by arms exports.

The experiences of countries with extremely limited access to military technology from the industrial countries illustrate the extent to which external supply and internal capacity are still closely linked. Partly because of its political isolation, Iran produces almost none of its own weapons. Although this in part stems from the way its industrialization has been stunted by years of domestic and regional instability, it also suggests the limitations of defense industrial progress that is based on technology purchased from private sources or renegade countries.

The following sections describe the three missile development strategies by examining programs in India, South Korea, and Iraq and Iran. Readers must keep one caveat in mind, however. The secrecy that surrounds most countries' missile programs makes precise assessments of their capabilities difficult. Published information is scarce, not always reliable, and subject to constant revision. The difficulty is further complicated because some governments exaggerate the scope of their missile programs for political reasons.

Adaptation of Space-Launch Vehicles: India

Ballistic missiles are closely related to space-launch vehicles in design and performance. The two differ in the payloads they can carry, their trajectories, and, to a lesser degree, the kinds of guidance and control they require.[32] According to the Arms Control and Disarmament Agency, however, "the only major difference between the space and missile variants is that the final boost stage of the ICBM is terminated earlier, before the payload has achieved enough velocity to enter orbit, resulting in its return to earth."[33] Early models of intercontinental ballistic missiles developed by the United States, such as the Titan II, were, except for the reentry vehicle they required, virtual duplicates of the space rockets used in the Gemini program. Similarly, the Soviet Union converted SS-5 and SS-6 ICBMs into space boosters.[34] In principle, space-launch vehicles may require less accuracy than missiles, but their guidance systems are similar and thus potentially convertible for use in missiles. Indeed, with the arguable exception of Japan, no country has invested in the production of space-launch vehicles solely for nonmilitary objectives.

Along with Israel, India leads the industrializing world in manufacturing space-launch vehicles and components. This situation is the result of three decades of investment in infrastructure facilitated by extensive assistance from West Germany, France, the United States, and the Soviet Union. West Germany, in particular, may have been pivotal in bringing about the technical progress that made India's Agni program possible. Although the United States has been increasing its involvement in India's space and defense industrial programs recently, its role as a supplier has been relatively modest since the mid-1960s.[35]

To accommodate its cooperative space ventures with advanced countries, India established the National Committee for Space Research as part of its Department of Atomic Energy in 1962. The space sector expanded steadily. The Indian Space Research Organization, in charge of sounding-rocket experiments, was established in 1969, and in 1972 the cabinet-level Department of Space, which was heralded as highlighting "the transition of the space effort from a scientific undertaking of limited magnitude to a coordinated program with specific goals and time-bound projects in space applications and technology."[36] India's Defense Research and Development Organization, established in 1958 to oversee defense industrial investment, was explicitly linked with the space sector when missile production efforts became part of the space enterprise in 1983.

India began working with the Soviet Union on experiments with sounding rockets in the 1960s and on satellite launch vehicles a few years later. Moscow valued the cooperation as an important instrument for expanding Soviet influence in this strategic third world country. The extent of Soviet involvement in India's space modernization efforts has not been replicated in any other developing state.[37] But although it was traditionally extremely careful in controlling access to advanced military technology, the Soviet Union apparently did not fully anticipate that

India would use the space technology and expertise to such effect.[38] By contrast, India's development of an independent defense industry, based on the production of Soviet weapons under license, experienced slower progress because the range and quantity of equipment manufactured was subject to strict control.[39]

In 1971 the Soviet Union and India signed an agreement for joint development of a satellite that culminated in the first successful launch by the Soviets of the Indian satellite *Aryabhata* in 1975.[40] Most of the subsystems in the *Aryabhata* were manufactured in India, although the Soviets provided some key elements.[41] The Soviet launch of the follow-on *Bhaskara* in 1979 established the foundations for more independent Indian efforts the following year.

Both the *Aryabhata* and the *Bhaskara* launches experienced major technical difficulties: the *Aryabhata*'s power supply systems failed, and the *Bhaskara* lost a crucial monitoring capability. Both required Soviet booster rockets to achieve orbit. Still, the joint experiments conducted as part of these ventures, including systems manufacturing and satellite tracking and monitoring, gave Indian scientists sufficient expertise to design and build their own solid-fuel rocket by late 1979.[42]

After one abortive test flight, the Indian-built, four-stage SLV-3 launched the *Rohini* satellite into near-earth orbit in mid-1980, making India only the seventh nation to have achieved this capability independently. As one commentator noted, "The magnitude of this achievement becomes apparent when one considers that Japan, a technologically advanced nation, was unable to put a satellite into space until its fifth attempt."[43] In the next two years, India tested the SLV-3 two additional times, with mixed results.

The SLV-3 program was expensive. In 1979, when it had been under way for eleven years, an estimated forty-five Indian industries and institutions were involved, directly employing some 300 scientists and engineers.[44] Despite its high cost, imperfect performance, and limited payload capacity, however, the SLV-3 is believed to have been invaluable to subsequent missile designs. The SLV-4, or augmented satellite launch vehicle, tested in 1986, was based on the SLV-3, with two solid-fuel boosters and improved guidance added to the original model.

Despite its success, the new ASLV program exemplifies the difficulties India encountered in trying to develop an independent space-launch capability through protracted trial and error. In its first test, the ASLV crashed 160 seconds into flight because of ignition failure in the first stage. It failed again in a test in 1988, reportedly for the same reason.[45] Still, it is serving as the basis for the ambitious polar satellite launch vehicle, which will have four stages and six SLV-3 rocket boosters and is designed to carry a 2,200 pound payload, a long step from the 77 pound *Rohini*.

Indian officials announced in October 1989 that they had successfully tested the first-stage booster of the PSLV, which is scheduled for launch in 1991.[46] The PSLV is to be succeeded by the geostationary satellite launch vehicle, designed to carry a 5,500 pound payload into geostationary orbit. The GSLV is following an accelerated development and testing schedule, with test launches beginning early in the 1990s and completion slated for the end of the decade.[47] The GSLV is considered particularly important to Indian advances in systems design because it is said to include an improved rocket engine based on cryogenic techniques that combine liquid oxygen and liquid hydrogen. According to Abdul Kalam, former director of launch vehicle development at the Indian Space Research Organization and the principal designer of the Agni, India is particularly interested in perfecting cryogenic engines, believing them to be more effective than other types of liquid- or stored-fuel rockets because they can provide greater thrust and can potentially reduce the size of the launch vehicle.[48] France is reported to have offered to sell India advanced technology on cryogenic rocket engines.[49]

Western European assistance has been crucial to India's technological advancement in the past two decades, overshadowing the assistance given by the Soviet Union in developing India's military space potential. But unlike the Soviets' caution about technology transfer, West Germany and France have provided equipment and expertise directly relevant to ballistic missile production. France assisted India in coproducing Centaure sounding rockets in the late 1960s and in developing an indigenous version of the French Viking liquid-fuel engine (used on the Ariane space launcher) in the 1970s. In several cooperative programs, German engineers have helped with rocket testing, guidance, and the application of composite materials.[50]

Although New Delhi continues to portray the space program as a peaceful scientific venture, Indian officials have referred to its military potential since at least the early 1970s.[51] The formal separation maintained between the space program and the Defense Ministry was criticized by one Indian military analyst in 1979 as a potential obstacle to realizing India's strategic goals. "If . . . national security goals someday

Figure 3-1. *Ranges of Third World Ballistic Missiles, by Type and Country*[a]

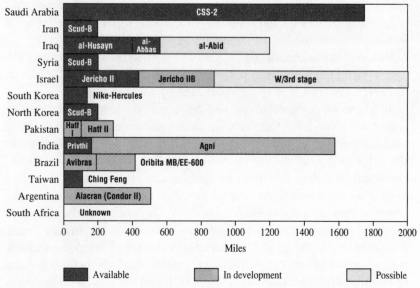

Sources: See text and table 4-2.

a. Intermediate-range Nuclear Force Treaty limits ranges to less than 300 miles. MTCR limits ranges to less than 186 miles and payloads to less than 1,100 pounds.

dictate a reconsideration of strategy, then it is clear that the potential of the space programme can be tapped if, and only if, the activities of [the Space Department and Defense Ministry] are coordinated."[52]

In the early 1980s, space-related missile efforts were formally integrated into India's national defense planning. In 1983 the government established the Integrated Guided Missile Development program, which is run under the auspices of the Defense Research and Development Organization and includes plans for a series of missile systems to be developed in coming years. According to one estimate, the DRDO operates more than forty-five defense-related plants and research facilities, of which nineteen are engaged specifically in various aspects of missile design.[53]

The missile program has generated two ballistic systems, the Agni and the shorter-range Privthi (figure 3-1). In addition, some press reports have suggested India is working on a missile with an estimated range of 3,000 miles.[54]

The Privthi liquid-fuel missile was first test-fired in February 1988 and has since been tested several more times.[55] It is reported to carry 2,200 pounds to a range of 150 miles and is claimed to be the first Indian system to have inertial guidance produced indigenously. Indian officials also claim they have succeeded in achieving a high degree of accuracy, a CEP of 250 meters, but these estimates are widely considered exaggerated. The Privthi is supposed to be deployed in 1991.[56]

The Agni, a two-stage system, has a payload of 1,000 pounds and a range of 1,500 miles. The first stage is apparently derived from the SLV-3 and uses solid fuel. The second stage is liquid fueled and believed to be adapted from the Privthi, but it has a reentry payload structure. It is guided by on-board twin microprocessors that India also claims to have manufactured.[57] It should be noted that Dr. A. P. J. Kalam, the missile's designer, previously served as director of the SLV-3 program.

In a recent publication the quasi-governmental Indian Institute for Defence Studies and Analysis reiterated that both the Privthi and the Agni are based on components produced by Indian engineers. According to the institute's director, the Privthi has a propellant tank and missile frame made of aluminum alloys developed locally, and "virtually none of the components for the engine or other parts were imported." Similarly, the Agni is portrayed as representing a significant advancement in Indian guidance technology and reentry and heat-shielding capabilities; the carbon heat shield is reported to be "completely indigenous."[58] Some observers charge that these claims are patently false. In addition to West German assistance in developing nose cones and engine nozzles, for instance, German microprocessors and software developed jointly with India in 1982 are believed to be the basis of the Agni's guidance system. According to Gary Milhollin, "the evidence is strong that the Agni owes its brain to German engineering."[59]

India continues to seek imports of gyroscopes, test-range instrumentation radar, and other sophisticated components from the United States, Germany, and France, and is involved in ambitious codevelopment projects for other kinds of advanced weapons that could provide spin-offs to the missile programs.[60] Although the U.S. refusal to sell the CAVCTS missile-testing device in 1989 prompted India to claim that it could produce the device without American help, the government is apparently seeking to purchase the equipment elsewhere.[61] Just by having succeeded in putting a satellite into low earth orbit, however, India has made clear that it possesses sensitive instruments useful for long-range missile guidance, whatever limitations may remain.[62]

India's ability to produce nuclear weapons-grade materials and nuclear explosives has been known since at least 1974, which means that
the country might soon be able to develop an operational nuclear missile
force. New Delhi's denials notwithstanding, this is a frequently stated
objective of Indian military planners. As an Indian military publication
stated in 1981, the country "must possess adequate capability for
strategic long-range strikes in the form of MRBM/IRBMs equipped with
nuclear warheads, a strategic air strike and interdictor force, and
adequate air defence, all equally complementary and coordinated."[63]
Bharat Wariavwalla, a scholar at the Institute for Defense Studies and
Analysis, reinforced this view after the Agni test: "Like good Hindus
and Pacifists, we say the program is only for peaceful uses." But the
Agni is, in every sense, a delivery system for nuclear weapons."[64]
Although the government denies plans to arm the Agni with anything but
a conventional warhead and may not even proceed with its deployment,
India is clearly experimenting with technologies that would be pertinent
to a nuclear missile force and has a program to develop its own mobile
missile launchers.

India's investment in space programs has thus proved useful in helping
it acquire expertise in techniques pertinent to missile development and
in building the modern scientific and industrial infrastructure needed for
more ambitious military endeavors. As officials have stated repeatedly,
India must develop advanced weapons, including ballistic missiles, to
maintain its technological and military stature and keep pace with
changing international technology trends.

India's space research and development facilities have served as a
conduit for foreign experts to train local engineers and scientists and for
imports and technical agreements that could be claimed as necessary for
peaceful scientific research, despite their latent military applications.
Unlike the growth of its defense industry, the steady expansion of India's
military space potential has occurred until recently without much active
scrutiny from more advanced nations. Under the peaceful cast of
civilian research, the nation had considerable latitude to acquire needed
technologies and expertise through routine and unpublicized channels.
India's space sector thus demonstrates how technology and expertise
with military applications can diffuse even when there are formal
prohibitions against outright transfers of military products. As a study
prepared for the Defense Department commented, even relatively unso-

phisticated ventures such as the production of sounding rockets can contribute to military industrial potential:

[A sounding rocket] agreement permits continuous discussion under official auspices between missile engineers and scientists in the supplier and recipient countries. Second, an agreement can have the effect of establishing a cadre of rocket personnel in the recipient country whose interest in further rocket or missile activity is aroused. . . . Third, it is obvious that development and production experience can be gained. . . . Fourth, the teams at the launch site become familiar with test procedures, have a reason to acquire increasingly more sophisticated test instrumentation, and acquire a practical engineering and operational knowledge of rocketry which cannot be duplicated merely at the scientific level.[65]

Now that India can build ballistic missiles, the question for the United States and other industrial countries is how much they will assist or impede future development efforts and in what way. Despite its public denunciations of the Agni missile test, Washington has expressed keen interest in deepening ties with India, including sharing advanced military and dual-use technology. This larger objective is unlikely to be vitiated by efforts to halt India's missile programs, although U.S. policy is explicit in its opposition to the country's amibitions for nuclear weapons and ballistic missiles. Some Bush administration officials, in fact, believe it is better for the United States to participate in Indian military modernization than to antagonize this regional power with export restrictions. "India is like a juggernaut that just won't be denied," one said. "It is in the U.S. interest that they be self-sufficient and beholden to no nation, and we would rather help them get there. It is better to be friendly to someone who is strong than not."[66] Others, of course, disagree, and chronic delays and controversies over pending sales of advanced technology have resulted as U.S. policymakers struggle to resolve internal disputes.[67]

Given the counterweight that the missile forces would pose against China, the Soviet Union may have less interest than the United States in dissuading India's missile-building efforts. It has, however, discussed with New Delhi the disposition of Soviet-origin technology and its potential application to missile programs, and has since become an informal adherent of the Missile Technology Control Regime.[68] In 1986 General Secretary Mikhail Gorbachev urged India to develop an international space-launch center, including a facility for commercial space launches to made available to other countries. Implying an offer of assistance for the civilian space program, the Soviet government apparently hoped to retain some measure of influence over India's military aspirations.[69]

Development of Defense Industries: South Korea

South Korea's ability to produce ballistic missiles is a by-product of the expansion and refinement of its defense industry that began in the 1960s. In contrast to India, which obtained most of its missile expertise through foreign assistance for its space program, South Korea obtained most of the technologies and expertise needed for its missile program from U.S. imports and technical assistance associated with coproduction of other weapons and with maintenance agreements. And it not only developed the expertise in explicitly defense-related facilities in which American influence was pervasive, but also pursued its program despite formal restrictions on access to ballistic missile technologies and over the strenuous objections of its major supplier.

The South Korean government has long had the goals of deploying sophisticated armaments produced or coproduced domestically, to show independence from the United States, hedge against the possibility of alterations in the U.S. commitment to its security, and capture what it considered the political and economic benefits of modernizing its defense industry. South Korea has developed a diversified scientific and production base and can equip its forces with all but the most sophisticated military technologies. It is rapidly gaining expertise in avionics, electronics, and other important fields. In particular, the government strongly supports the aerospace industry, which has steadily expanded its capabilities by aggressively pursuing weapon coproduction ventures with ever-higher levels of local participation in advanced technological activities.[70]

South Korea's investment in its defense industry has followed a pattern common in other developing states, moving from importing finished equipment, to establishing maintenance and overhaul facilities that allowed for modest participation in manufacturing spare parts, to assembling and manufacturing weapons under license, and finally to designing, developing, and building its own weapon systems. Progress from stage to stage has not, however, been sequential for all categories of weapon systems, and for some all four stages still exist side by side.

Korea still imports components to build highly advanced systems, as well as some finished equipment it prefers not to produce indigenously.

South Korea's efforts to achieve an independent defense industry owe their impetus to American encouragement. Although weapon coproduction contracts with American firms began in the mid-1960s, the industry got its first major boost during the Nixon administration as part of U.S. policy to provide military manufacturing technology to friendly states to encourage greater self-reliance as U.S. troop deployments declined. The transactions gradually evolved from licensed production of simple munitions to significant Korean participation in the manufacture of advanced systems such as fighter aircraft.

After steady expansion under President Park Chung Hee in the late 1960s and early 1970s, South Korea's defense industry crossed a new threshold in 1978 following President Carter's abortive decision to reduce U.S. troop levels. In the effort to assuage Korean dismay at the possibility of such retrenchment, the United States provided $800 million in arms transfers in 1978. And despite the Carter administration's policy of prohibiting coproduction with most developing countries, many of these transfers included coproduction and technology-sharing arrangements for major military items. South Korean technicians subsequently reverse-engineered or copied technology data packages and equipment to produce what were thereafter designated as indigenous products.[71]

For two decades South Korea has wanted to develop a long-range surface-to-surface missile that could reach Pyongyang to counter the threat posed by North Korea's deployment of Soviet-origin Frog-7 and Scud missiles and to offset the north's quantitative military superiority.[72] Despite the active opposition of the United States and limited support from the South Korean military, President Park staked his personal prestige on developing an indigenous ability to build ballistic missiles and invested significant funds in a program run by the Defense Ministry's Agency for Defense Development. Conducted clandestinely, the program persisted throughout the late 1970s and the 1980s, albeit with frequent interruptions and setbacks and despite its adverse effects on other military priorities.[73]

South Korea's exposure to techniques pertinent to missile development began under the auspices of the U.S. Military Advisory Group in 1972, when Korean engineers became involved in maintaining the Hawk and Nike-Hercules surface-to-air missile systems. The program led to the establishment of a commercial maintenance facility directed by a local firm, Gold Star Precision Industries, where South Korean personnel were trained in missile maintenance by the U.S. military and American companies.[74] As part of the program, the personnel were provided with technical specifications for upgrading missile reliability, including electronics improvements, techniques for improving conventional warheads, and information pertinent to converting the system to a surface-to-surface mode.[75] U.S. technical assistance in aircraft coproduction also improved the expertise of South Korean engineers in avionics, airframe design, and other areas relevant to missile development and operations. And Korea has imported a variety of U.S. missiles, which, given its noted ability to reverse-engineer products, may have provided additional experience in basic missile design.[76]

South Korea's ballistic missile program is based on the conversion of the U.S. Nike-Hercules surface-to-air missile to a surface-to-surface configuration. Under the aegis of the Agency for Defense Development, its engineers improved the missile's electronics, guidance, and warhead packaging. Based on these modifications, South Korea subsequently developed two versions of a surface-to-surface missile that it claims is of indigenous design. Designated the NH-K, it is a two-stage, solid-fuel system, one version with a range of 110 miles and the other 140 to 160 miles (see figure 3-1). Both can apparently carry nuclear warheads.[77]

After the first successful test flight of the NH-K in 1978, the Defense Ministry noted that South Korea had achieved a new status, joining the six other nations that could produce their own missiles.[78] In official pronouncements, Seoul has gone to great lengths to obscure the degree to which this achievement derived from U.S. expertise, heralding it as a important symbol of technological independence.[79] The NH-K was supposed to go into mass production in the late 1980s, but this has not been confirmed.[80]

South Korea has also begun to invest in space research and intends to launch a research satellite into low earth orbit by 1996 using a Korean-produced rocket.[81] Further research efforts that could improve missile technology include an accelerated program to develop rocket launching technologies and guidance. If the program achieves its long-term goal of developing a space launcher, Korea could feasibly build missiles that have ranges far longer than the NH-K.

South Korea has been a signatory to the Nuclear Non-Proliferation Treaty since 1975, despite evidence of its interest in nuclear weapon development that has surfaced periodically.[82] It may also have a chemical weapon program and has at least the latent capability to make such weapons should there be sufficient incentive, such as the deployment of chemical weapons by North Korea.[83]

South Korea thus illustrates the limited influence a supplier can have even when the supplier is the main source of military technology and is the recipient's closest security partner. For a country whose dependence on the United States has been integral to its security, South Korea's willingness to incur the costs of circumventing U.S. policy demonstrates the degree to which it has accorded the acquisition of a ballistic missile sovereign importance. This importance has had far more to do with political symbolism—demonstrating independence and nationalistic pride—than with any objective calculation of military utility.

South Korea's behavior also illustrates the difficulty of controlling technological developments in a country once it has acquired the capacity to engage in independent or quasi-independent weapon production. Although the United States thought it was restricting access to technology pertinent to ballistic missiles, its investment in South Korea's defense industrial base unavoidably aided independent research and development efforts. Once a state can purchase manufacturing technology, efforts to restrict its access to weapons or critical components become less effective and may only delay rather than terminate programs that the local government values.

In fact, as has proved true of states with latent nuclear programs, South Korea may have actually gained leverage over the United States through its determined efforts to develop ballistic missiles. In trying to persuade it to abandon its missile project, the United States granted Korea access to a wide range of advanced technologies that it may have not otherwise have received. Some of these agreements may in turn have indirectly helped Seoul continue the missile program. Similarly, the latent threat to produce and deploy other destabilizing systems may help South Korea discourage U.S. policy alterations that it opposes, such as reducing troop strength in the peninsula.

Despite recent considerable progress, self-sufficiency in defense production continues to elude South Korea. Aside from easing fiscal constraints, importing U.S. material has symbolic and military importance, reaffirming close security ties with the United States. As long as the United States continues to provide relatively liberal access to coproduction and coassembly arrangements and continues to support Seoul's objectives, the costs of actions that risk terminating the relationship likely will outweigh any apparent benefit.

Still, South Korea's deployment of missiles and the possibility that it may export them holds the potential for serious friction between the allies. Although there is no evidence yet of ballistic missile exports, Seoul has long felt hampered by U.S. interference in its quest for export revenues and has repeatedly violated the U.S. prohibitions against the transfer of American-made equipment to third parties. Many South Korean officials believe that the United States is obligated to assist Korea in developing and protecting its defense industry, an industry the United States has had the greatest role in fostering. This includes the right to export weapons.

South Korea has been trying to rid itself of the renegade reputation it has earned as an arms supplier, but its dependency on exports makes this difficult, especially as production expands and diversifies into more advanced systems. In the past, Seoul directed exports toward countries that for one reason or another could not buy weapons from the United States or Western Europe or even the Soviet Union, including pariah states, such as Taiwan and South Africa, or countries at war, such as Iraq and Iran. In the absence of cooperation to help stem the proliferation of destabilizing weapons, South Korea's efforts to expand its share of the high-technology market may at some point include missiles. It is still not too late, however, to elicit Seoul's support for international missile export restraint, albeit at the cost of other forms of compensation and more accommodating policies that reflect the genuine interdependence between the two security partners.

Missile Importers and Modifiers: Iraq and Iran

Although both Iraq and Iran have acquired the technology to begin indigenous or quasi-indigenous missile programs, neither has a defense industry nearly as sophisticated as South Korea's or India's. What is significant about their missile programs, however, is that both have been able to purchase missile-related technologies even though they are subject to international strictures supported by the majority of industrial countries and some industrializing ones.

Figure 3-2. *International Arms Trade in Ballistic Missiles, Condor Program*

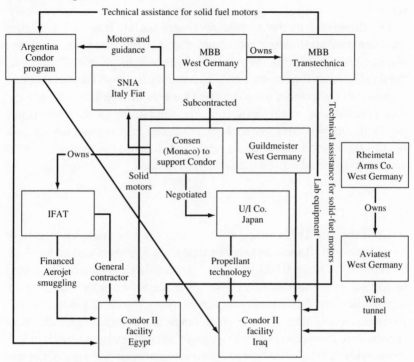

Source: Northrop Analysis Center, 1989.

The development of missile programs in Iran and Iraq underscores the inherent limitations on supplier export controls when there is a high demand for combat systems and countries have the financial resources to attract suppliers to meet that demand. In particular, Iraq's participation in the Argentina-based Condor missile consortium in the mid- to late 1980s provides a glimpse into the unprecedented complexity of the arms supply relationships that operate outside the influence of industrial nations' policy controls or established international law.

Initiated in Argentina in the mid-1980s and involving Egypt as well as Iraq, the Condor program attempted to develop a ballistic missile with a range of up to 560 miles by using technical assistance largely from West German and Italian engineers.[84] Iraq is believed to have lent financial support to the program until 1988.[85] As figure 3-2 shows, the patterns of trade involved in the development of Condor give no evidence of traditional industrial-country influence over international arms transactions.

Developments in the missile programs within Iraq and Iran also illustrate the attenuating influence of industrial countries over the disposition of weapons they have transferred to clients. During the Persian Gulf war, the combatants acquired missiles from various sources, regardless of pressures from the great powers to stop the transactions. Any comfort one might draw from the limitations of Iran and Iraq's production capabilities, as such, is tempered by the evidence of how readily the market can accommodate the demand for missiles and fill voids left by the advanced industrialized nations.[86]

Iraq

Until the late 1970s Iraq's military arsenal was made up largely of Soviet materiel. It included short-range Frog-7 rockets and an unspecified number of Scud-B ballistic missiles. Baghdad had apparently sought to purchase the more advanced Soviet-made SS-12, which has a range of 560 miles, but the request was denied. Since the early 1980s, Iraq has purchased equipment from a wider range of countries, with the most sophisticated weapons, including fighter aircraft, supplied by France.[87] Arms sales to Iraq were barred by an international embargo beginning after its invasion of Kuwait in August 1990, causing all significant military trade to cease for the forseeable future.

The attenuation of Soviet influence over Iraq in the past decade exemplifies the limitations of seeking political influence through technological coercion. To express its dissatisfaction with the quality of Soviet weapons and Soviet restrictions on their supply, Iraq began to reduce its dependence on the Soviet Union in the early 1980s. In the early phases of the Iran-Iraq war, for instance, Soviet reluctance to provide needed materiel led Iraq to increase imports from other suppliers. Recognizing that their partial embargo was ceding export contracts to other states, the Soviets resumed exports to Iraq in 1986, including an estimated 300 Scud missiles. But Iraq continued to turn to other suppliers. Dependent on Arab economic support to sustain the war, it found that its benefactors had even less interest in buying into the web of political interference associated with Soviet arms supplies.[88]

By the end of the war, Iraq was equipped with Brazilian armored cars,

French fighters, Austrian artillery, and Scuds that it had modified and improved without Soviet sanction, reportedly with the help of German and Egyptian engineers, some of whom may have been associated with the Condor program.[89] Iraq apparently also received shipments of Brazilian Astros-2 artillery rockets.[90]

Iraq's efforts to develop missiles apparently began in the early 1980s and have since flourished in ambitious efforts to produce a range of systems.[91] The earliest production programs were based on modifications of the Scud-B. Iraq has two such systems, the al-Husayn, with a 375 mile range, and the al-Abbas, reported to have a potential range of 560 miles (an unmodified Scud has a range of 190 miles). Both systems have been tested successfully, and Baghdad used approximately 190 al-Husayn missiles against Tehran in the 1988 "War of the Cities."[92]

The greater range of the al-Husayn was apparently achieved by reducing the size of the warhead from 800 kilograms to 190 and increasing the fuel capacity by 20 percent. The al-Husayn also appears to use improved guidance technology, not the original Scud package, and the Iraqis have claimed it has a CEP of 500 meters, half that of the unmodified Scud-B. This claim has been widely challenged, however.[93]

The al-Abbas apparently is an improved version of the Al-Husayn. Some analysts claim that, unlike the al-Husayn, it does not have a reduced payload, but this assessment has since been challenged.[94] Iraq has claimed an extremely high level of accuracy for the al-Abbas as well—a CEP of 300 meters—which is also very much in doubt because the Scud-B's accuracy would had to have undergone a tenfold improvement and the guidance package used in the al-Husayn would had to have been substantially altered.

Other Iraqi missiles include improved versions of the Frog-7 and the Laith–which have a longer range (70 miles) and carry cluster or chemical munitions—and a series, designated Fahd, under development as follow-ons to the al-Husayn; little is known about the Fahd system.[95] At the end of 1988, Iraq announced that it had successfully tested an antitactical ballistic missile, the Faw-1, but claims about its ability to intercept missiles are believed exaggerated.[96] Before its military occupation of Kuwait in August 1990, Iraq had a cooperative program with Brazil for missile development, which included training several hundred Iraqi engineers there.[97] It also had plans for two longer-range missiles, the Tammuz-1 ballistic missile and the al-Abid satellite launch vehicle, each with a range of 1,200 miles or more. Baghdad claimed to have succeeded in launching a three-stage rocket into low earth orbit in December 1989, which would suggest a nascent space program, but the claims have been refuted.[98] Still, Iraq apparently hopes to become the first Arab nation to achieve such a capability, which could give it a basis for developing an intermediate-range ballistic missile.[99]

Before the outbreak of hostilities with Iran, Iraq's defense industrial base was not very advanced, and it is still not considered capable of producing advanced weapons without some external assistance. The development and production of the al-Husayn, for example, involved hundreds of foreign nationals and relied on imported gyroscopes, among other vital technologies. Iraq apparently can, however, manufacture subcomponents pertinent to advanced missile design, including some used in guidance technology and reentry vehicles.[100]

Before August 1990 Iraq had focused on establishing an ambitious network of research and development facilities for advanced weapons, including missiles, rockets, and chemical weapons. The two most important facilities are the Sa'ad 16 project, located near Mosul, and Project 395. The country has received technical assistance on these projects from the Soviet Union, the United States, China, West Germany, Egypt, Brazil, and Argentina.[101]

Sa'ad 16 is an extensive enterprise that is reported to have already cost $200 million. It contains more than fifty laboratories concentrated in one installation controlled by the military under the aegis of the Military Industries Organization, directed by the son-in-law of President Saddam Hussein. This installation houses computers, radar stations, wind tunnels, and other advanced design and testing equipment.[102] It was built with West German and, in one instance, American assistance. Despite a ban on military and dual-use exports to the combatants in the Persian Gulf war that the U.S. government imposed in 1980, Hewlett-Packard sold computers and other electronic equipment to Iraq in 1985–86, some of which is useful for missile development.[103]

Iraq has also been building three factories to produce solid-fuel rockets, part of a program codenamed Project 395. Originally thought to be part of Iraq's participation in the Argentine-Egyptian Condor II program, Project 395 involves some of the same West European enterprises as the Condor consortium. With the long-term objective of developing intermediate-range missiles, Project 395 is providing Iraq with incipient production capabilities for solid-fuel engines, rocket components, and test facilities.[104]

Iraq also has a history of research and development on nuclear and chemical weapons. Its nuclear program was the subject of considerable publicity in the 1970s and again in 1990, following U.S. intelligence reports in November that it had achieved a capability to assemble a crude nuclear device "within six months."[105] The Osiraq reactor, purchased from France in 1976 and widely agreed to be for warhead production, was considered sufficiently advanced to warrant a preemptive attack by the Israeli air force in June 1981 (at the time, Iraq was involved in negotiations to purchase a heavy-water power reactor from Italy as well as a reprocessing facility).[106] The successful destruction of the Osiraq delayed but certainly did not terminate the country's plans to become the first Arab nuclear state. Many analysts believe it could have an enrichment capability to produce nuclear weapons comparable to Pakistan's by the end of the century.[107]

In the meantime, Iraq has stepped up production of chemical weapons. In April 1990 President Hussein threatened to use chemical weapons against Israel if it ever attacked Iraq, prompting a flurry of attention on Iraq's chemical weapon program.[108] In August 1990 it was reported that Iraq had loaded chemical weapons on aircraft for possible use against international forces moving into the region in defense of Kuwait and Saudi Arabia, a rumor that was never confirmed. The Iraqis are believed to have five chemical warfare facilities, including a major installation at Sammara that produces nerve agents, and they may be developing a chemical warhead for ballistic missiles.[109]

Iraq's establishment of a defense industrial infrastructure helped it attract foreign investment for missile and other defense production efforts, for at least as long as it can pay for these ventures. Foreign involvement in Sa'ad 16 illustrates the complicated network of commercial interests, involving companies from more than a half-dozen countries, that such a program can engender. Sometimes technology provided to Iraq has been transferred through firms from different countries operating as industrial mercenaries. Sometimes technology has flowed from an industrial supplier without the apparent sanction of the supplying country.[110]

Iraq's activities demonstrate how porous the international system of technology controls can be in the face of commercial enterprises determined to circumvent export laws. Despite West Germany's extremely restrictive formal arms export policy, it was West German firms that most aided Iraq's missile programs. Only recently, after repeated

American complaints and considerable publicity, has the German government, an MTCR signatory, begun to tighten its export enforcement laws.

Given the ravages of a protracted war in the 1980s and Iraq's weak industrial infrastructure to begin with, its investments in missile programs reflect the inordinate priority it has given to military needs. For the foreseeable future, however, the destruction of Iraqi military facilities in Operation Desert Storm and its progressive international isolation will hobble its military industrial progress. The economic and political costs of the military crisis will undermine economic recovery, and could ultimately force Baghdad to abandon or scale down its military production programs.

Iran

Iran's defense industry owes its genesis to the accelerated program of military modernization undertaken in the 1970s by the Pahlavi regime and assisted by the United States. Although the United States sold it a substantial amount of sophisticated arms, Iran did not have the industrial base to begin any major programs of weapons coproduction (although several were under consideration before the revolution).[111] The abrupt termination of relations with the United States in 1979 severely hampered defense capabilities, including access to critically needed spare parts for U.S. systems. Israel may have supplied some parts in recent years, but sources remain inadequate.[112]

Since the revolution, Iran's weapons have been procured from the Soviet Union and from China, North Korea, and other third world countries. Tehran turned to Libya for Scud-B missiles in 1984, for instance, and North Korea has been a significant supplier of arms and technical assistance since 1980. North Korea may have been the source of the Scuds Iran purchased during the last phases of the Iran-Iraq war, permitting it to attack Iraqi population centers. There is also evidence of an Iranian–North Korean effort to produce modified Scuds, apparently involving an Iranian pledge to provide funds and technology in return for North Korean–produced missiles. North Korea may also have helped Iran launch its chemical weapons program.[113]

The Soviet Union has proved incapable of stemming the flow of Scuds into Iran through its close clients, Libya and North Korea. These transfers allowed Iran to continue prosecuting the war against another Soviet client immune from Soviet pressures.[114]

Since 1985 China has also been a major supplier of arms to Iran. In 1989 it was reported that Tehran had reached an agreement with Beijing to buy components useful in developing a medium-range missile and that China was helping build production facilities in Iran. Among the programs cited as the result of Iranian-Chinese cooperation are a surface-to-surface missile, designated the Iran-130, with a range of 80 miles; the Oghab, a tactical rocket with a range of 25 miles; and a new version of the Scud-B with a range of 180 miles.[115] Iran purchased the Silkworm missile from China and is reportedly interested in purchasing China's M-9 missile, a medium-range (350 miles), mobile, solid-propellant missile with inertial guidance.[116] Requests for the CSS-2 missile that China has sold to Saudi Arabia have thus far not been granted.[117]

In October 1988 Iran held a military exhibition in Tehran to demonstrate the defense products it claimed to have developed indigenously. All the missiles on display were of short range and, aside from the Oghab, are thought to still be under development. Iranian officials, prone to hyperbole, have claimed that more than 80 percent of the missiles it used against Iraq were manufactured independently.[118]

Iran has acknowledged that it can make chemical weapons and is thought to be planning mass production with assistance from West German companies and from North Korea.[119] Israel has charged that Iran is engaged in "adapting combat-proven chemical warheads to its missiles and is developing a biological warfare capability as well."[120] This charge has not been substantiated. Iran had a fledgling nuclear weapon program under the shah, but it has been set back radically; for now there is no prospect of an Iranian nuclear armed missile.[121]

In May 1989 Iran's deputy foreign minister announced plans to diversify arms supply relationships: "If we depend on one particular country or bloc," he argued, "then they take advantage of the situation. . . . They want to impose their own ideology on us."[122] The statement may have been a reference to Tehran's ongoing negotiations with Moscow for advanced weapons, including fighter aircraft. Given their delicate balancing act involved in trying to sustain relations with both Iran and Iraq, the Soviets have apparently proved too reluctant a supplier to satisfy even the Iranian government.

Iran is, then, at such an early stage of missile development and has such obviously aggressive ambitions that international cooperation to slow or stop its programs may be both feasible and desirable. As the collapse of the Condor program illustrated, the costs of missile development in countries with undeveloped industrial sectors or with severely limited resources can be raised to unacceptable levels by the concerted efforts of suppliers. Because all the industrial powers have expressed a direct interest in containing military developments in Iran, an international cartel could be very effective, albeit only if it is also supported by China. Although states such as North Korea likely would try to exploit market opportunities resulting from other suppliers' restraint, their production capabilities are still limited and could themselves be subject to international sanctions.

Summary

The various acquisition strategies that countries have chosen for missile development are the result of both domestic and international influences. Countries seem to have adapted to the opportunities and constraints of the international market to acquire missile technology, but the ways they have done so represent differences in their ambitions and industrial and military priorities.

India seems to have used its civilian space program to evade international restrictions on the supply of military manufacturing technology and to achieve the international status accorded states with advanced satellite (and missile) capabilities. Demonstrations of its technological prowess, both civilian and military, are part of its broader strategy to challenge the enduring stratification of the international system that it believes has deprived it of its rightful status as a regional superpower.

Efforts to interfere with India's missile program have proved controversial. And any attempt by a supplier cartel to impose strict restrictions on dual-use exports, though it would probably be effective in temporarily slowing India's progress, could backfire. Indeed, New Delhi's reaction to the international denunciations of the Agni test reflects the degree to which India finds foreign intervention a catalyst to its aspirations for greater independence. As one Indian commentator proudly asserted, "every one of the success stories in self-reliance [in India] has come in the teeth of foreign pressure."[123] Another Indian analyst went further, threatening that if the United States considered trade strictures or "reducing aid to India [it] should give thought to the possibility that

India might be compelled to sell technology, including various kinds of weapon technology."[124]

How the United States and other industrial suppliers will balance their interest in containing adverse military developments in the region and their interest in strengthening ties with India remains to be seen. But they need to recognize the endurance of Indian ambitions for technological and military self-sufficiency, political and economic obstacles notwithstanding. If India's missile programs illustrate how difficult it is to control the diffusion of technology even when there are significant trade barriers, they also constitute an object lesson in how important it is for a supplier to be attentive to the national goals and internal developments of client states if it wants to influence their outcome.

India's aspirations for missiles have been evident for years, but not until recently have the great powers taken them seriously. To be effective, future efforts to elicit cooperation from states such as India will require a greater understanding of their objectives and an appreciation of the likely costs of infringing upon what they perceive to be their sovereign interests. At a minimum, countries with advanced technologies must explicitly agree that the benefits of export controls and trade sanctions outweigh the disadvantages of the political and economic frictions that will inevitably be engendered. Other instruments may be required to bring influence to bear in cases such as India's, instruments that more accurately reflect the interdependence that has emerged between this regional power and the industrial world.

Unlike India, South Korea has been able to exploit liberal U.S. policies toward sharing defense technology to acquire a measure of independence in weapon research and development, which it has then used to pursue nationalistic objectives. Whatever other objectives they may serve in the future, South Korea's efforts to develop ballistic missiles constitute a strong political statement. They reflect its long-standing aspirations to independence and a more equitable relationship with the United States. Military utility aside, its missile program heralds a renewed assertion of South Korea's sovereignty and technological prestige.

For Iran and Iraq, investments in missile programs have a more proximate, military cause. Although the programs may be valued as indicators of modernization, the efforts are directed toward use in combat, and are not especially intended as engines of industrial development.

To acquire missiles and the technology to make them is not a transitory or easily reversible impulse in any of these countries, but the extent to which the impulse may be susceptible to international influence varies. It may not be possible to slow technological progress very much in states like India; indeed, interference could prove a quixotic pursuit. Cooperation, not just coercion, is probably the only way to bring about restraint in Indian missile development and deployment. This is equally true for South Korea, where efforts to encourage caution in both missile deployment and export policies will require some kind of reciprocity.

The wisdom of cooperation does not, however, mean laissez-faire policy for transfers of missile technology. The observation is meant rather to underscore the potential limitations of a supplier export regime that tries to impose coercive restraints against countries that have already demonstrated their ability and willingness to spare no costs in eluding such strictures.

Iran and Iraq are in a different category. Their war not only alerted the world to the special dangers of ballistic missiles in third world hands, but also to the extent industrial countries were losing control over the pace and content of their own arms transfers to say nothing of those of other countries in the international arms market. This lesson has been reinforced all too starkly in the current Iraqi crisis.

Several countries, including West Germany, have moved to reform their export control apparatus to restrain their own nationals. Even China seems to be showing signs of moderation in missile sales, or at least to have been alerted to its inadvertent diffusion of technology. These reforms reflect the degree to which governments rightly feel they must have an interest in exerting some control over the disposition of certain kinds of technology, however difficult this goal may be.

CHAPTER FOUR

The Military Significance of Ballistic Missiles

BALLISTIC MISSILES possess certain characteristics that have traditionally accorded them special status as military instruments, including their
speed in striking targets, their ability to penetrate defenses, and their
perceived usefulness for nonconventional operations. But the characteristics that make missiles attractive to military planners also generate
concerns about their effects on military stability.

U.S. policy has tended to reflect the belief that the growing availability
of missiles in the third world inherently increases the likelihood and
lethality of regional conflicts. A study prepared by the Congressional
Research Service, for example, argues that the global spread of missiles
portends "greater destruction and loss of civilian lives in future regional
conflicts as adversaries become more likely to fire missiles, possibly
armed with chemical or even nuclear warheads, into the cities of their
opponents."[1] This view is implicit in the logic of the Missile Technology
Control Regime.[2] Whether the assessment is accurate, however, is
uncertain. Few doubt that the spread of nuclear weapons would alter
regional balances severely. But how much non-nuclear third world
ballistic missiles in themselves presage significant changes in regional
combat, whether the spread of such other delivery systems as advanced
aircraft may be equally significant, or if the development of certain kinds
of missile forces may actually help states deter aggression under certain
circumstances is unclear.[3]

Much of this debate is necessarily based on conjecture. The limited
use of ballistic missiles in regional conflicts thus far provides few lessons
about the effects of missiles on the likelihood or outcome of war.[4] The
evidence suggests that conventionally armed short-range missiles of the

kind used in the Iran-Iraq war did not decisively change the outcome of the conflict.[5] Concerns about ballistic missile programs tend to focus on possible technological trends, such as the use of ballistic missiles with chemical warheads.[6]

The key question addressed here is whether missiles accord states combat capabilities that would not be possible with other delivery vehicles. As a corollary, can possession of ballistic missiles alter the likelihood and character of regional conflicts?

Military Effectiveness: Operational Criteria

One way to assess the effect of ballistic missiles on military capability is to compare the performance characteristics of missiles with those of other weapon systems available in the third world. The characteristics can be assessed at least approximately on the basis of range, payload, speed of delivery, and accuracy. Although these variables are highly interdependent, they are discussed separately for the purpose of analysis.

Range

Achieving the ability to launch ballistic missiles to intercontinental range was a critical threshold in the nuclear rivalry between the super-powers, making it possible for each side to target the other with weapons deployed within their own territories. Developing countries also need missiles of sufficient range to target adversaries and to be able to deploy and launch them from secure sites. But the importance of range depends on geography, including the distance between adversaries, the size of the territory being defended or attacked, and the proximity of population centers and key military targets to an adversary's forces.

In the third world, where many antagonists share a common border, traditional definitions of short-, intermediate-, and long-range missiles developed in the U.S.-Soviet context have limited pertinence.[7] Given the proximity of many third world targets to opposing military forces, even missile systems classified as short-range (less than 300 miles) could reach deep into the territory of an adversary. Most third world missiles, moreover, are mobile. For countries aiming to achieve longer-range systems, even a system such as the Agni, which has a range of 1,500 miles—still well short of the ranges of missiles considered strategic in the U.S.-Soviet context—could extend India's reach outside the region. Both Israel and India already have missiles that can reach targets within the southern territory of the Soviet Union, for example.[8]

Ballistic missiles can provide the means to deliver munitions to greater distances than is possible with artillery, which is designed for battlefield use at very short ranges.[9] But most combat aircraft found in third world arsenals, with average combat radiuses of 370 to 1,500 miles, can already achieve far greater ranges than most third world ballistic missiles (table 4-1).[10] Because of the growing spread of in-air refueling capabilities, moreover, the range of aircraft in third world arsenals could increase significantly.[11] Still, missiles under development in India, Israel, and perhaps Iraq eventually may achieve ranges of 3,000 miles or more and thus exceed the reach of all but the most advanced aircraft available to the third world. Missiles of this range raise concerns that they will expand the scope of conflict beyond the territories of the combatants, and could even pose risks to the industrial powers.

Increasing the range of systems, however, does not automatically accord greater military capability. Longer missile ranges place higher demands on accuracy and make it more difficult to carry large warheads because missiles must then have either additional fuel. To compensate for reductions in accuracy, countries must either increase the number of missiles, target them less precisely, or use unconventional warheads with greater destructive capability.

Payload

A missile's destructive capability depends in part on the size of warheads it can carry. Most observers believe that to serve as a delivery vehicle for a nuclear warhead, a missile has to be able to carry a minimum payload of 1,100 pounds. Conventional high-explosive warheads typically weigh between 1,100 and 2,200 pounds. Smaller payloads are possible—by using advanced submunitions, for example—but most missiles in third world arsenals or under development can carry 1,100 to 2,200 pounds (table 4-2).[12]

The payloads of missiles are much greater than those of artillery

Table 4-1. *Third World Aircraft and Missile Performance, by Country and Type of Weapon*

Country	Weapon	Range[a] (miles)	Payload[b] (pounds)	Accuracy[c] (CEP)
Iran	F-4 D/E aircraft	504	12,980	n.a.
	F-5 E/F aircraft	186	7,040	n.a.
	Scud-B[d]	190	2,200	908 yds
Iraq	Su-24 aircraft	678	17,600	n.a.
	al-Husayn	375	400	1–2 mi
	al-Abbas	560	n.a.	2–3 mi
Israel	F-15 A/B/C/D aircraft	864	23,540	n.a.
	F-16 A/B/C/D aircraft	558	11,880	n.a.
	Jericho II	900	226?	n.a.
	Lance	80	600	400 yds
Syria	Su-24 aircraft	678	17,600	n.a.
	MiG-23 BN aircraft	570	6,600	n.a.
	Scud-B[d]	190	2,200	980 yds
	SS-21	75	1,000	330 yds
India	MiG-29 aircraft	715	12,760	n.a.
	MiG-27 aircraft	360	9,900	n.a.
	Prithvi	150	2,200	n.a.
	Agni	1,500	2,000	n.a.
Pakistan	Mirage V aircraft	808	9,240	n.a.
	F-16 C aircraft	558	11,880	n.a.
	Hatf-I	50	1,100	n.a.
	Hatf-II	187	1,100	n.a.
North Korea	MiG-29 aircraft	715	12,760	n.a.
	Su-25 aircraft	342	19,360	n.a.
	Scud-B[d]	190	2,200	980 yds
South Korea	F-16 C/D aircraft	575	11,880	n.a.
	F-5 A/E aircraft	186	15,400	n.a.
	NH-K	160	n.a.	n.a.

Sources: International Institute for Strategic Studies, *The Military Balance 1988–89, 1989–90* (London: Brassey's, 1989, 1990); Christopher Chant, *Compendium of Armaments and Military Hardware* (London: Routledge and Kegan Paul, 1987); Renato Contin, "MiG-29: A New Step in 'Mirror Policy,' " *Military Technology* (April 1987), p. 129; and Sheila Tefft, "India Steps Up Arms Race," *Christian Science Monitor*, April 25, 1989, p. 1.

n.a. Not available.

a. Radius of action carrying standard warload.

b. Maximum payload.

c. The CEP for aircraft varies widely and is dependent upon the type of weapon carried and other operational factors.

d. The Arms Control and Disarmament Agency lists the payload of the unmodified Scud-B missile as 1,100 pounds. However, it is widely believed to be able to carry 2,200 pounds.

systems, most of which have capacities well below 220 pounds, but combat aircraft can carry significantly heavier loads and more diversified types of ordnance.[13] Most combat aircraft in developing countries' arsenals can carry bomb loads ranging from 3,000 pounds to more than 20,000 pounds, although usually they carry 1,100 to 1,200 pounds.[14] As

Seth Carus has argued, "to deliver the same ordnance as a single aircraft flying one mission might take as many as eight Frog-7s or four Scud-Bs. It would take 10 Iraqi al-Husayn missiles, which have warheads of only 180–190 kg. of explosives, to equal the payload carried by a single F-16."[15]

Carus also notes, however, that the destructive capability of missiles is not just a function of the size of payload, but is affected by the speed at which they travel. "Supersonic speeds impart considerable energy to ballistic missiles when they land. . . . The Scud-B travels at three times the speed of sound when it lands, not only exploding unexpended fuel but causing considerable damage with the impact of its two-ton missile fuselage."[16]

To increase destructive capability (and compensate for inaccuracy), missiles can be equipped with nonconventional munitions, including nuclear or chemical warheads. Unlike nuclear weapons, however, which are truly "weapons of mass destruction," chemical weapons are far less effective against military targets. As Thomas McNaugher has argued, "chemcial weapons used tactically fall somewhere between high explosives and battlefield nuclear weapons, but closer to conventional ordance."[17]

Historically, missiles have not been considered a particularly efficient way to deliver chemical weapons. As one analyst stated, "Aircraft, when air defenses are not insurmountable, and multiple launch rockets, when their range is sufficient, can place [chemical agents] on target much more accurately and effectively."[18] The effectiveness of missiles in delivering nuclear weapons depends to a great degree on the sophistication of the missile system and the confidence a country has in its performance and reliability. As one analyst argued, new missile producers, "may well find it inadvisable to utilize relatively unreliable tactical missiles or their own untried versions for delivering nuclear strikes. Rather, it will seem to be more prudent to rely on well proven aircraft, made by reputable world manufacturers. . . ."[19]

Several countries are developing chemical warheads for their missile forces, and others, including India and Pakistan, appear to be developing nuclear-capable missiles as well, as Israel has already done.[20] Whether or not missile delivery of nonconventional munitions is as efficient as air delivery, missiles' speed and ability to elude air defenses could make them valued instruments for certain military operations, especially surprise attack.

Table 4-2. Third World Ballistic Missile Performance, by Country and Type of Weapon

Country and type	Payload (pounds)	Range (miles)	Accuracy (CEP)	Propulsion	Source	Status
Middle East and Africa						
Egypt						
Frog-7	1,000	40	440 yds	solid	USSR	Deployed
Scud-B[a]	1,100	190	980 yds	1-stage liquid	USSR	Deployed
Vector	1,000	500–600	n.a.	solid	Egypt/Argentina	R&D
Sakr 80	450	50	n.a.	2-stage solid	Egypt/Iraq/North Korea?	Deployed
Scud-B	2,200	190	980 yds	1-stage storable liquid	Egypt/North Korea?	R&D
Iran						
Scud-B[a]	1,100	190	980 yds	1-stage solid [sic]	USSR or North Korea	Deployed
Oghab (Eagle)	n.a.	25	n.a.	n.a.	Iran/North Korea	Deployed
Iran-130	n.a.	80	n.a.	solid	Iran/China	Deployed
Iraq						
Scud-B[a]	1,100	190	980 yds	1-stage liquid	USSR	Deployed
Scud-B (al-Husayn)	n.a.	375	1–2 mi	1-stage liquid	?	Deployed
Scud-B (al-Abbas)	n.a.	560	2–3 mi	1-stage liquid	?	R&D
Condor-II	1,000	500–600	n.a.	solid	Argentina/Egypt/Iraq	R&D [sic]
Israel						
Jericho	n.a.	400	n.a.	2-stage solid	Israel	Deployed
Jericho follow-ons	n.a.	900	n.a.	2-stage solid	Israel	Tested
Lance	600	80	400 yds	liquid	United States	Deployed
Libya						
Frog-7	1,000	40	440 yds	solid	USSR	Deployed
Scud-B[a]	1,100	190	980 yds	1-stage liquid	USSR	Deployed
SS-21 (?)	1,000	75	330 yds	solid	USSR	n.a.
n.a.	n.a.	300	n.a.	n.a.	West German design	R&D
Saudi Arabia						
CSS-2 (DF-3A modified)	4,500	1,600–1,860	1.5 mi	1-stage cooled liquid	China	Deployed
Syria						
Frog-7	1,000	40	440 yds	solid	USSR	Deployed
Scud-B[a]	1,100	190	980 yds	1-stage liquid	USSR	Deployed
SS-21	1,000	75	330 yds	solid	USSR	Deployed

System				Propellant	Origin	Status
Yemen						
Frog-7	1,000	40	440 yds	solid	USSR	Deployed
Scud-Bᵃ	1,100	190	980 yds	1-stage liquid	USSR	Deployed
SS-21	1,000	75	330 yds	solid	USSR	Deployed
Far East and Southwest Asia						
India						
Prithvi	2,200	150	n.a.	liquid	India	Tested
Agni	1,500–2,000	1,550	n.a.	2 stage liquid/solid	India	R&D
Korea, North						
Frog-7	1,000	40	440 yds	solid	USSR	Deployed
Scud-Bᵃ	1,100	190	980 yds	1-stage liquid	North Korea	Deployed
Korea, South						
Honest John	n.a.	25	Unguided	solid	U.S. and South Korea	Deployed
Korean SSM	n.a.	110–160	n.a.	2-stage solid	South Korea	Deployed
Pakistan						
Hatf I—King Hawk	n.a.	50	n.a.	1 or 2 stage	Pakistan w/technology from	R&D
Hatf II—King Hawk	n.a.	187	n.a.	1 or 2 stage	China and West Europe	R&D
Taiwan						
Green Bee (Ching Feng)	n.a.	60	n.a.	solid	Taiwan	Terminated
Sky Horse	n.a.	620	n.a.	n.a.	Taiwan	Terminated
South America						
Argentina						
Condor I	880	60	n.a.	1-stage solid	Argentina	R&D
Condor II	1,100	500–600	n.a.	2-stage solid	Argentina/Egypt/Iraq/West European consortium	R&D
Brazil						
MB/EE-150 (Orbita)	1,100	90	n.a.	solid	Brazil	R&D
MB/EE-350 (Orbita)	n.a.	215	n.a.	solid	Brazil	R&D
MB/EE-600 (Orbita)	n.a.	370	n.a.	solid	Brazil	Concept
MB/EE-1000 (Orbita)	n.a.	620	n.a.	solid	Brazil	Concept
SS-300 (Avibras)	2,200	185	n.a.	solid	Brazil	R&D
SS-1000 (Avibras)	n.a.	740	n.a.	solid	Brazil	R&D

Source: Arms Control and Disarmament Agency, *World Military Expenditures and Arms Transfers, 1988* (1989), pp. 18–19.

Speed and Ability to Penetrate Defenses

Two characteristics particularly distinguish the performance of missiles from other delivery platforms: the speed at which they travel and their ability to elude air defenses. Speed enhances a country's ability to launch surprise attacks and aids the invulnerability of missiles to any air defenses currently deployed. Combat aircraft cannot execute surprise attacks against countries with competent air defenses, although this may change as new aircraft technologies become available. A recent study conducted by analysts at Stanford University, for example, argues that "modern strike aircraft are designed to overcome air defenses, given that the proper equipment and tactics are used. As for early warning, it is probable that a well-handled low altitude strike aircraft, such as the BAC Tornado, using terrain masking, will give as short a notice of its arrival in the vicinity of the target as a tactical ballistic missile."[21]

For many third world countries, however, conducting sophisticated air operations of this type will not be possible for the foreseeable future.[22] According to Seth Carus, operating aircraft in a highly defended environment is even difficult for advanced countries:

Air operations are affected by the need to penetrate air defenses at acceptable loss rates. This means that strike aircraft may be supported by large numbers of air defense suppression aircraft, command and control airplanes, etc. For example, one source indicates that the U.S. Navy used more than 70 aircraft in its attacks on Libya in 1986, but only 14 actually dropped bombs on targets in Libya. Almost the same number of planes were used for defense suppression, and others provided electronic jamming, command and control, tanker support, and air cover for the strike aircraft.[23]

With the continued sophistication of air defenses in the third world, the cost of conducting military operations with aircraft may increase to a point at which missiles become a competitive alternative.[24] The disparity in cost between missiles and aircraft—an estimated $1 million for the Scud, for instance, compared with more than $20 million for even relatively nonadvanced aircraft–reinforces this point.[25]

Accuracy

Compared with the current generation of missiles produced in the industrial world, some of which have accuracies of a few feet, most models in third world arsenals are very inaccurate. As discussed in chapter 3, an unmodified Scud-B has a CEP of 980 yards, and the

CSS-2 a CEP of 1.5 miles. Only the Soviet SS-21 in Syria, with a CEP of 330 yards, is considered relatively accurate (table 4-2).[26] By contrast, modern fighter aircraft can deliver high-explosive munitions with CEPs of 5 to 15 meters.[27]

Most analysts believe that because of their relative inaccuracy, missiles in the developing world are suited only for nonconventional operations against airfields, troop formations, and other unprotected military targets, or for terror campaigns against civilian populations. Aaron Karp has argued, for example, that without nuclear weapons, inaccurate ballistic missiles are reduced to "appurtenances of the battlefield."[28] In the absence of greater accuracy, it is difficult to iden- tify other missions that are better carried out with missiles than with aircraft.

Coupled with advanced conventional warheads such as fuel-air explo- sives or cluster munitions, however, ballistic missiles with high accuracy could be effective against a wide range of military targets. The implica- tions of such highly accurate systems capable of precision strikes against military targets have been discussed in the U.S.-Soviet context for many years. Analysts generally assume that the combination of low yield and high accuracy in a ballistic missile would raise incentives to use these systems, including use in preemptive operations. As Henry Rowen and Albert Wohlstetter noted in 1977, "greater accuracy improves effectiveness in destroying targets because more bombs hit the target, and reduces collateral damage, because fewer bombs miss the target and hit civilians and fewer and smaller bombs can be used. Within given political constraints, this greatly increases mission effectiveness; it is likely to increase the speed and even the likelihood of a decision to release weapons for use, especially if it is a question of using nonnuclear weapons."[29]

Systems currently being developed by the United States that fit this category include the advanced tactical cruise missile. The ATCM is expected to have an accuracy three times better than that of the Lance missile (which has a CEP of 400 yards), carry almost 1,000 pounds of payload, and, according to one estimate, is less than half the cost of a Scud-B.[30] The technical difficulties involved in developing or even acquiring such a system, however—which presumably will not be made available for export to third world countries—suggest that developing countries will not have these capabilities for some time. The challenge of producing such systems could be compounded by operational impediments. Accuracy is not only a function of the technical characteristics of the missile itself; it may be affected by the structure of the command and control system, the level of training of operators, and the availability and reliability of targeting information. In actual conflict, accuracy is also likely to be affected by the "fog of war," the confusion, misinformation, and mistakes endemic to combat that make it difficult to forecast effects on weapon performance very precisely.

With the exception of Israel, most developing nations have only embryonic capabilities in such vital areas for missile performance as command, control, communications, intelligence, training, and operational experience in modern tactics. A former commander of the Strategic Air Command described the importance of these factors for strategic nuclear operations:

Strategic warfare is a highly complex and involved science which demands a vast and unprecedented global support organization, staffed by tens of thousands of experienced specialists. Therefore even the most revolutionary strategic weapon system—be it a bomber, an ICBM, or a missile-firing submarine—does not, by itself, represent strategic capability, just as a destroyer or cruiser by itself does not represent naval power. . . . Strategic capability is achieved only through the effective integration of weapon systems, organization, and men into a harmonious and centrally controlled entity. If this cannot be achieved, new strategic weapon systems will add little to the Nation's offensive strength and, conceivably, even detract from it because they will compete with instead of supplement existing weapon systems.[31]

Other Considerations

Countries will no doubt continue to try to improve the range and accuracy of their missiles, and new systems, such as highly accurate ballistic and cruise missiles carrying advanced ordnance, may reduce operational limitations. Currently, however, most third world missile models may be assigned missions that could be carried out as well or better by aircraft.[32] Missiles also have some additional distinct disadvantages. Whereas aircraft, unless shot down or disabled, can make repeated bombing rounds, missiles can only be used once. Aircraft also can carry more diversified ordnance.[33]

A more important disadvantage may stem from the provocative signal sent by missile deployments in areas of pronounced tensions. Missiles may actually reduce security by putting a premium on preemptive operations and by impeding the flexibility of leaders to deploy forces in a manner that demonstrates defensive rather than offensive intent. And missiles cannot be recalled in the event of accidental or mistaken launch and cannot be used for demonstrations of force aimed at containing crises. As a study prepared for the Defense Department stated,

It is important that national force structures provide the ability to communicate degrees of intent between disputants in the most varied and flexible manner—by displaying power without committing it, and by starting small rather than major actions. In some cases, jet fighter forces have provided alternatives to more extensive forms of war when vital interests were threatened. The deployment of ballistic missiles in regional disputes may, to some degree, lead to more rigid strategies. Present-day missiles require a target with a value commensurate to the system cost. They also lack the visibility and variation in alert status provided by combat aircraft in the regional environment.[34]

Generalized comparisons of weapon capabilities, however, can be misleading. The combat effectiveness of missile systems does depend on the number and capabilities of missiles available to each side, nature of the targets, rate at which missiles can be fired, presence or absence of defenses, types of warheads being delivered, duration of conflict, and other technical considerations. But it also can depend on far more subjective criteria, such as the level of training of the military or the coherence of a country's military objectives.

Most analyses of performance characteristics assume that military technology and conflict (or conflict avoidance) are linked, suggesting that the type of military technology available can serve as an independent variable in analyzing the determinants of war. A causal connection between the content of arsenals and the proclivity for or against military aggression is difficult to demonstrate empirically, however. Although states with long-standing enmities account for a good part of the recent interest in ballistic missiles in the third world, the incentives for investing in missile programs may not correlate directly with military threats or reveal much about military intentions.

The acquisition of more sophisticated weapons may give developing countries greater latitude in choosing how to pursue military ambitions or how to resolve disputes by violent means, but the conditions for conflict precede the acquisition of arms and differ widely among countries. The interaction between advanced weapon technologies and the prospects for, duration of, and intensity of military confrontation is a complex web of political, economic, and operational factors that requires analysis case by case.

Case Study Assessment

Assessing the significance of ballistic missiles for regional military balances is complicated by the lack of a precise and commonly accepted definition of military effectiveness. A traditional measure of effectiveness is the degree to which a weapon accords a state the ability to wage selective attacks on an adversary's force structure and other military assets—its so-called counterforce capability.[35] Non-nuclear weapons that can inflict indiscriminate damage on civilian targets and a limited number of unprotected military targets may heighten tensions and increase casualties but cannot alter basic power relations.[36] Such systems are relegated to a status of "terror weapons," not decisive military instruments.

To some, however, the effectiveness of missiles does not necessarily derive from the ability to wage precise attacks on military targets. As Seth Carus has argued, "The perception . . . that if the missiles cannot be used in tactical or operational military roles, they do not contribute to the winning of a war . . . seems somewhat narrow. If the missiles can be used in strategic attacks in ways that lead the opponent to act in desired ways, then the missiles have utility."[37] Thus even highly inaccurate, conventionally armed systems such as the modified Scud-Bs used in the Iran-Iraq war are said to be militarily effective if they cause the other side to alter tactics or temper hostilities. Moreover, some civilian targets might be considered militarily significant in certain regional contexts. According to Aharon Levran, chemical attacks on Israel's population centers could fundamentally alter the character of a regional war. In this context, a surface-to-surface missile "that is armed with a chemical warhead or is used against civilian targets, is no longer tactical but a strategic weapon."[38]

For the purpose of this analysis, missile forces are considered to be significantly altering a regional balance if their introduction can be seen as affecting military acquisitions, tactics, and overall preparedness among rivals. As Uzi Rubin has written, "A new weapon (or new way of using an existing weapon) can shift a balance of power if its effect is so decisive that it forces an antagonist to implement major and time-consuming changes in his tactics, strategy or force structure."[39] Accordingly, both real and perceived changes in military threats are taken into account. The perception of heightened threats posed by missile forces may be as important a determinant of nations' behavior, in both peace-time and crisis, as more technical assessments of military capabilities.[40]

Israel and Syria

Widely defined, the Arab-Israeli conflict encompasses states from North Africa to the Persian Gulf. Of all the countries near Israel, Egypt is the only one to have reached a peace settlement with it and currently poses no direct military challenge. If Iran is counted as a possible military antagonist, five states (the others are Syria, Saudi Arabia, Libya, and Iraq) are potential belligerents in a war with Israel, and all possess ballistic missiles.

Israel's military planning takes into account the collective capabilities of its potential adversaries. Saudi Arabia's acquisition of missiles, for instance, though it has never posed direct military challenges, has added to Israel's perception of vulnerability. The Chinese-supplied CSS-2 in the Saudi arsenal, which has a potential range of 1,500 miles, can hit any part of Israeli territory, albeit with very low accuracy.[41] Emerging missile states that have a history of conflict with Israel, such as Iraq, pose a more direct challenge, if they have not been destroyed by U.S. air strikes. The al-Husayn missile, with a range of 375 miles, could have reached targets throughout Israel if launched from sites in Iraq's western territory.

Syria, however, poses by far the most important long-term threat to Israel's security. Aside from Iraq, it exhibits the greatest hostility toward Israel; for example, Syria was the last Arab state to continue shunning Egypt for having reached peace accords with Israel in 1979. Iraq's preoccupation with the effects of military crisis in the Gulf, Saudi Arabia's traditional reluctance to become involved in wars with Israel, and Egypt's posture of conciliation all suggest that Syria is the regional power most likely to renew armed aggression against Israel after the conclusion of the Gulf conflict. Given its involvement in the Lebanese war fighting Israeli-backed Christian forces, Syria has a proximate cause for the potential escalation of tensions. And following Jordan's decision in the summer of 1988 to renounce all territorial claims to the occupied West Bank, Syria is also the only state with which Israel has an outstanding territorial dispute.[42]

INVENTORIES. Israel possesses a significant arsenal of ballistic missiles, including the U.S.-supplied Lance, which has a range of 80 miles, and the indigenously produced Jericho I, with a range of 400 miles, and Jericho II, with a range of more than 900 miles.[43] Characteristics of the Shavit rocket, used to launch a satellite in September 1988, suggest that Israel could achieve ranges of 1,500 to 2,200 miles if this system were converted for use as a ballistic missile.[44] A second satellite launch, using the three-stage Shavit, was reportedly scheduled for early 1990, although this was denied by the Israeli government.[45]

With U.S. assistance, Israel's arsenal maintains a significant qualitative edge over those of its Arab adversaries. Its military establishment is recognized as the most sophisticated in the region in equipment, quality of personnel, overall level of scientific and technological advancement, and virtually every other measure.[46] Israel has a sophisticated arms industry and has participated in collaborative ventures with the West in work on a wide variety of highly advanced technologies, including combat aircraft, missile and satellite technology, and an antitactical ballistic missile system, the Arrow, currently under development.[47]

Israel's planners have strongly emphasized developing a highly advanced and complex operational infrastructure for modern warfare. The country's command, control, intelligence, and logistical capabilities far surpass those of any Arab state. Most important, Israel has a nuclear arsenal, believed to consist of 100 to 200 weapons.[48] The combination of nuclear weapons and advanced delivery systems, including ballistic missiles, guarantees it an absolute retaliatory capability against any act of aggression.

Syria's missile arsenal reflects an almost total reliance on the Soviet Union for military equipment. It includes Soviet-supplied Frog-7 unguided missiles, which have a range of 40 miles, the Scud-B, with a range of 180 miles, and the more accurate SS-21, with a range of 75 miles.[49] Syria's total Soviet-supplied missile inventory is estimated at 200 systems. Although it has limited financial resources, Syria is apparently intent on achieving greater independence from the Soviet Union: press reports have cited attempts to purchase the Chinese M-9 ballistic missile, with an estimated range of 372 miles, and possible collaboration with North Korea to acquire their modified Scuds.[50]

Syria has almost no defense industry and thus cannot produce or modify missiles. Nor does it have nuclear weapons or a program to acquire them. It may, however, have substantially increased its capabilities to produce chemical agents, including the nerve agent Sarin, since the Lebanon war, and it possesses chemical warheads. Chemical weapon production facilities near Damascus and possibly in Homs may have been built with the help of companies in Western Europe. Syria may also be receiving equipment related to chemical weapon manufacture from Eastern Europe.[51] If combined with Syrian ballistic missile forces, this new capability could begin to undermine Israel's decisive military superiority in the region.[52] Although chemical weapons are no match for Israel's strategic nuclear deterrent, they open up new conflict scenarios in which Syria could conceivably make some tactical gains.

In the past, Syria has been unable to prevail against Israel in combat. Its air defenses were no match to the Israeli air force in the 1982 Lebanon war, for example, and it suffered a major defeat in the 1973 war. Unable to pay hard currency for weapons, Syria depends on Soviet concessionary aid, and is hence hostage to the Soviet government's reluctance to supply advanced weapons, as well as the relative inferiority of those weapons when compared with Western systems.[53]

ROLE OF BALLISTIC MISSILES. The spread of ballistic missiles in the Middle East significantly heightened Israel's perceptions of military vulnerability, as revealed by its reactions to Iraqi Scud attacks in January 1991. The small size of Israel's territory, which means that strategic targets are within reach of even short-range systems, the concentration of its population and industrial centers, which increases their susceptibility to surprise attack, and its reliance on national mobilization to mount military operations, which could be disrupted by surprise attacks on population centers, all suggest that a preemptive Syrian missile attack, if mounted effectively, could limit Israel's ability to retaliate. Terror attacks on Israeli population centers, moreover, would have profound psychological effects in a country that has such severe sensitivity to casualties.[54]

Some analysts believe that the threat of missile strikes by Arab neighbors could undermine Israel's doctrine of "preemptive counterforce," which aims to limit damage by moving conflict to adversaries' territories and promptly and decisively destroying their ability to wage war.[55] If Syrian missiles were successful in disabling airfields and thus interrupting air operations during the first hours of a surprise attack, Israel could find it impossible to use its superior airpower to provide support for its ground forces and to defend against Syrian aircraft. Under such conditions, Syria could not only move to recapture the Golan but could penetrate into Israel itself.[56]

Figure 4-1. *Ranges of Israeli, Saudi Arabian, and Syrian Missile Systems*

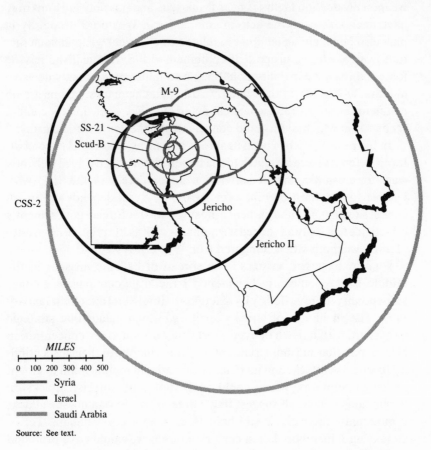

MILES

0   100 200 300 400 500

—— Syria

—— Israel

—— Saudi Arabia

Source: See text.

Given the geography of the region, ballistic missiles are potentially effective even without long ranges. Damascus and Tel Aviv are less than 60 miles from the countries' common border. Missiles can be fired from any site inside Syria and reach all but the extreme southern tip of Israeli territory (figure 4-1). With these distances, warning times of missile attacks would be extremely short.[57]

At present, Syrian missiles would also be able to penetrate Israeli air defenses, something Syria could never accomplish in any significant way with aircraft. In the past the superiority of Israeli air defenses, along with the limitations of Syrian air defenses and the proven talent of Israeli pilots for evading them, accorded Israel a decisive military advantage.

Israel has long relied on its ability to defend against air strikes, an ability in which it has invested heavily. It is taking additional defensive measures to protect against missile attacks, including the effort to develop the Arrow antitactical ballistic missile system, a program to improve its ability to detect and destroy missile launchers, efforts to harden key military installations, and a national program of civil defense.[58]

Unless and until effective Israeli defenses are developed, however, ballistic missiles provide Syria with at least a putative ability to launch a successful surprise attack. According to Aharon Levran, "given the estimated number of accurate SS-21 missiles and launchers in Syria, and adding the less accurate Scuds, whatever their effectiveness, the Syrians, without taking physical risks, can cause significant damage for a limited period of time to vital Israeli military installations, particularly with their SS-21s."[59]

If combined with chemical warheads, Syria's current missile inventory could enable it to launch a preemptive attack against a number of important civilian and military targets. Chemically armed Scuds could terrorize Israeli population centers, while the more accurate SS-21s could disable airfields or staging grounds. According to some analysts, a first strike of this sort could provide Syria with the time to mount a successful ground assault on Israel's northern border to reclaim the Golan Heights.[60] Combined with large-scale investment in defenses and artillery deployments between Damascus and the Golan Heights, Syria could have "the requisite confidence that it can initiate cost-extracting warfare against Israel without intolerable risks to itself."[61]

Although such operations may be possible in theory, and have imposed additional burdens on Israel's defense planning, other factors may mitigate any decisive military advantages that otherwise might accrue from Syria's possession of ballistic missiles. Israel's highly advanced intelligence network, for instance, provides it with strategic warning. Syria would have to prepare a ground offensive before a missile attack if such an operation were to be exploited effectively, and this would permit Israel to mobilize and disperse its aircraft before the attack.

Moreover, projecting a major attack assumes that Syria would be willing to risk the consequences of Israeli retaliation, which could range from conventional strikes against its economic and industrial infrastructure and its army to the selective use of nuclear weapons.[62] Thus one significant military effect of Israel's missile forces is that they imply the possibility of prompt nuclear retaliation, regardless of what Syria may do with air defenses. As such, they deter the likelihood of a surprise attack. It is difficult to envision the stakes that would make Syria consider incurring the risks of such retaliation. Preemptive attack also assumes that Syria would be willing to sanction heavy Arab casualties in the effort to achieve a fairly limited objective.

Still, some analysts argue that Syria's ability to launch a missile strike means it could impose unacceptably high casualties and complicate a prompt response, thus undermining Israel's confidence in its deterrent. This situation could lead Israel to prepare for preemptive action to destroy Syrian missile launchers upon strategic warning of a possible attack, because it would be too late to disarm Syrian missiles after hostilities begin.[63] Facing such a threat, Syria could be expected to develop preemptive tactics as well, putting pressure on both sides to put missiles on hair-trigger alert and launch them quickly in a crisis, possibly even before intelligence of an impending attack could be verified.[64]

Its new ability to launch terror campaigns against Israeli population centers and possibly disable the Israeli air force on the ground may appear to Syria to provide a semblance of parity with Israel's military capability, including its nuclear arsenal. This is an important political objective, because Damascus has long believed that Israeli military superiority has accorded it undue political influence internationally.[65] Similarly, the ability to respond to an Israeli nuclear strike by launching a terror attack with chemically armed missiles may give Syria some additional measure of confidence in its ability to retaliate, further underscoring the perceived benefits of missile forces.[66]

Even before the outset of war in the Persian Gulf, the compensatory efforts Israel undertook to counter the risks of missile attacks from Syria (and other Arab states), including measures for both active and passive defenses, reflect the seriousness with which it takes this threat. Such perceptions obviously help deepen Israeli-Arab hostility. However remote the contingencies that would bring about their effective use, the spread of missiles in this region has brought a new dimension to Israeli perceptions of a threat, which have damaged prospects for broader Arab-Israeli conciliation.

There are other, more indirect political effects stemming from the deployment of missiles in the region. Israel's possession of systems that can strike targets in the Soviet Union, for instance, implies that it has a deterrent against any future Soviet support of traditional Arab clients in a war, a source of major concern in the 1967 and 1973 conflicts. Israeli missile forces also may cause the Soviet Union to lean more heavily on Syria and other Arab antagonists to advance the peace process and may encourage the Soviets to seek closer ties with Israel, a trend already developing under the new political leadership of the Soviet Union.

At the same time, Israel's concerns about the proliferation of missiles among Arab states may provide greater incentives to seek accommodation. For all the states in the region, the uncertainties associated with ballistic missile forces, underscored by the military instability created by Saddam Hussein in 1990, could also lend impetus for regional or bilateral agreements to reduce the risk of future military escalation or terrorism.[67]

Iran and Iraq

The Iran-Iraq war ended in a ceasefire in July 1988, leaving both sides economically and militarily exhausted but without having resolved the disputes that led to the hostilities.[68] Both sides incurred major losses. Iran suffered staggering civilian and military casualties, economic devastation, and Iraqi attacks with chemical weapons while the world turned a blind eye. In 1981 Iraq had started what it thought would be a quick and painless military excursion, only to spend seven years in an all-out war of survival that ended with its having barely recovered its original position, and at a very high price. Neither country achieved its aims. Iran did not succeed in overthrowing the government of Saddam Hussein and, some believe, suffered a humiliating defeat that has further attenuated its geopolitical status.[69] If Iraq's goal was to reclaim the entire Shatt al-' Arab waterway that separates it from Iran, a waterway now rendered useless because of sunken ships and silting, then it suffered a net loss in the war. It did manage to become a leading military power in the region, a status Baghdad sought to demonstrate by invading and annexing Kuwait in 1990.

Despite Iraqi overtures in August 1990 in a failed effort to elicit Iran's support for war aims against Kuwait and Saudi Arabia, Iraq and Iran remain actively antagonistic. And both states have hostile relations with other powers. Some experts have raised concerns that the military destruction of Iraq in January 1991 could tilt the regional balance of power and lead Iran to renewed aggression against its neighbor in the future.

Figure 4-2. *Ranges of Iranian and Iraqi Missile Systems*[a]

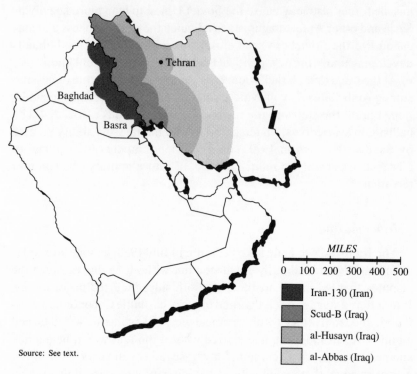

MILES

0   100   200   300   400   500

■ Iran-130 (Iran)

▨ Scud-B (Iraq)

▨ al-Husayn (Iraq)

▨ al-Abbas (Iraq)

Source: See text.

INVENTORIES. At the beginning of the Iran-Iraq war, Iraq's arsenal of missiles was limited, consisting of a small force of Soviet-supplied Scud-Bs and Frog-7s. As originally configured, the Scud-B, with a range of 180 miles, was unable to strike Tehran from Iraqi territory, a distance of 240 to 310 miles from the Iraqi border. In the early stages of the war, however, Iraq did use Frog-7 and Scud-B missiles against Iranian border towns.[70] Unable to obtain longer-range missiles from abroad, Iraq modified its Scud-Bs to extend their range: the Al-Husayn has a range of 375 miles and the al-Abbas 550 miles (figure 4-2). Iraq is also developing two 1,200 mile systems, the al-Abid and the Tammuz-1.

Until the beginning of hostilities over Kuwait, Iraq had a sizable inventory of modern combat aircraft, including Soviet-supplied MiG-23s, MiG-21s, and MiG-29s and the French F-1, which enabled it to maintain clear air superiority over Iran throughout the war, and had been trying to buy the more advanced French Mirage 2000 and the Soviet SU-24 long-range bomber.[71] Some of its recent arms agreements included coproduction contracts with Western countries. Iraq also had an embryonic arms industry that can produce a range of less advanced weapons, now believed to be effectively crippled by American airstrikes.

Although its nuclear program is still limited, Iraq was extremely active in producing chemical weapons. During the war, it made and used both mustard agents and nerve agents against Iranian forces. Iraq was also believed to be actively trying to produce biological weapons.[72]

As witnessed during Operation Desert Storm, the effectiveness of the Iraqi military has been impeded by the lack of an infrastructure for the modern command, control, intelligence, and logistics essential for operating sophisticated equipment. Its successes in the Iran-Iraq war can be attributed in large measure to the massive assistance it received from outside states intent on ensuring an Iranian defeat, its ability to use chemical weapons without fear of retaliation, and the isolation of Iran by the international community, which severely limited Tehran's access to external assistance. In the military operations being conducted over Kuwait, the Iraqi military proved no challenge to the international force, and was severely weakened within a matter of days.[73]

Iran's missile arsenal is less extensive than Iraq's. It did not obtain Scud-Bs until 1985, at first apparently from Libya and subsequently from North Korea. It has begun development of the Oghab missile, which has a range of 25 miles, and the Iran-130, with a range of 80 miles, for which it is receiving Chinese and possibly North Korean assistance (see chapter 3). It has not been able to build up a significant arms industry, although it was able to produce hundreds of Oghab rockets during the war.[74]

Although Iran's missiles have shorter ranges than Iraq's, the distances they need to travel to reach significant targets are also shorter. Baghdad is barely 95 miles from the Iranian border, and the second most important urban center, Basra, is less than 15 miles.

As a consequence of the war, Iran has stepped up its efforts to produce chemical weapons, and there is some indication it is trying to develop a chemical warhead for its ballistic missiles.[75] It is believed to remain highly dependent on foreign sources for the chemical weapon program, however.[76] Iran's plans for integrating chemical weapons into its forces are not clear, but it appears committed to taking any steps necessary to counter Iraqi chemical weapons.[77] It has no significant prospects for developing nuclear warheads but seems to be actively pursuing this option.[78]

Iran's current arsenal reflects the necessarily ad hoc manner in which it has acquired weapons since the overthrow of the Pahlavi regime and especially during the war. There is little compatibility among the weapons, which will make rebuilding its armed forces that much more difficult. In addition, the decision to divide the military between regular forces and the Revolutionary Guards, apparently inspired by the Khomeini government's distrust of the professional military, undercut the capabilities of the armed forces and left an organizational divide that has yet to be bridged.[79]

The Iran-Iraq war illustrates the importance of intangible factors in determining the outcome of conflicts. As Sharam Chubin has argued, "The failure of Iran . . . was due primarily not to any deficiencies in arms supplies or organization, doctrinal inadequacy or shortcomings in training, but first and foremost from a failure in strategy; the inability or refusal to formulate war aims or strategic goals that were attainable, that is, within its capacities."[80] Spurred by parochialism and chauvinism, the leadership's unrealistic goals undercut the strength of the professional military and vitiated the effectiveness of what limited advanced equipment it had at its disposal. Iran's status as a geopolitical pariah and its domestic weakness account for its defeat. Given current conditions there, such factors are likely to continue to determine its relative military strength far more than the status of weapon inventories.

ROLE OF BALLISTIC MISSILES. The success of ballistic missile strikes in the War of the Cities in 1988 that encouraged both sides to end hostilities was less the result of the strikes' military utility than their psychological effects in adding to the atmosphere of desperation and exhaustion that prevailed in both countries.[81] The use of ballistic missiles secured no military gains for either side. It seems instead to have brought home the futility of the enduring stalemate after seven years of combat and thus weakened support for continuing the conflict.[82]

The use of ballistic missiles in this conflict suggests that short-range, conventionally armed ballistic missiles are not a particularly effective military instrument. Still, one legacy was to accord a much more prominent role to ballistic missiles in both states' military modernization plans, opening new relationships with outside powers to supply missile modification and production programs, encouraging stepped-up programs for producing chemical weapons and, perhaps, influencing military strategies to accommodate a greater role for missile forces. For Iraq, at least, the war seems to have reinforced the legitimacy of a doctrine of first use of chemical and possibly biological weapons.[83] Partly because of Iraqi rhetoric, the threat of Iraqi missile strikes played a vital role in the preparation for and tactics of Operation Desert Storm, leading to massive targeting of Iraq's missile installations and launchers.

For Iran, some analysts have observed that missiles are a particularly attractive alternative to aircraft, in part because of the government's mistrust of the professional air force. Missiles provide a means to conduct long-range military missions without having to use trained pilots or maintenance crews, which are now extremely scarce as well as politically suspect. As one analyst remarked, "It is no surprise that the Scuds are in the hands of the most militant element of the armed forces, the Islamic Revolutionary Guard, rather than the army."[84]

For now, the military significance of ballistic missiles in a future conflict involving Iraq or Iran is questionable. Iraq's military objectives have been blunted for the forseeable future. But even if both were able to launch chemically armed ballistic missiles, their limited accuracy would narrow target choices to cities or troop concentrations, and the weaknesses of both sides' other military forces would make securing a decisive military advantage difficult. Although breakthroughs in missile accuracy cannot be ruled out, the pace of the missile programs in both states will be heavily influenced by financial constraints, the competing demands of economic recovery and, for Iraq, the effects of military devestation.

Before its invasion of Kuwait, Iraq was intent on developing a chemical weapon force, partly by investing heavily in its missile programs (see chapter 3). In early 1990 President Hussein threatened to use chemical weapons should Israel attempt to attack Iraq with nuclear weapons.[85] In so doing, Iraq established the precedent of threatening to use chemical weapons to deter nuclear threats, threats that are now hollow. But as an Indian observer noted, the linkage of nuclear and chemical weapons may affect attitudes "of many countries facing perceived nuclear threats and not having the capability or inclination to possess nuclear deterrence" and may undermine any potential support for an international ban on chemical weapons.[86]

The spread of ballistic missiles is increasing the costs and potential risks of the regional military rivalry, even if it is not according either side decisive military advantages. Iran's competition with Iraq seems to have entrenched its determination to develop modern missiles and chemical weapons. The possession of chemical weapons by Iran poses potential consequences for outside powers—not just Israel but all the states in the region—and could have the effect of legitimating their acquisition throughout the Arab world. Possession also raises the possibility of irrational or unplanned use in this highly volatile region where political control of military forces is uneasy and weapons may be diverted to terrorists or subnational groups. Iraq's venture into Kuwait demonstrates that missiles are yet to play a decisive role in regional military operations, but their presence in the Persian Gulf and the belief, however inaccurate, that they might be used to deliver chemical weapons severely heightened regional and international tensions.

India and Pakistan

The antagonism between India and Pakistan, underscored by three wars in less than forty years, stems from deep disparities in ethnic and religious affiliations, political ideologies, military objectives, and the sizes of their territories, populations, and armed forces. These disparities have left the two countries in an enduring state of imbalance.[87]

India sees itself as a regional power on a par with China and is determined to extend its political and military reach beyond the Asian subcontinent. As a senior diplomat in New Delhi has commented, "India's military expansion is not so much part of a strategic assessment as a view of India's proper place in the world."[88] Relations with Pakistan are only one factor in India's political and military calculations and, at least in some public declarations, not the most important factor by far. Nevertheless, in its effort to match the military capabilities of the Chinese, India has achieved the potential to defeat Pakistan at any level of military confrontation.

Pakistan views India's aspirations as a direct challenge to its sovereignty and security. The geography of Pakistan, including a concentration of population centers and major military installations near the Indian border and a lack of territorial depth, saddle it with intractable disadvantages.[89] Military planning in Pakistan is almost wholly directed at achieving some kind of parity with its eastern neighbor. But whereas Pakistan sees all military developments in India as potential threats, India dismisses Pakistan's concerns, emphasizing that its broader military aspirations cannot be judged from this parochial perspective.

Although officially nonaligned, India is tied to the Soviet Union through a treaty of friendship and cooperation and, until recently, received most of its advanced weapon systems from the Soviets. It has been engaged in a major program of military expansion since 1980, including efforts to produce weapons using Western technology and to enhance its nuclear weapons capabilities, which it first demonstrated in a "peaceful" explosion in 1974.[90]

Since the Soviet invasion of Afghanistan in 1979, Pakistan's access to U.S. assistance and arms supplies has been second only to that of Israel and Egypt.[91] Its nuclear weapon capability has been significantly advanced in the past few years, in part because the United States has suspended many of its more stringent strictures against Pakistan's nuclear program.[92] Pakistan's nuclear program is intended as a deterrent against India's overwhelming conventional and nuclear superiority.[93]

INVENTORIES. Both India and Pakistan have recently demonstrated their ability to build ballistic missiles. India has successfully tested the Privthi, with a range of 150 miles, and the Agni, which has a potential range of more than 1,500 miles with a payload of 1,000 kilograms (figure 4-3). Pakistan claims to have successfully tested two indigenously produced surface-to-surface missiles in February 1989, the Hatf I and Hatf II, with ranges of 50 and 186 miles respectively, and a payload capacity of 500 kilograms. Another system with a range of 372 miles is reportedly under development.[94] It is unlikely that any of these missiles have been deployed. According to Indian sources, the decision to go forward with mass production of the Agni is still pending, although the Privthi is reportedly slated for deployment in 1991.[95]

The two countries' abilities to project military power outside their territories is restricted for now to their combat aircraft. The Indian air force flies a wide array of Soviet aircraft in addition to some British Jaguar and French Mirage 2000 aircraft. The Soviet MiG-29, its longest-range fighter, has a maximum combat radius of 715 miles, which would allow it to cover all of Pakistan but falls far short of the range needed to reach strategic targets in China.[96] The Pakistani air force flies the U.S.-supplied F-16, the French Mirage III and Mirage V, and a number of obsolescent aircraft provided by China. Pakistan's longest-range aircraft, the Mirage V, has a maximum combat radius of 800 miles, which is insufficient to cover major targets in India.[97]

However ambitious their current plans, financial constraints are likely to slow the pace of Indian and Pakistani programs or force them to seek revenues from outside sources to offset increasingly prohibitive costs, or both. India announced in early 1989 that it was beginning a more aggressive arms export program, for example, while Pakistan is deter-

Figure 4-3. *Ranges of Indian and Pakistani Missile Systems*

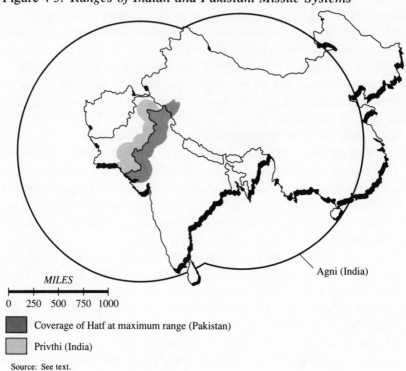

MILES

0	250	500	750	1000

■ Coverage of Hatf at maximum range (Pakistan)

☐ Privthi (India)

Source: See text.

mined to become a major arms producer for the Arab world, which is already a critical source of funding. Because of financial pressures, Pakistan is also believed to have signed an agreement to train Iranian nuclear engineers.[98]

ROLE OF BALLISTIC MISSILES. The addition of the Privthi and Agni missiles to India's arsenal could provide it with various new military options. Both systems could circumvent Pakistani air defenses in a surprise attack and could reach virtually all of Pakistan's important industrial and population centers, which are located along its eastern border with India. The range of the Agni would allow India to reach targets in China, the Arabian peninsula, and the southern Soviet Union as well (see figure 4-4). Agni missiles armed with high-explosive or chemical warheads could disrupt airfields and destroy other military installations throughout Pakistan, assuming the missiles achieve sufficient accuracy. The range of the Agni, moreover, makes it possible for

India to base it in the south, beyond the range of current Pakistani aircraft or missiles.[99]

The deployment of the Hatf missiles would not extend Pakistan's reach deep into India; indeed, the Hatf I, with its range of 185 miles, could barely reach the outskirts of New Delhi. A system with a range of 372 miles could reach the capital and other population centers. The deployment of the missiles it has actually developed could ensure Pakistan's ability to deliver munitions on Indian soil, but with limited military effect unless they were armed with nuclear warheads.

The inaccuracy of the models now being developed by both sides suggests that they would be useful only as delivery vehicles for nonconventional weapons. The Indian government maintains that both the Privthi and the Agni will be sufficiently accurate to be effective as conventional systems, but this is doubtful. And the commander-in-chief of Pakistan's army said in late 1989 that the new longer-range missile Pakistan has under development "is not so sophisticated in terms of guidance because we don't have [the] technology."[100] Neither state seems to be interested in acquiring chemical weapons for their own forces, although both could produce chemical agents.[101]

Given the balance in the region and India's clear superiority, the military significance of deployments depends largely on whether the missiles are armed with nuclear weapons. Advances in conventionally armed missiles eventually could prove militarily significant, but only over the very long run. Some Pakistani analysts have expressed concern about the consequences of a continued technological rivalry between the two states that would lead to wider diffusion of highly sophisticated conventional capabilities.[102] But the crucial matter now is the connection between missile and nuclear proliferation.

If Indian and Pakistani missile development hastens the pace of nuclear deployments, the consequences for regional and international stability could be important, depending on whether forces were deployed survivably and with sufficient assurances that they would not be used preemptively. Nuclear deployments in the region may or may not be inherently destabilizing, but neither India nor Pakistan has sufficient experience in doctrine or command and control to ensure stable deterrence.[103] Nuclear-armed Hatf missiles could allow Pakistan to retaliate against industrial centers in northern India and thus deter Indian aggression. With its entire territory within range of Indian missiles and aircraft, however, Pakistan could not be assured that its nuclear forces would survive an Indian first strike. If Indian missile deployments intensify fears of a preemptive attack on missile installations, Pakistan could be induced to adapt preemptive strategies as well.[104]

The proliferation of missiles in the subcontinent could have even more important international consequences. India's interest in developing long-range missiles stems more from its concerns about China than about Pakistan. India does not need long-range missiles to attack Pakistan, for which it has more than enough advanced strike aircraft. The deployment of missiles with the range of the Agni puts a number of important Chinese industrial and military centers within India's reach. If based in the far eastern Indian state of Arunachel Pradesh, the Agni would put Beijing within reach. Were India to improve the accuracy of its missiles to be useful against hard targets, it might be able to attack Chinese missiles with conventional as well as nuclear warheads.[105] This is still a distant technological prospect, however.

An Indian threat to Chinese missile forces could lead to far-reaching instabilities. It would impinge on relationships throughout the region and would necessarily involve the Soviet Union because India could theoretically alter the Sino-Soviet balance. China might then take action against what it perceived to be provocation by India that could pose risks to Pakistan as well.

In addition to seeking a counterdeterrent to China's nuclear forces, India's efforts to develop its own missiles reflect the complexity of its regional relationships. The recent movement toward Sino-Soviet rapprochement may have encouraged New Delhi to seek greater independence in defense capabilities, including missile production, in anticipation that ties with Moscow might weaken. China's sale of CSS-2 intermediate-range missiles to Saudi Arabia, which the Indian government viewed as Beijing's way of strengthening Saudi-Chinese ties and indirectly threatening India because of the close relations between Saudi Arabia and Pakistan, may also have reinforced Indian resolve. And China's ongoing relationship with Pakistan may suggest that Beijing would be willing to intervene in a war between Pakistan and India, a development that India might hope to forestall by developing a missile force capable of striking targets within Chinese territory.[106]

A missile force could also help India project more influence in the Indian Ocean. New Delhi has long objected to the presence of American nuclear forces there, and officials have sometimes complained that India is encircled by the three nuclear powers—the United States, the Soviet

Union, and China—operating in the region. As one analyst noted, intermediate-range nuclear missiles, "which would nominally extend India's reach from Beijing to the Persian Gulf, could serve as a political counter to these pressures and unambiguously establish India's credentials as a regional superpower."[107]

India's military ambitions impinge so directly on interests outside the region that the consequences of missile proliferation cannot be gauged by the effects on Pakistan alone. Any alteration of the Indo-Pakistani military balance is outweighed by the overall pace of nuclear proliferation on the subcontinent and the tensions that might be engendered elsewhere, particularly in China. The significance of India's missile capability thus stems from its association with India's nuclear program, which together could enable the country to project a nuclear force over a large part of the Eurasian land mass.

North Korea and South Korea

North and South Korea are almost as antagonistic today as they were just after World War II. With U.S. troops and nuclear weapons stationed in South Korea to act as a tripwire for American involvement should conflict break out, and with the Soviet Union and China supporting the North to some degree, the stakes of a military confrontation between the two adversaries could be very high. The delicate balance means that Moscow, Beijing, and Washington have an inherent interest in avoiding war in the Korean Peninsula, given the clear likelihood of escalation to a major, and possibly nuclear, conflict.[108]

The ceasefire negotiated at the end of the Korean War in 1953 established a demilitarized zone two kilometers on either side of the border between the two countries. South Korea maintains defenses thirty miles deep along the entire length of the DMZ, while North Korea concentrates its defenses just north of the Uijongbu Corridor, a strategic choke point along the border.[109]

Aggression from the North through direct conflict or, as is more likely, through infiltration or subversion, preoccupies South Korean security planners. Because of Seoul's proximity to the DMZ, South Korea also is concerned about its vulnerability to a surprise attack. It has always maintained a highly prepared, very high quality military force to offset the disadvantages of geography and the North's quantitative strength.

North Korea remains committed to violent reunification of the Korean peninsula. Because of its repressive and bellicose regime, it has become progressively more isolated internationally and in recent years has quarreled with China and the Soviet Union, its major suppliers, about its military objectives.[110] Its ability to impose extreme austerity on its population has allowed the government to devote more than 20 percent of the national budget to military priorities, resulting in an armed force disproportionate to its resources (and defensive needs).[111]

Both sides maintain large military establishments and weapon inventories. North Korea has larger ground forces, with more than 3,000 Soviet-supplied battle tanks and a large number of combat aircraft, including the advanced Soviet MiG-29. South Korean forces are technologically superior and include various U.S.-supplied combat aircraft such as the F-16. South Korea's defense industry, which has developed significantly since the 1970s, can produce relatively sophisticated equipment.[112]

INVENTORIES. South Korea began to develop its own ballistic missiles in the mid-1970s. It converted Nike-Hercules surface-to-air missiles supplied by the United States into two versions of a surface-to-surface missile, with ranges of 100 miles and 136 to 156 miles. It also has the U.S. Honest John unguided missile with a range of 24 miles.

North Korea was first reported to have acquired Scud-B missiles in 1988. Although they were originally thought to have come from the Soviet Union, analysts now believe they were acquired from Egypt. North Korea has since begun producing its own version for domestic use and export markets. With technical assistance from China and financial support from Iran, it is reported to be developing a version of the Scud with a range of 270 to 280 miles. It has also imported the Soviet Frog-7, with a range of 40 miles, which it has reverse-engineered.[113]

ROLE OF BALLISTIC MISSILES. Given the size of North and South Korean military forces and the operational constraints on ballistic missiles and the limited numbers of models currently available, possession of the missiles by either side does not now decisively alter the regional balance. Neither state's missiles extend their combat reach. With a radius of 575 miles, the South Korean F-16 fighter can cover all of North Korea, while the North's MiG-29s, with a radius of 715 miles, can reach all of the South and almost to Japan.[114]

Ballistic missiles may become significant, however, because of their potential to penetrate air defenses and deliver nonconventional warheads. North Korea has a chemical weapon production program, and South Korea is believed to be seeking to acquire such a capability.[115] Both have expressed interest in nuclear weapons, a development forestalled in the South by the U.S. military commitment and diplomatic persuasion, and slowed in the North by Soviet pressure and limitations on access to nuclear materials, although regional and international concern about the North is very high.[116]

Because both Seoul and Pyongyang fall within the ranges of existing missiles, the possibility of a preemptive attack on population centers is feasible. An attack on Seoul has inherent military significance for South Korea—this is where it maintains military headquarters. Other military targets could also be vulnerable. Except for Pusan, where U.S. military personnel are stationed, almost all of South Korea's air bases are within range of the Scud-B (figure 4-4).[117] The Scud-B might be able to reach the military installation at Kunsan, where U.S. nuclear artillery shells and aerial bombs are alleged to be stored.[118] Because of the short distances, the speed of ballistic missile attacks could further seriously undermine stability. A Frog missile launched from bases in North Korea could reach Seoul in eight minutes; a Scud could reach major industrial areas in Ulsan and Pusan in thirty.[119]

For now, the significance of ballistic missile development in the two Koreas is more political than military. Both have demonstrated their willingness to defy the strictures of suppliers and pursue missile programs as a symbol of sovereignty and military independence, their pronounced dependency on their respective benefactors notwithstanding.

Seoul's aspiration to develop a missile that could hit Pyongyang is an important indicator of its willingness to risk friction with the United States on behalf of a nationalistic ambition. Its pursuit of this development program, moreover, has been an important barometer of its capabilities in military research and development. Seoul has also found that it could use the threat of continuing or accelerating such activities, as with its latent nuclear ambitions, to gain important concessions from the United States in weapon and technology transfers.

Similarly North Korea's acquisition of Scud-Bs was not sanctioned by the Soviet Union and represented the first significant breach between the two states over military policy. North Korea's modification of the Scud for export and its sales to Iran, among others, have proceeded despite Soviet efforts to stop these activities.[120] The Soviet Union is also finding itself pressured to provide other kinds of armaments to North Korea to maintain some measure of influence.[121]

The attenuation of superpower influence over the Koreas and the

Figure 4-4. *Ranges of North Korean and South Korean Missile Systems*

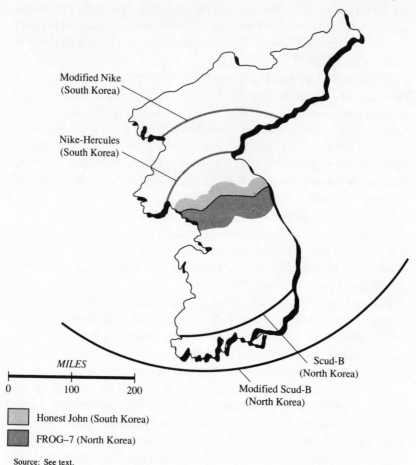

Modified Nike
(South Korea)

Nike-Hercules
(South Korea)

MILES

0   100   200

Scud-B
(North Korea)

Modified Scud-B
(North Korea)

Honest John (South Korea)

FROG–7 (North Korea)

Source: See text.

willingness of Seoul and Pyongyang to pursue military programs that could prove destabilizing might well become a problem. Despite periodic evidence of Seoul's clandestine efforts, the United States has so far been successful in dissuading South Korea from pursuing a nuclear program by offering sufficient compensation or threatening sanctions. But as South Korea becomes a more fully independent economic and military power, such measures may prove less effective, especially if the United States begins to reduce its troops on the peninsula. U.S. troop withdrawals could be stalled if opposition from the South Korean government is accompanied by threats to develop destabilizing forces.

The estrangement of the North Korean regime from the Soviet government, and Pyongyang's increasing willingness to pursue independent military objectives may also threaten the stability of the region. North Korea's interest in using missiles as an export commodity could help it strengthen bonds with like-minded states, as well as add to the availability of missile technologies internationally.

Given the risks of aggression by either party, their development of missile capabilities, even combined with chemical warheads, does not necessarily raise the likelihood of war. But should the North Korean regime develop a better ability to launch surprise attacks and should it believe that the attacks would cripple a prompt and effective response from the South and the United States, the threat of aggression may rise. The acquisition of missiles could contribute to such a North Korean perception. Similarly, if North Korea can acquire the requisite materials, missile forces could speed nuclear deployments in the North, which would also contribute to regional instabilities. Indeed, by providing incentives for South Korea and Japan to acquire nuclear weapons, nuclear-armed missiles in the North could have tremendous regional and international consequences.

Conclusion

By traditional measures of utility, most ballistic missiles in third world arsenals are of limited military significance. The systems are generally too inaccurate to strike at military targets effectively or to give aggressors confidence that such attacks could result in decisive military gains. Operational limitations, limits on the quantities available through purchase or indigenous production, and the presence of other military forces to deter their use combine to make the systems little more than symbolic augmentations of nations' military sovereignty.

This conclusion, however, may change in the coming years. Improvements in missile accuracy, aided by the diffusion of guidance technology from the industrial countries, technological breakthroughs on the part of emerging producers, and the commercial availability of satellite imagery to assist in targeting are already on the horizon.[122] If third world states couple accurate delivery with nuclear or advanced conventional weapons, the global military calculus could alter dramatically.

Although high costs and technical constraints have already pushed some states to their technological limits, the potential availability of lower-cost alternatives, including cruise missiles adapted from drones and remotely piloted vehicles, could extend the proliferation of missiles well beyond the regions and countries now under consideration.[123]

As third world missile forces improve, and especially as longer-range systems become more widely available, regional demarcations between combatants may become blurred, so that these missile forces may begin to pose consequences far beyond their borders. The Indian Agni, for instance, can reach targets in China and the southern territory of the Soviet Union. Missiles being developed by Israel could reach even further into the Soviet Union. CIA Director William Webster has claimed that six countries will have missiles with ranges of more than 500 miles by the end of the century, and three may have missiles with ranges of up to 2,500 miles.[124]

The global proliferation of missiles may increasingly impinge on the superpowers' ability to reduce their own militaries and may create new incentives for them to deploy strategic defenses. Proliferation may also fuel the interests of other states to acquire defenses, including the kind of antitactical ballistic missile forces being developed by the United States and Israel. Such a development might prompt the kind of competitive offensive and defensive deployments that have been discussed in the strategic context and could prove destabilizing in certain regions.

As seen in the recent Persian Gulf operations, industrial countries' forces and bases could become increasingly susceptible to perceptions of risks posed by third world powers, with uncertain consequences. The greatest risk may be the legitimation of chemical weapons as an alternative or counter to nuclear weapons. At a minimum, this would impose higher economic burdens on the industrial states to protect their populations and adapt military countermeasures to reduce the threat posed by new, chemically armed missile powers. A key concern of the U.S. military as it moved to counter Iraqi aggression in Kuwait was the fear that Baghdad would use chemical weapons, a contingency that could severely hamper U.S. military operations in future conflicts.

It is possible to identify the outlines of what is required to create conditions of stability between military antagonists, or at least to extrapolate these from the superpowers' experience since World War II. According to the traditional logic of deterrence, there are five essential requirements: neither antagonist should see advantages from striking the other preemptively; both sides should have stable command and control systems under competent political authority that can function effectively even under the stress of crisis; forces operating in peacetime should be configured in a manner that does not signal provocative intent; confidence-building and verification agreements should be concluded to reassure an adversary that no clandestine efforts are being undertaken that could significantly alter the balance; and the fear of inadvertent or accidental launch, including launch as a result of terrorist action, should be reduced to a minimum.[125]

In light of the volatile political-military conditions in most developing regions, one cannot say that these requirements for deterrence exist today or that they will be easy to create in areas of marked tension. Aside from the fact that the superpowers' experience pertained to a bipolar system that had the benefit of agreed territorial boundaries, the superpowers have had four decades to manage their transition to relative equilibrium.

Heightened military and political tensions associated with missile deployments may be transitional phenomena, the price paid by countries as they develop modern military forces. The consequences of these tensions for regional and international stability are not predictable. They will depend on the countries in question and the policies they pursue. Managing the complexities of a multipolar deterrent structure, however, will certainly be more complicated than has been anticipated by most industrial governments and may require them to take the third world seriously for the first time.

CHAPTER FIVE

The Proliferation of Conventional Technology: The Bureaucratic Dimension

THE TRANSFER of military technology to allied and friendly states has been an integral part of U.S. policy for more than four decades. In addition to exporting finished weapon systems, the United States has sold or otherwise supplied blueprints and technical data, manufacturing equipment and expertise for assembly, and entire production lines for weapon development and manufacture.

But how America treats technology transfers varies according to the U.S. and world economic and political climate, and the content, type, and destination of the exports. The United States has aggressively promoted the sale of advanced military technology to Western Europe since the 1960s, but has subjected technology diffusion to the Soviet Union and Eastern Europe to an elaborate system of restraint since the 1940s. Transfers to the developing world, although increasing in quantity and sophistication throughout most of the postwar era, have been encouraged or controlled depending on the political environment prevailing in the United States and the international or regional circumstances. Some exports, such as components and materials related to nuclear weapons, are subject to almost blanket prohibition under international agreement. Some highly advanced weapons considered vital to maintaining U.S. technological superiority, such as low-observable (stealth) technology, are controlled unilaterally. In short, there are almost as many means by which technology is transferred or controlled as there are types and sources.

This chapter describes the elements of the U.S. and international

98

systems for controlling transfers that affect the direct or indirect diffusion of missile and other advanced military technologies from industrial countries to the developing world. The institutions for managing this trade cover two categories of transfers: security assistance and military investment that flow directly from industrial to developing countries, and technologies transferred from the United States to other industrial states that may be deliberately or inadvertently retransferred. Although the two categories are intricately interrelated, they are discussed separately here to clarify their special roles.

Describing the regime for controlling the diffusion of technology internationally poses a number of definitional problems. U.S. policy on technology transfers is fragmented intellectually and institutionally. It cuts across traditional demarcations of economic, military, and diplomatic interests, and it impinges on such disparate elements of broader domestic and foreign policies as commercial investments and export promotion, management of the domestic defense industrial base, strategic trade controls, development and security assistance, and international trade cartels for controlling technologies used in nuclear and chemical weapons.

There is a tendency among analysts to discuss the process for regulating technology transfer as if it consisted of distinct formal policy instruments operating independently, a bias replicated in the bureaucracy. Efforts to control technology flows to the third world, for example, have not been coordinated systematically with export controls on flows to the Soviet Union and Eastern Europe, despite the increasing overlap in the two spheres as advanced technologies diffuse globally. Similarly, the potential contribution of civilian investments in technology, subsidized by multilateral lending institutions, to developing countries' defense production capabilities has rarely been taken into account, even if the components or processes may be used in military programs. Despite their apparent significance to emerging missile programs, for example, transfers of so-called dual-use technologies through commercial channels were only recently recognized as warranting greater control.

Weaknesses in U.S. policies regulating technology transfers have been accentuated by the rapid changes and growing complexity of the international technology market. Commercially available components of military significance, including guidance and telemetry equipment, satellites, and computer technology, have contributed to developing countries' capacity for independent or quasi-independent weapon production. The military production programs of a growing number of countries have also benefited from an expanding international system of commercial entrepreneurs involved in military trade that operates outside direct U.S. control.

The evolution of the international technology market has not been accompanied by commensurate changes in the bureaucratic apparatus regulating it. Complex jurisdictional structures established for promoting or restraining transactions have evolved into a highly stratified bureaucratic system rife with discontinuities and contradictions. For instance, a decision in 1986 to sell advanced computers to India through commercial channels, heralded as "a major opportunity to increase American influence in that nation at the expense of the Soviet Union," was followed in 1989 by concerns about India's potential use of supercomputers in its missile development program, a program the United States is trying to discourage.[1] Similarly, the effort to dissuade countries from acquiring nuclear technology, which has usually involved compensatory transfers of conventional weapons and production technology, has provided these same countries with the ability to produce the advanced technologies needed to develop and deliver nuclear forces. Tel Aviv's ongoing effort to acquire a supercomputer from the United States has encountered vigorous opposition from those in the executive branch and Congress, who see the acquisition as contributing to Israel's nuclear weapons capability. Supporters of the sale argue that denial of the transaction would not only lose business for American companies but reduce what leverage the United States retains over the direction of Israel's nuclear program.[2]

The disparities in objectives and practices among agencies that oversee technology transfers impede the implementation of coherent guidelines. Even the modest guidelines of the Missile Technology Control Regime, for example, have provoked protracted interagency disputes over interpretation. And a common feature in discussions about controls imposed through the Coordinating Committee on Multilateral Export Controls (COCOM)—internecine controversies among the Commerce, State, and Defense Departments, and between Congress and the executive branch, not to mention among allies—have plagued efforts to implement coherent export controls for decades.[3] Recent efforts to revise COCOM guidelines and related U.S. policy to better reflect altered relations between East and West have prompted many of the same divisions, with even greater vitriol.[4]

These altered relations and other changes in the international environment have, however, pointed up the need for a more comprehensive and integrated decisionmaking apparatus for controlling military trade. In 1988 a task force report for the House Foreign Affairs Committee urged that the Foreign Assistance Act of 1961 be completely revised to define "a new framework, and a new purpose." The report described the legislation regulating U.S. security and economic assistance as "strewn with obsolete, ambiguous and contradictory policies, restrictions and conditions."[5] A 1988 report for the Department of Defense urged a major reorientation of U.S. security programs. It charged that ineffectual policies on acquisitions and on funding research and development had meant that the United States "lagged in fielding weapons systems needed to cope with the increasingly capable forces of the . . . lesser adversaries of the Third World" and had failed to meet the security requirements of friendly developing states.[6]

Attention to these problems does not suggest a consensus about means for reforming U.S. policy nor that there are political foundations for major alterations. Disaffection with current policy, however, is widespread and is based on a common perception that the U.S. technology transfer regime is conceptually adrift. The first step, then, toward reform requires an understanding of the structure of the existing apparatus. Proposals for reforms, based on an analysis of current inefficiencies and contradictions, are presented in chapter 6.

Security Assistance

For most of the 1950s and early 1960s, the United States used grant aid and transfers of military materiel to help promote the recovery of Western Europe and advance the policy of global containment. Recipients of U.S. weapons and technology were close allies, and decisions about transfers were guided by considerations of U.S. force planning, which were based on assessments of how recipient countries could supplement an American military response in the event of aggression by the Soviet Union in a general conventional war.[7] Exports were concessionary—mostly obsolescent equipment. Assisting countries to develop defense capabilities was seen as a way to recreate in the non-Communist world a system of collective security unified against a common threat.

Aid to developing countries during the Truman and Eisenhower administrations was overshadowed by the priority given to Europe and was largely symbolic. Although the Truman administration's Point Four program pledged a bold new effort to make "the benefits of our scientific advance and industrial progress available for the improvement and growth of underdeveloped areas," its purpose was to encourage political support for the United States, not to promote the military modernization of sovereign countries.[8]

As U.S. assistance extended beyond Western Europe to countries outside the immediate arena of U.S.-Soviet military rivalry, rationales for providing aid expanded accordingly. The Kennedy administration's concerns about internal security in Latin American and Asian countries provided a more explicit basis for military aid. As an element of the nation-building approach to the third world epitomized by the Alliance for Progress, the administration reoriented security assistance programs to include economic assistance, assistance for counterinsurgency efforts, and other measures to improve the stability of friendly regimes. In addition to promoting the compatibility of the arms used by a recipient's military forces, weapon transfers became means to influence a country's political and economic evolution. The transfers signified American support for a country's regime and implied reciprocal obligations for the recipient to pursue policies consistent with American interests.[9]

Throughout the 1950s and 1960s the superpowers dominated the sale of military technology. As the United States bolstered Western European defenses, the Soviet Union transferred arms to improve the defense capabilities of Warsaw Pact allies, although the transfers were intended to reinforce their status as Soviet military surrogates. Following a sale of arms to Egypt in 1955—its first outside the Warsaw Pact—Moscow began to rely on arms transfers to forge political relationships with newly independent states. Offers of weapons to countries in the Middle East, in particular, became a way to establish an international political and military presence and to try to discourage the creation of American bases in countries proximate to its southern flank.[10]

Both the United States and the Soviet Union based their use of military transfers on the largely unquestioned premise that recipient countries would remain loyal to their supplier. Given the marked dependency of these countries on many forms of outside assistance and their limited ability to purchase arms from other sources, the assumption

Figure 5-1. *Arms Transfer Agreements with the Third World, Selected Years, 1975–89*

Billions of constant 1989 dollars

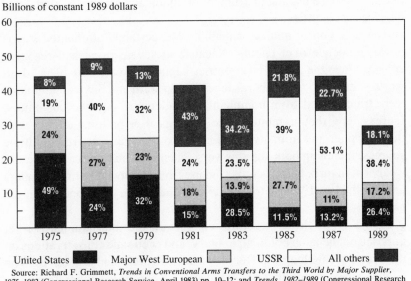

United States ■ Major West European ▨ USSR ☐ All others ■

Source: Richard F. Grimmett, *Trends in Conventional Arms Transfers to the Third World by Major Supplier, 1975–1982* (Congressional Research Service, April 1983) pp. 10–12; and *Trends, 1982–1989* (Congressional Research Service, June 1990), tables 1A and 1B.

a. Western Europe includes France, the United Kingdom, West Germany, and Italy.

was reasonable. By the mid-1970s, however, intense competition among all the Western industrial countries (and some industrializing countries such as Israel) to sell advanced armaments to an ever larger number of clients had breached the superpower monopoly (figure 5-1).

The beginnings of the transformation of the international trade in technology were marked in 1969 by the advent of the Nixon Doctrine, which announced changes in U.S. arms transfer policy. The declared objective of the policy was to promote self-reliance among friendly countries in place of continued dependence on U.S. interventionary forces. But it also tacitly recognized a growing necessity to accommodate developing countries' demands for greater autonomy in military matters and recognized a corresponding weakening of the effectiveness of traditional instruments of diplomacy, particularly U.S. overseas troop deployments and concessionary military programs. As the patterns of trade between industrial and industrializing countries shifted to emphasize the competitive selling of technology either for cash or resources, recipients' dependency on suppliers and suppliers' influence on recipients diminished accordingly. Once perceived as an instrument solely of the superpowers' commitment to security relations, the sale of advanced military technology, including production technology, evolved in the 1970s as a leading instrument of diplomacy among industrial and developing countries.

The diffusion of military capability has certainly attenuated super-power influence over clients. Because of severe fiscal and resource constraints in the industrial countries beginning in the mid-1970s, third world states with more liberal access to Western and Soviet technology were transformed from compliant dependents to coveted customers. Increasingly, they exhibited little ideological or political affinity with their supplier and in many cases began to receive arms from multiple sources, including both superpowers. Their new ability to manufacture weapons, in turn, helped convert many from clients into arms suppliers and, by the late 1980s, into commercial and military competitors of the great powers.

In the 1980s these structural changes in the international market imposed challenging political, military, and economic considerations on the use of technology transfers for advancing national objectives. The common assumption that industrial states would inevitably retain suffi-cient technological superiority to vitiate potential threats from develop-ing nations began to be tested more seriously. Attacks on military forces of the industrial powers by third world forces armed with fairly sophisticated weapons occurred several times in the mid- to late-1980s: Argentinian pilots operating aircraft armed with French-supplied Exocet missiles attacked British forces in the Falklands in 1982. Iran attacked U.S. tankers in the Persian Gulf during its war with Iraq. Libya launched Scud-B missiles against a U.S. military base in Italy in 1986. New producers of weapons also developed their own arms sales relationships, often despite superpower opposition (see chapter 2). And America's concerns about its loss of technological and commercial competitive-ness, which had focused on exports of technology and expertise by other industrial states, began to include industrializing states as well.

The formal criteria guiding U.S. security assistance have remained more or less the same since the 1960s, with administrations adopting particular emphases according to their political biases and objectives. As a practical matter, the criteria for approving or denying transfers have been defined so broadly that they can cover a multitude of contingencies. For example, official policy encourages the sale of military technology to "strengthen an ally, [enhance] free world defense, aid internal security, increase standardization, obtain U.S. military rights, foster U.S. influence, indicate support for collective measures, and promote cordial relations.'' The criteria for denying sales, equally vague and all-encompassing, include whether a proposed transfer could "promote nuclear proliferation, increase chances of hostilities, upset the balance of power, promote arms races, risk compromise of classified U.S. information, risk loss of technical advantage, create an excessive economic burden, add overly sophisticated weaponry, or arm a dictatorship.''[11] Even when guidelines were tightened during the Carter administration, the bureaucracy was left to work out the relative importance to be given particular criteria in adjudicating proposed sales.

In practice, the sheer volume of requests for the approval of arms sales has meant that most military licenses granted each year are approved or denied with little scrutiny or debate. Of the 80,000 license requests or agreements processed annually through the State Department's Office of Munitions Control (renamed the Center for Defense Trade in January 1990), for example, probably less than 20 percent are referred to other agencies for review and less than 1 percent to Congress.[12] And most decisions are approved or denied on the routine recommendations of mid-level personnel; only rarely are they examined by more senior officials.

In controversial cases the review process becomes a diffuse mix of technical, political, and military judgments that derive as much from transitory political considerations and agencies' various interpretations of policy as from any formal statutes or precedents. Although some export guidelines, such as prohibitions on the transfer of nuclear weapons or the embargo on the sale of arms to South Africa, are enduring and clear-cut, interagency deliberations about significant transactions are rarely driven by objective assessments of long-term national security.

Even if detailed formal criteria existed to guide decisionmaking, they would conflict with the array of military, political, and economic interests brought to bear in considering major arms sales. The irrelevance of formal guidelines is illustrated in the list of countries eligible by law to receive U.S. military equipment, which, the Congressional Research Service notes, includes one country that "no longer exists as such (the Republic of Vietnam) and several for which sales have been suspended or no longer appear to support U.S. security or world peace (such as Cambodia, Laos, Ethiopia, Libya, Afghanistan, Iran, and Nicaragua). There is no requirement that such countries be determined ineligible by the President or removed from the list.''[13] Similarly, the Export Administration Act stipulates that commercial exports must be controlled if they might compromise national security but not at the expense of the U.S. economy. Vague guidelines and contradictory directives leave wide latitude to subjective judgment in deciding the merits of proposed sales.

The recurring patterns of interagency disputes, reflecting long-standing institutional biases, are far more important determinants of policy than formal criteria. Although in theory all agencies are supposed to operate with a coherent and consistent concept of "the national interest," this is not the case. The State Department is typically most concerned about political and diplomatic effects of arms transactions; the Department of Defense and its constituent agencies, about the effects on recipients' military capabilities and the benefits of arms exports for U.S. military planning. The Commerce Department, which has become a more prominent interpreter of policy as commercial technologies have commanded a larger share of military trade, tends to protect American economic competitiveness and often opposes export controls on these grounds.[14]

The outcome of deliberations on arms sales is often influenced by the clout of the agencies involved, the perceived importance of the recipient in domestic politics, and even the expertise or endurance of the agencies and officials involved in evaluating cases. Bureaucratic warfare rather than analysis becomes the modus operandi in what is often a protracted process of plea bargaining and political compromise that may or may not reflect long-term national objectives. This is particularly the case when there is no unanimity about U.S. objectives at the highest levels of policymaking, as typically has been true of arms transfer policy.[15]

Approving Arms Sales and Security Assistance

The imprecision of the criteria for approving or denying arms sales derives in part from the disparate interests of the agencies that make the decisions. Some, such as the Defense Security Assistance Agency, which helps to facilitate the purchase of American military equipment by clients overseas, are concerned primarily with promoting exports. Others, such as the Arms Control and Disarmament Agency or the Defense Technology Security Administration in the Pentagon, are preoccupied with trying to control arms sales that may violate policy.[16]

Security assistance is a label applied loosely to a wide variety of military programs promoted by the executive branch, including government-to-government Foreign Military Sales (FMS), licensed commercial sales, the Military Assistance program (MAP), the International Military Education and Training program (IMET), peacekeeping operations, and Economic Support Funds (ESF). In addition, concessionary aid granted under the Development Assistance program and implemented by the Agency for International Development and by multilateral lending agencies has helped subsidize flows of advanced technology to the developing world.[17]

The most significant of these instruments for the diffusion of military technology are the Foreign Military Sales program and commercial sales, overseen by the State Department. In recent years, dual-use technologies that are sold through commercial channels have been recognized for their potential contribution to weapon production programs and are subject to controls exercised by the Commerce Department. Nuclear-related exports, subject to laws prohibiting access to materials, equipment, and technology that could assist countries in developing nuclear weapons, are overseen by various agencies in the State, Defense, and Energy Departments, the Nuclear Regulatory Commission, and the Arms Control and Disarmament Agency.[18]

The Foreign Military Sales program promotes government-to-government sales for which the U.S. government serves as the middleman between defense contractors and recipient states. In addition to arranging for the purchase and transfer of technology from companies or defense stockpiles, the government negotiates payment options for weapon purchases and provides long-term maintenance for equipment, among other services. In the past few years FMS has become a credit extension program in which countries receive loans to purchase equipment either at a subsidized rate or at the prevailing Treasury interest rate.[19] Commercial sales, by contrast, are initiated directly by private firms, subject to licensing by the government. Sales of major equipment developed for the U.S. military are usually approved by FMS procedures, and sales of less sophisticated equipment and products developed independently are approved through licensing procedures operated by the State Department's Office of Defense Trade Control; but this is by no means always the case. At an annual average of $10 billion in transactions between 1982 and 1989, the Foreign Military Sales program has long overshadowed commercial military sales, which averaged less than $2 billion annually.[20]

Together with dual-use commodity sales, however, the commercial sales may grow in significance in the coming years.

Reflecting concerns that the United States was becoming overly permissive about arms sales, Congress passed the Arms Export Control Act in 1975 to ensure more careful political scrutiny. The act imposed new eligibility guidelines for arms recipients and additional mechanisms for monitoring arms transfer requests, including stricter controls on transfers of major military equipment and prohibitions on retransfers of equipment to third parties.[21]

To ensure that arms sales were guided by foreign policy objectives, the Arms Export Control Act vested formal authority for approval in the Department of State, acting on behalf of the president. The operational management of arms sales is under the under secretary of state for security assistance, science and technology, who is assisted by the staff of the Bureau of Political-Military Affairs. The Center for Defense Trade in the bureau handles FMS and grant requests; the Office of Defense Trade Controls reviews commercial sales. Commercial exports are subject to the restrictions outlined in the Munitions List of military hardware and services compiled by the State Department and the Department of Defense. In addition, dual-use technologies are controlled by the Commodity Control List and the Militarily Critical Technologies List. Although statutorily under the jurisdiction of the Commerce Department, the lists are based on guidance from the Defense and State Departments, which specify items that should be subject to control because of national security or foreign policy concerns.[22]

Transfers of space-related technology are of increasing importance to ballistic missile programs and are influenced by NASA, which has a mandate to promote international cooperation in space. The recently established National Space Council in the White House is periodically consulted about pending transfers of space technology that could pose national security problems and adjudicates disputes among NASA, Commerce, Defense, and State.[23]

Economic assistance provided by the Agency for International Development and through such multilateral agencies as the World Bank and the Export-Import Bank is a more indirect way for countries to acquire advanced technologies. Despite some statutes requiring coordination with other agencies, these institutions usually do not concern themselves with the potential effects of their programs on a recipient's military capability. The activities of a country's military sector, even when they involve significant efforts to enlarge a defense industry, are generally considered outside the purview of lending agencies' authority. The World Bank, for example, lists military imports and exports as a separate category of trade that is not part of its evaluation of a country's eligibility for credit. World Bank country reports, which assess every other aspect of economic potential and performance in detail, are strangely silent about the benefits or costs of defense sectors. Because the contributions of defense industries to national investment, export revenues, and overall economic growth are increasingly important in developing countries, to ignore them seems atavistic and misleading. In 1989, after the Export-Import Bank provided Iraq credit insurance for nonmilitary exports, one senator proposed amending the Export-Import Bank Act to require closer scrutiny of the uses to which the bank's funding and credit insurance are being put.[24]

Implementing a sales agreement can involve reviews by many agencies and cabinet departments, depending on how sensitive or significant they consider the transaction. Arms sales requests and license applications that could conflict with the guidelines of one policy or another are sent for review to those agencies that may have an interest in the matter, including State's regional bureaus, the Human Rights and Humanitarian Bureau, and the Arms Control and Disarmament Agency. The requests can also be referred to the Departments of Defense, Commerce, Energy, and Treasury; NASA; the Central Intelligence Agency; and, in rare cases, the National Security Council. Requests to sell dual-use technology that originate in the Department of Commerce and that could have policy implications are referred to the State and Defense Departments by Commerce officials.

In the Department of Defense, sales can be reviewed by civilian staff in the Office of the Assistant Secretary for International Security Affairs, by the secretaries of the various armed services, by the Defense Technology Security Administration in the Office of the Assistant Secretary for Security Policy, and by the Defense Security Assistance Agency, which is the executing agency for all foreign military sales. Further review by military authorities can pass through the military departments, the Joint Staff, and the regional commanders in chief. An estimated average of 270 days was required to approve an FMS contract in 1986, and some seemingly uncontroversial licensing requests have taken two years before they were finally approved or denied.[25]

By executive order, the secretary of defense has the authority to execute arms sales, giving the Department of Defense a powerful effect on policies. Although it has no formal policymaking authority, the Defense Security Assistance Agency can decisively influence the content and pace of military assistance programs. As the coordinating agency between foreign governments and various elements of the executive branch, the DSAA prepares the security assistance budget based on its assessment of the requirements of potential recipients, U.S. budgetary priorities and funding limits, and regional and country precedents. Because concessionary aid has been severely limited in recent years, the agency's recommendations about which countries should receive FMS credits, the types of technologies to which they should have access, and the terms it sets out to facilitate purchases through other means determine in major ways the direction of policy.[26] Similarly, the military assistance and advisory groups, which operate as part of overseas missions and are staffed by military officers, help the local U.S. ambassadors and the regional commanders-in-chief to coordinate—and often initiate—foreign governments' requests for military equipment. As the element of the government that is most active in implementing military programs overseas, advisory groups are important catalysts for U.S. military sales and are the repositories of expertise about recipients' military requirements and objectives.

Until 1988 the formal mechanism for interagency policy coordination was the Arms Transfer Management Group, previously known as the Arms Export Control Board. Chaired by the under secretary of state for security assistance, science, and technology, the group included senior representatives from the Office of the Under Secretary of Defense for Policy, the Office of the Assistant Secretary of Defense for International Security Affairs, the Joint Chiefs, the Defense Security Assistance Agency, the Departments of Commerce and Treasury, the Agency for International Development, the Arms Control and Disarmament Agency, the Central Intelligence Agency, and the National Security Council. Meetings, however, were infrequent, and then only to adjudicate major disagreements; the group is now moribund. For policies on nuclear and missile nonproliferation and other specific matters, working groups known as policy coordinating committees have met more regularly, although most of the routine decisionmaking on these matters continues to be decentralized.[27] New analytical support and policy advisory mechanisms have been established recently for the management of the Missile Technology Control Regime, discussed later in this chapter.

To all these reviewing bodies one must also add Congress. The 1975 Arms Export and Control Act gave Congress authority to review and veto proposed sales in excess of $25 million or any sale of a major item of defense equipment valued at more than $7 million. These levels were doubled in 1981 to $50 million and $14 million. Although the act requires agencies to send routine reports to Congress about impending arms sales and security assistance programs, the number of major sales requiring advance notification has been declining; it was fewer than eighty in 1986.[28]

Congress finds it difficult to override the executive's traditional prerogatives in approving weapon sales. In the fifteen years since the passage of the Arms Export Control Act, it has formally forced the withdrawal of only two proposed sales. On three other occasions it placed conditions on or eliminated specific weapons or capabilities that were part of larger transactions. In recent years, however, Congress has been able informally to force the withdrawal or modification of proposed sales by making it clear they would face concerted opposition. All these instances involved proposed sales of weapons to Arab or Persian Gulf nations.[29]

Congress is often more influential in heightening the political sensitivity of impending transactions, either to promote or discourage the sales. Its actions have, for instance, made the executive branch and the public more concerned about missile proliferation, even if it has not been entirely successful in imposing new requirements on the executive branch to penalize countries or companies that traffic in missile and other sensitive technologies.

The major source of congressional influence on security assistance transactions continues to be its power to approve appropriations, especially through earmarking Foreign Military Sales credits and concessionary aid for favored recipients. Because of growing fiscal constraints and dwindling political support for security assistance to any country, Congress has cut overall funding and apportioned the bulk of FMS credits to fewer than a half-dozen countries. More than 50 percent of the credits go to Israel and Egypt.[30] Congressional intrusions into security assistance decisions have been widely criticized for limiting the flexibility of the government to use this instrument in support of foreign policy.[31]

Administering Security Assistance

The executive branch and Congress have been accused of a multitude of sins in administering security assistance. Depending on the source of the criticism, the decisionmaking process is either too cumbersome and thus overly restrictive or too cumbersome and thus unable to impose meaningful restrictions. Defense manufacturers have charged that the excessive bureaucratization of the technology transfer process needlessly and capriciously delays and sometimes denies sales. Congress or the executive branch, they complain, have undercut U.S. economic and military strength, ceding markets to competitors without gaining commensurate benefits for U.S. foreign policy. Conversely, those concerned about the dangers of technology diffusion charge that arms exports have been too strongly promoted, that short-term political or economic interests have satisfied the demands of arms clients at the expense of global stability. They have also argued that the layers of bureaucracy have not prevented inadvertent or unwarranted technology diffusion because they have failed to monitor its disposition once it is sold.

These otherwise clashing perspectives agree that there is not enough routine attention paid to the terms of collaborative weapon production agreements. The transfer of weapon production technology to developing countries epitomizes the tensions between promoting exports of U.S. technology and controlling its disposition and use. In the late 1970s the United States had coproduction agreements with just six developing countries: Taiwan, South Korea, the Philippines, Argentina, Brazil, and Israel. The technologies involved were relatively unsophisticated, and the extent of local participation in the manufacturing process was modest and carefully restricted. By the early 1980s, however, more than a dozen developing countries had coproduction or licensing agreements, including contracts that permitted access to a range of processes for making sophisticated armaments.[32] The potential for trouble had increased enormously.

It is now estimated that the United States has entered into eighty-seven government-to-government weapon production agreements with nineteen countries since 1960.[33] There is no official tabulation of how many less formal arrangements have contributed indirectly to such programs; indeed, the number is probably inestimable. In addition, transfers of information, technical data packages, and components for producing U.S. equipment have become a routine element of U.S. relations with a growing number of countries and have often proceeded with little scrutiny.

Coproduction agreements have always been a double-edged sword. The agreements can be useful for government because they improve foreign relations and to business because they mean profits. But granting third world countries the right to produce weapons poses serious dilemmas. U.S. companies may profit, but they may also be creating future competitors. Policymakers may be gaining friends abroad, but they may also lose control over the direction and content of recipients' production and export programs once these countries possess sophisticated manufacturing capabilities. As a report from the Defense Science Board Task Force stated in 1976, "control of design and manufacturing know-how is absolutely vital to the maintenance of U.S. technological superiority. Compared to this, all other considerations are secondary."[34]

U.S. defense industry representatives have increasingly complained about lax enforcement of end-use requirements in such countries as Korea and Taiwan. The laxness, they claim, has permitted U.S. technology and expertise to be used for indigenous production and export programs and illegal commercial gains.[35] Aside from assisting potential competitors, coproduction agreements have been criticized as contradicting the idea that arms exports strengthen U.S. security by reducing the unit costs of domestic weapon production. The agreements also increase the risk of compromising the security of U.S. technology through industrial espionage or as a result of political upheaval that replaces a friendly regime with one hostile to the West.[36]

It is axiomatic that once transferred, technology and expertise cannot be retracted. An obvious corollary, then, is that coproduction contracts are an inherently inflexible instrument of policy. Increasingly, however, acceding to these agreements has been less a matter of choice than of necessity. Faced with a client that insists on sharing production as the price of signing a contract, the United States will typically "agree to coproduce the item rather than lose the entire sale to another country."[37] Or, as a Korean defense official candidly explained, the United States became more permissive toward cooperative weapon ventures with Korea not just because America "inevitably needs multinational cooperation" in the changing international technology market, but because "Korea will foster its defense industry independently of the U.S. intent, i.e., even without U.S. assistance."[38]

In a 1989 report the General Accounting Office accused the Defense and State Departments of failing to monitor compliance with U.S. restrictions on production levels and end-use in cooperative weapon contracts or to enforce sanctions when violations were evident. In the eighteen programs it reviewed, the GAO charged that "DOD had relied on the foreign countries to report on production quantities and had not verified the information it had received. Although the DOD relied on U.S. embassy offices to inform it of noncompliance, these offices were not tasked with and did not consider themselves responsible for oversight or management of coproduction programs to ensure compliance." The State Department's Office of Security Assistance and Sales, the report went on to say, "tends to favor officials of recipient countries more than it does protection of its own national interests and balance of payments."[39]

Countries can also acquire sensitive, militarily significant information from a wide variety of other sources, many of them legal. Iraq, Israel, Pakistan, India, South Korea, Taiwan, and even Bulgaria have gained access to sensitive Department of Energy data related to nuclear weapons. The DOE's nuclear weapons laboratories, from which the information was purchased, have faced a fundamental dilemma. The 1978 Nuclear Non-Proliferation Act and other laws require controls on the dissemination of unclassified information related to nuclear weapons, but as the GAO discovered, the laws also require DOE and the weapons laboratories "to collaborate with the private sector to disseminate unclassified research results." Of an estimated 39,000 research reports produced by DOE laboratories in 1986–87, about 60 percent were unclassified and available for sale.[40] Like NASA, the Commerce Department, and other agencies with jurisdiction over technical information that has potential military applications, the Department of Energy is expected both to control and disseminate its products.

The options available to the government to enforce restrictions on the use of U.S. technology are relatively few, particularly because most punitive measures would incur substantial political costs. Aside from outright abrogation of a security relationship, the United States can threaten to suspend financing for foreign military sales and impose trade sanctions, or it can denounce the perpetrator through diplomatic channels. When the country guilty of a violation is a close security partner, monitoring agencies, Congress, and the president more and more often look the other way unless infractions are so egregious or politically explosive they could become public *causes célèbres*.

The Case of Missiles

The evolution of the Missile Technology Control Regime illustrates the difficulties the United States faces in trying to impose controls on the trade in military technology. Since the inception of the regime, disputes among agencies and between Congress and the executive branch over proposed transactions that might run afoul of its regulations have been common. The problems of defining and implementing even the modest restrictions in the MTCR demonstrate the complexities created by the competing jurisdictional alignments within the U.S. bureaucracy, let alone those created by attempts to coordinate activities with other countries.

Efforts to launch the MTCR began in the early 1980s when policymakers realized that despite long-standing controls on sales, third world countries could still gain access to components and expertise needed to build ballistic and cruise missiles. Prompted by the concern that many of these states were also incipient nuclear powers, U.S. officials presented the MTCR as the next logical step in efforts to control the proliferation of nuclear weapons. The formal announcement of the regime in April 1987 depicted it as the next phase in the progression of policy moves that had helped establish the International Atomic Energy Agency in the 1950s, the Non-Proliferation Treaty in the 1960s and the nuclear supplier cartel, formed as the London Suppliers' Group, in the 1970s.[41]

In practice, the MTCR has evolved into an instrument that aims to contain the worldwide diffusion of technologies for ballistic and cruise missile systems. Although much attention has been given to the missile programs of India, Israel, and other emerging nuclear powers, the focus of the MTCR is directed as much toward countries without existing nuclear capabilities, including Saudi Arabia, Iran, and Libya.

The United States had initiated discussions with its six economic summit partners (Canada, the United Kingdom, France, West Germany, Italy, and Japan) in 1982 to develop coordinated guidelines for exports of missile-related components and technology. According to participants, the discussions were contentious and protracted. As was the case with COCOM after World War II, the United States took the lead in selling the concept of a supplier cartel, emphasizing the severity of the threat of ballistic missile proliferation and offering detailed proposals about the types of technology that it believed should be controlled.

Although the regime was not formally announced until 1987, the partners agreed to implement its strictures informally in 1985.[42] In technical documents known as the "Equipment and Technology Annex," two categories of missile-related technologies are subject to restraint (figure 5-2). Category I covers missile systems and complete subsystems, including ballistic and cruise missiles, space-launch vehicles, sounding rockets, target and reconnaissance drones, and other unmanned vehicles that can deliver 500 kilograms of payload more than 300 kilometers.[43] Category II covers propellants and propulsion systems; materials, instruments, flight control systems, and avionics equipment; launch- and ground-support equipment and facilities; and certain kinds of computers and software, test equipment, and related production equipment and technology. These technologies are to be subject to case-by-case review and, in the event of approval for transfer, the negotiation of strict end-use assurances with recipients. The regime does not cover other forms of nuclear delivery systems, such as manned aircraft, or other types of missiles. Indeed, as was pointed out in testimony in 1989 by a Defense Department official, the MTCR was designed specifically not to interfere with the trade in missiles that fall below the range or payload specifications—which includes most air-to-air, sea-launched, or surface-to-air missiles—nor with trade in antitactical ballistic missiles.[44]

The jurisdictional lines for MTCR implementation involve most of the agencies that help oversee security assistance, but the regime has elevated the Commerce Department to a more important policy role. Many category II items include commodities with potential civilian applications and thus fall under the jurisdiction of Commerce. According to testimony by a department official, Commerce received "several thousand" export license applications in 1988 and determined that fewer than one hundred were related to missile programs.[45] Although the official estimate is that only 20 to 30 percent of all export requests with potential applications for missile development originate in the Commerce Department, this still represents a voluminous case load for the department to review.

The Commerce Department reviews cases according to four criteria: whether the item proposed for export appears in the "Equipment and

Figure 5-2. *Missile Technology Control Regime Guidelines*

Category I[a]

Scope: Unmanned capability to deliver 500 kilograms to 300 kilometers

Complete systems
  Rockets
    Ballistic missiles
    Space-launch vehicles
    Sounding rockets
  Air vehicles
    Cruise missiles
    Target drones
    Reconnaisance drones
Complete subsystems
  Rocket stages
  Reentry vehicles
  Solid- or liquid-fuel rocket engines
  Guidance sets (CEP 10 kilometers at 300 kilometers)
  Thrust vector controls
  Warhead safing, arming, fusing, and firing mechanisms
Specially designed production equipment and facilities
Technology for design and production

Category II[a]
  Propulsion components
  Propellants and constituents
  Propellant production technology and equipment
  Missile structural composites: production technology and equipment
  Pyrolytic deposition/densification technology and equipment
  Structural materials
  Flight instruments, inertial navigation and production
  Flight control systems
  Avionics equipment
  Launch and ground support equipment and facilities
  Missile computers
  Analog-to-digital converters
  Test facilities and equipment
  Software and related analog or hybrid computers
  Reduced observables technology, materials, and devices
  Nuclear effects protection

Source: "Equipment and Technology Annex."
a. See text for explanation of categories.

Technology Annex," whether the country of destination has a missile program, whether this program is "a project of concern," and whether the item would "make a significant contribution to a missile development program." In the last case, some officials in Commerce seem to have interpreted "missile development" to mean development of a nuclear delivery system only.[46]

If any of these criteria apply, cases are referred to the State Department, along with the Commerce Department's assessment of whether it intends to approve or deny the transfer. If an item appears in the "Annex" but Commerce analysts do not think it will make a significant contribution to a missile program, the department requests a recommendation from the State Department. If the export is destined for a country with "a project of concern" but is not necessarily destined for that project, Commerce refers the case to State to get assurances about the application and disposition of that technology from the recipient before granting a license. In theory, the MTCR has codified restrictions that were already part of the Export Administration Act's list of controlled technologies and has simply granted Commerce the right to expand these restrictions to cover missile-producing countries in the third world, as well as the Soviet Union and other traditional U.S. adversaries.

In the State Department, the Office of Defense Trade has routine jurisdiction over missile-related export requests. To coordinate the interagency review procedures imposed by the MTCR, the department established the Missile Technology Export Control Group (MTEC), which includes representatives from the Departments of Defense and Commerce, NASA, the Arms Control and Disarmament Agency, the Customs Service, and the intelligence community. The group examined an estimated 200 cases between June and October 1989 and, according to a State Department official, developed "systematic procedures for reviewing both Commerce and State cases."[47]

To supplement its analytical staff, the State Department established the Missile Trade Analysis Group in 1989 to track foreign participation in missile programs of concern. The Office of Weapons Proliferation Policy in State's Office of Political-Military Affairs was also established in 1989 to coordinate chemical and missile nonproliferation initiatives.[48]

Late in 1989 the Department of Defense announced similar innovations. Under a new deputy for nonproliferation policy, who reports to the assistant secretary for international security affairs, activities related to MTCR are to be coordinated closely with overall regional security and nonproliferation policy. As one of the prime forces behind the formulation and implementation of the MTCR, the Defense Department has been the most forceful defender of comprehensive export controls and is the only department on record to recognize the value of using trade sanctions against violators of the regime. The deputy for nonproliferation has testified that violators could be subject to punitive action under the existing defense federal acquisition regulations, which allow for government contracts to be denied to domestic and foreign companies if they fail to comply with proliferation-related laws and regulations.[49]

In addition to seeking more authority over proposed international collaborative ventures for weapon production, the Defense Department tried for several years to gain the right to have all licenses handled by the Commerce Department referred to Defense so that Pentagon officials could decide which they should examine more closely. Until recently, referral was left to the discretion of Commerce officials. Off the record, some Defense officials believe that Commerce is lax in its interpretation of MTCR guidelines, a belief that has already caused friction between the two departments.

Prompted by Defense Department officials, Congress included in 1989 legislation a statute requiring the Commerce Department to submit a list of pending export licenses to DOD. The action prompted instant opposition from Commerce. According to James M. LeMunyon, deputy assistant secretary of commerce for export administration, this initiative "would delay some 40,000 to 50,000 license applications each year for enhanced technical review in Commerce. About 10,000 of those would be further delayed by referral to State and Defense, overloading their systems. . . . Contrary to the intent of Congress as expressed in the 1988 Trade Act, it would delay legitimate U.S. exports unnecessarily, thus hindering the ability of U.S. firms to win in the global market place."[50]

Interagency wrangling over missile-related exports has reflected familiar institutional biases. When the sale of electronic equipment for Iraq's missile-development complex was proposed in 1989, the Commerce Department argued that it had no statutory authority to deny the transaction, in part because MTCR guidelines could not be applied to contracts that had already been negotiated. Defense officials countered that the MTCR was official U.S. policy at the time of the contract award and thus could be applied retroactively. The issue had to be decided by the National Security Council, which sided with the Defense Department.[51]

There also are disputes about the relative significance of different kinds of equipment and whether they should be controlled. In a protracted debate about the proposed transfer to India of a reentry vehicle heat and vibration simulator that some believed could be useful for missile testing, the Commerce Department dismissed the equipment as not particularly critical to missile design, the Defense Department was firmly in opposition, and the State Department waffled before finally siding with Defense. The transfer was eventually denied.[52]

Despite the rhetorical commitment of the administration to missile nonproliferation, the recent establishment of new bureaucratic mechanisms to implement the policy is partly the result of congressional pressures. Four pieces of legislation were introduced in 1989 and 1990 that would have imposed trade sanctions on companies and countries supplying technology banned by the MTCR, whether or not they are adherents to the regime. One amendment introduced by Congressman Howard Berman passed the House by an overwhelming majority in the fall of 1989, and a version of it was adopted as an amendment to the fiscal year 1991 Defense Authorization Act, including provisions to impose sanctions on companies that violated MTCR guidelines.[53] The message to the administration was clear. Missile proliferation was being taken seriously by a bipartisan congressional coalition and could result in the imposition of more comprehensive protectionist measures if the administration failed to act.

Quite apart from dealing with congressional grievances, the Bush administration is fighting an uphill battle to sustain the viability of the MTCR in the face of continued missile exports by other countries, including MTCR adherents. Even as it tried to convince additional countries to participate in the regime, the administration has had disputes with allies about proposed sales that it believes are prohibited by the MTCR.

One particular sticking point has involved the future of peaceful cooperative ventures in space technology with third world countries. Because the technology for producing space-launch vehicles is virtually indistinguishable from that for producing ballistic missiles, prohibitions on transfers of the technology potentially disrupt ventures to which some suppliers, especially France, attach great importance. The United States has tried to emphasize international cooperation in space exploration and the availability of commercial space-launch services to replace exports of space-launch vehicles, but has clung tenaciously to its sovereign right to assist nations bilaterally and has persisted in negotiations with Brazil and India to sell liquid-fuel rocket propulsion equipment.[54]

Even within the United States there is some dispute about the scope of MTCR restraints on such items as remotely piloted vehicles. Although these appear as a category I commodity subject to a "strong presumption of denial," many of the vehicles do not have the range or payload capacity to fall under MTCR strictures. However, with the advent of the U.S. Global Positioning Satellite system, the Soviet GLONASS, and other commercially available satellite navigation services, countries conceivably could improve the accuracy of the vehicles and use them for military purposes. In other words, the technologies used to build systems that do not have the range or payload characteristics covered by the MTCR are of concern because they could be used to produce systems that would be covered.[55]

Another potential controversy involves U.S. assistance to Israel to develop an antitactical ballistic missile, the so-called Arrow program. Although the administration's position has been that this collaborative venture falls outside MTCR limits, other countries that might be induced to join the MTCR, including other Middle Eastern powers, could challenge the assertion and cause difficulties for U.S. military planning and frictions in relations with Israel.[56]

Debates on the MTCR have also helped highlight the difficulty of assessing the risks and benefits of those advanced technology exports that could make an indirect contribution to missile programs. The most important item of equipment under scrutiny is the supercomputer, for which requests from India, Brazil, and Israel—all of them missile producers—were pending in mid-1990. Supercomputers are not vital for missile development, but they can be useful in accelerating the pace and scope of testing programs. Moreover, they can be linked through commercial computer networks, potentially giving a state the ability to conduct nuclear research beyond its borders.[57] In the ongoing disputes, the Defense Department and the Arms Control and Disarmament Agency have opposed sales to Brazil and Israel; State and Commerce have favored them.

Aside from clarifying technological guidelines, the regime's most pressing need is to bolster its crediblity by expanding its membership. Spain joined in early 1990, as did Belgium, Luxembourg, and the Netherlands. Eliciting the support of the remaining members of the EC is particularly urgent as it approaches the removal of all intra-European trade barriers in 1992. According to Assistant Secretary of State Richard Clarke, "Unless [the other members of the EC] are brought in, an MTCR member in the EC after 1992 might not be able to control an export to a non-MTCR EC country, and the item could go from that non-MTCR nation to a missile program of concern to us."[58]

Regardless of the composition of its membership, the MTCR will likely remain the basis of U.S. policy on sensitive missile-related exports, if only because the regime codifies longstanding American restraint in these matters. It may be premature to make predictions, but the management of the MTCR will probably coincide with current patterns of export restraints, balancing technical stipulations and political considerations. Countries with which the United States and its allies have limited or hostile relations are likely to bear the brunt of MTCR restraints, while countries perceived as more vital will continue to receive the kinds of technologies that would have been permitted before the regime's inception. Although this outlook is at odds with the more strident view of legislators such as Senator John McCain, who has stated bluntly that "there are no good proliferators" and that no nation should be exempt from the regime, experience indicates that this perspective will not prevail in the bureaucracy.[59]

East-West Industrial Country Military Trade

Despite the common perception that the MTCR is a major policy innovation, the United States and its allies have had four decades of operational experience with trade controls to protect national security. Beginning with the Battle Act in 1951, which imposed an embargo on exports of "arms, ammunition, and implements of war" to U.S. military adversaries, any commodity that could "materially aid" the Soviet Union or its allies has been subject to an elaborate system of restraint. Yet although the objectives of East-West trade controls have received enduring support, implementing controls has engendered many of the same kinds of controversies stirred up by the MTCR.

In spite of their obvious relevance of East-West controls, however, the applicability for the emerging missile cartel of experiences in administering them has only recently been acknowledged by policymakers, partly because of ideological biases. Supporters of strict East-West controls have been preoccupied with advances in Soviet military technology and have not taken advances in the developing world too seriously.

Moreover, many policymakers have considered that controlling the spread of military technology is an arms control issue unrelated to broader issues of U.S. trade policy.

But the questions raised have far more to do with the management of international trade than with arms control. Concerns that were voiced in the MTCR or in COCOM are beginning to converge as developing countries become more industrialized and areas for potential policy coordination emerge. The potential effects of the changes currently being implemented in COCOM for industrializing countries, and for the overall future of export controls, may be far more significant than any other alteration in U.S. policy.

For four decades, trade between NATO allies and the Soviet bloc has been managed by the informal Coordinating Committee with seventeen industrial country members. Like the Missile Technology Control Regime, COCOM is consensual and imposes no treaty obligations. That it has endured through all the policy shifts in U.S.-Soviet and NATO–Warsaw Pact relations is a minor miracle. It did so largely because guidelines were sufficiently flexible to permit sovereign countries to pursue their vital economic interests and because of a common concern about the Soviet military threat.

The United States has been the most vociferous defender of restraints in matters of sensitive exports to the Soviet Union and Eastern Europe and has typically found itself at odds with allies when it tried to impose limitations multilaterally. And control efforts were sometimes pushed to absurdity, as apparently occurred in 1948 when the Defense Department proposed an embargo on exports of baseball bats to the Soviet Union because they could boost the morale of Soviet troops.[60]

Despite agreement about the objectives of trade controls, there have been strong differences among governments and domestic agencies over the implementation of COCOM guidelines. The differences have resulted from varying economic and political objectives, diverse perceptions of the Soviet threat, and shifting concepts of how best to restrain Soviet military ambitions. Controversy has been particularly intense with respect to the types of technologies that warranted control and the extent to which nonmilitary commodities—everything from wheat to supercomputers—should fall under the regime. The most common complaint of COCOM's supporters as well as its detractors has been that the list of controlled commodities is far too comprehensive, forcing debate over trivial infractions and distracting attention from potentially more serious compromises of advanced technology. Despite major reforms of COCOM lists in 1990, these disputes will undoubtedly endure.

The content and extent of export controls have been altered periodically to reflect changes in the climate of East-West relations. After a brief period of liberalization during the heyday of détente, Congress granted successive administrations increasing authority to control both military and dual-use exports to the Soviet bloc. In 1979, for example, the Export Administration Act mandated that national security and foreign policy controls should be established on a wide range of exports. The act created two mechanisms, the Militarily Critical Technologies List (MCTL), and the Commodity Control List (CCL), to designate the exports warranting careful scrutiny. The MCTL identified technologies deemed vital to U.S. technological superiority; the CCL controlled commodities that were considered potentially valuable to hostile states.[61] By the mid-1980s, the CCL included more than 200 categories of commodities and services, each comprising dozens of items subject to control for reasons of national security or foreign policy. Any item on the list automatically required an export license, which generated an estimated 120,000 requests a year, less than 1 percent of which were subsequently denied.[62]

The comprehensive nature of the CCL and MTCL was challenged from many sides. American business interests felt unduly penalized by their own government, and a 1986 report by the House of Representatives charged that perhaps a third of the commodities subject to control, including personal computers and calculators, common household products, and a wide variety of other readily available goods, were not militarily significant. Among many examples of bureaucratic excess, licenses for urinalysis equipment and gloves for meat cutters were denied because the sales would compromise national security.[63]

In the 1980s, greater attention to commercial exports thought to be useful for Soviet military modernization led the Reagan administration to impose an ambitious and controversial system of export restraints operated by the Defense Department. Although the Commerce Department is legally in charge of commercial trade, the Pentagon gained significant powers of oversight beginning in 1984. A Defense Department directive stated that the Pentagon had the authority to "treat defense-related technology as a valuable, limited national security resource to be husbanded and invested in the pursuit of national security objectives." The directive led to the establishment of the Office of Technology

Security under the assistant secretary for international security policy, an operation that grew from six employees to almost 300 in the same year.[64]

Many U.S. contractors complained that the imprecision of the criteria for monitoring license requests and the inevitable delays incurred as the requests moved through successive layers of the new bureaucracy penalized American industry for no legitimate reason. The sudden urgency to expand the technology security program had brought in untrained personnel who were unfamiliar with the technologies and the procedures they were being asked to oversee. Given the all-encompassing nature of the program's mandate, even routine licenses for exports to countries outside the Warsaw Pact were caught in the bureaucratic web. To cynics the program was a way of practicing arms control by other means, stifling U.S. military exports far more successfully than the deliberate system of restraints the Carter administration had tried to impose. Considering that the Reagan administration was committed to deregulation and privatization, not to mention promoting U.S. military assistance worldwide, the enterprise appeared anomalous and self-defeating.

In the mid-1980s, a French defense official, pointing to his country's success in promulgating new coproduction ventures around the world during this period of American extremism, suggested that France should erect a statue of Richard Perle, the assistant secretary of defense for international security policy, to demonstrate its gratitude.[65] Americans alleged that U.S. export controls on technology widely available internationally had contributed to the rise of competitive electronics industries in Asia and even Eastern Europe, with Korean, Japanese, and Polish companies actively selling clones of U.S. computers throughout the world.[66] A report by the National Academy of Sciences estimated that the effort to control technology dissemination to the Soviet bloc had not only failed, but was costing the U.S. economy $9 billion a year. The report urged lifting controls on commodities readily available from other sources and focusing only on highly advanced military technologies, such as those involving stealth and antisubmarine warfare, that were critical to U.S. defense.[67]

Since the late 1980s, the progressive economic integration of Western Europe, the reemergence of sovereignty in Eastern European countries and their opening to the West, and the unification of Germany have forced major alterations in technology trade policies among industrial countries. The United States, however, has been the most reluctant actor in this regard. As recently as July 1989 a dispute between the secretary of defense and secretary of commerce publicly dramatized the domestic controversy and highlighted the extent to which U.S. preoccupations were out of date with the realities of the international technology market. Having determined that eleven countries, many of them not members of COCOM, were capable of making high-quality personal computers, Commerce Secretary Robert Mosbacher moved to lift restrictions on a sale of early-1980s-vintage computers to the Soviet Union. Secretary of Defense Richard Cheney, apparently as angered over Commerce's failure to consult him as over the actual decision, tried to block the sale on grounds of national security, but won only a minor compromise on the range of items to be released.[68]

The Cheney-Mosbacher dispute was symptomatic of a profound confusion in the United States about broader issues of U.S.-Soviet relations, trade policy, and how to manage rapidly diverging U.S. and allied interests. A common caricature of the differences of approach had the United States clinging to export controls to retain some semblance of protectionism against the East, while the allies rushed to exploit new commercial opportunities in any communist nation that had money. In a COCOM meeting in October 1989 the United States once again found itself the lone advocate of export controls that its allies were rejecting as useless and atavistic. Led by West Germany, which was anxious to promote its highly competitive machine tool industry in Eastern Europe, the other allies pushed for relaxation of export restraints across a wide front. Excessive controls were retarding economic progress in Eastern Europe, they argued, and some charged the controls were being maintained strictly to protect lagging sectors of U.S. industry.[69]

In early 1990 the Bush administration took steps to accommodate these pressures and realign U.S. policy more closely with that of the allies. Noting that American interests were best served by helping rebuild the economies of former Eastern bloc countries—almost the antithesis of COCOM's original mandate—the administration proposed to eliminate thirty technologies from the COCOM control list and to cut controls severely on thirteen others. At the High Level Meeting in June 1990, COCOM members pared the list even further, focusing especially on computers, telecommunications, and machine tools. Although critics argue that the list is still unnecessarily long, COCOM is moving toward a more manageable interpretation of technologies deemed militarily significant. According to Dennis Kloske, under secretary of commerce for export administration, the actions taken in June amounted to "removal of about 50 percent of our licensing case level."[70]

The decisions to alter the scope and content of COCOM restrictions suggest that there will be a fundamentally new approach to technology export controls in the future. With fewer controls on the supply, COCOM is focusing on protecting the uses to which technology is put. Increasingly, this will require cooperation from client states. As was discussed in the June 1990 meeting, for example, Czechoslovakia, Hungary, and Poland are to receive especially liberalized access to technology if they can provide sufficient assurance that they will prevent its misapplication or reexport. To this end, they must adopt "adequate export control systems, on-site verification and a national commitment to ensuring that strategically relevant technology is devoted exclusively to civilian purposes."[71]

There is still no consensus in the United States about the desirable limits of trade liberalization with Eastern Europe and the Soviet Union, and the future of COCOM as an institution is not entirely clear. Despite the strains, however, most COCOM members still seem to believe it advantageous to have some measure of export coordination. But the weaknesses of the regime may be exacerbated by the growing number of states that export military technology and are not members of the committee. At some point, countries like Korea, Singapore, Brazil, and Argentina will have to become part of a consultative mechanism about technology exports if COCOM is to survive. Even in the most optimistic of scenarios about the future global environment, some technologies vital to the West's technological edge will need to be protected from market forces. Possible reforms of COCOM to accommodate the changes in the international technology market are discussed further in chapter 6.

U.S.-Allied Military Trade

Military trade among the United States and its close allies in NATO and East Asia would on the surface not appear to be a controversial policy matter. Sharing advanced technology to reduce the costs of maintaining a common defense is a goal that goes back to the earliest days of the alliance. In practice, however, collaboration on weapon production and other efforts to promote standardization and interoperability of allied forces have not been very successful and have engendered chronic disputes.

One impediment to more effective cooperation has been disagreements between the United States and the allies over export rights for systems produced collaboratively. To retain indigenous defense industries, all the industrial countries have become dependent on military exports. Because the transatlantic market has long been dominated by the United States, the allies have been forced to market advanced technologies to the developing world while trying to increase their competitiveness in the industrial market, an effort in which they have been increasingly successful.

U.S. restrictions on retransfers to third countries of weapons that contain U.S. technology have been a source of constant irritation to the allies, who view them as discriminatory and economically painful. For instance, efforts during the Carter administration to forge a series of collaborative ventures under the rubric of "families of weapons" were hampered by repeated disputes over potential retransfers.[72] Partly in response to such perceptions of U.S. technological discrimination, the European countries have been moving steadily toward greater intra-European defense integration, launching new collaborative efforts and strengthening institutional arrangements to promote European cooperation. The Independent European Program Group, for instance, comprising all the NATO defense ministers except for those of the United States and Canada, has a mandate to define, develop, and procure weapon systems, and has launched about twenty all-European programs. In addition to reducing costs and achieving economies of scale, the IEPG hopes to create a more competitive export base for Europe that is unhindered by American interference.[73]

With the elimination of commercial trade barriers planned for 1992, greater European defense integration will further attenuate U.S. influence over the disposition of advanced military technologies. And given the severe fiscal constraints faced by all the industrial countries, the need for export revenues will exert steady pressures for still more liberal export policies, even when such actions encourage the diffusion of advanced technology with military applications.

In both Europe and Japan, the United States is faced with having to share technology more freely if it is to retain some measure of influence over and revenues from overseas defense programs, or having to continue retrenching from economic competition, which could leave it with even less stature. U.S.-Japanese technological cooperation, in particular, may be a crucial means of keeping the Japanese from becoming serious competitors in the military technology market.[74] Japan has not only outstripped the United States in producing semiconductors, machine tools, a range of advanced electronic products, and other components necessary for making modern weapons, but has achieved such a high degree of excess capacity in its defense-related industries that military exports may become a structural imperative.[75] As long as Japanese prohibitions on military exports remain in place, the United States has the opportunity to develop a comprehensive strategy for U.S.-Japanese defense cooperation and trade policy that serves both countries' interests.

In the final analysis, the key question for U.S.-allied defense cooperation is a priori a domestic one. The management of cooperation among the allies on matters of defense is inseparably linked to U.S. macroeconomic policy and decisions about how America will adapt to changing economic realities to restore its competitive stature. A critical challenge is the growing importance of commercial technological innovations vital to military modernization and the extent to which other countries, especially Japan, have begun to eclipse the United States in producing these innovations.

Observers agree that U.S. investment in technology needs to be reorganized to reduce an excessive reliance on funding by the Defense Department and that policy will have to be reformed to revitalize both the defense industrial base and U.S. commercial capacity. There is no consensus about the means to achieve this, but few would dispute that American security will increasingly have more to do with economic and technological prowess than with military capacity per se.[76]

Summary

The accelerating diffusion of ballistic missile technology is symptomatic of the weaknesses in the existing apparatus for managing the trade in military technology. For reasons far more pressing than the threat of ballistic missiles, significant reforms may be required to develop institutions and policies that can cope with the challenges of a rapidly changing international market.

The difficulties of identifying technologies that warrant control and of coordinating the activities of the agencies with jurisdiction over the trade are likely to place severe demands on governments. As has occurred with respect to nuclear proliferation, policies to control the diffusion of conventional weapons are focusing on earlier stages of the production cycle: instead of aircraft and missiles, for instance, guidance and propulsion technologies. Gradually, the content of trade will move toward more intangible elements of the manufacturing process, including technical data packages and expertise.

This movement is contributing to a progressive attenuation of traditional levers of supplier control. End-use assurances, for instance, have little relevance to complicated manufacturing processes such as integrated circuitry, where the ultimate destination of the products cannot be monitored. The international commercialization of high-technology industries, moreover, may further blunt the ability of governments to influence other countries' exports and imports. And no one has devised effective barriers to the diffusion of scientific and technical knowledge, which recognizes no national borders.

Efforts to manage military trade between developed and developing nations are impeded by the geopolitical diversity of the regions and the absence of any common agreement among exporters about the desirability and effectiveness of alternative diplomatic instruments. The relatively modest prohibitions of the Missile Trade Control Regime have already demonstrated the difficulty of implementing comprehensive technical controls in an international system marked by such diversity.

Over the long term the MTCR is only one of several instruments that will have to be brought to bear to control diffusion. In addition to efforts to encourage political accommodations among potential adversaries and to contain the incidence and scope of regional conflicts, the transition to a more complex international system will require far greater integration of industrial countries' domestic policies. At a minimum, governments must recognize that the various agencies guiding security and economic assistance, international space cooperation, and trade and industrial policy cannot continue to operate as if they were separate entities. The global diffusion of advanced technology impinges on all these areas, cutting to the heart of military preparedness, economic capacity, technological innovation, and diplomatic stature.

CHAPTER SIX

Toward an International Technology Security Regime

IN THE AUTUMN OF 1989, American and Japanese officials held meetings to discuss their countries' bilateral trade imbalance and ways to reform Japanese trading practices, which Washington considered discriminatory. Wearying of U.S. complaints about its domination of trade in high-technology products, Japan countered with a detailed critique of U.S. economic and industrial failings. Fading American competitiveness stemmed less from Japanese actions, the officials stated flatly, than from the years of U.S. mismanagement of its economic, industrial, and educational systems.[1]

Although the litany of Japanese recommendations for improving the American economy included many reforms that U.S. experts had long advocated—reducing the budget deficit, increasing government incentives to corporations to undertake more long-term research and development, restructuring the educational system—the significance of the critique was less its content than its source. Having traditionally looked to the United States for leadership, Japan had come of age and was exercising the prerogatives afforded by its new status as an economic superpower.

Japan's behavior illustrates the kinds of challenges the United States can expect to encounter more and more frequently in its international relationships. In a world of rival, technologically advanced industrial powers, its international economic strength has been steadily undermined by internal weaknesses.[2] As a corollary, its latitude for pursuing foreign policy objectives has been circumscribed by constraints imposed by domestic economic ills and an industrial sector of declining competitiveness. The division between foreign and domestic policy has become

131

blurred, and the United States, along with other advanced nations, is being called upon to define its interests and objectives in the international arena even before it has reached consensus at home about how best to do so. America must now adapt not only to a world in which it has lost technological preeminence, but to one in which the very concept of technological sovereignty has changed. With the ever quickening pace of innovation and dissemination, geopolitical boundaries no longer coincide with the boundaries of the international technology market. The internationalization of high-technology industry has undercut traditional relationships between countries, according much greater latitude to commercial activities, with significant implications for defense capabilities.

New security challenges, from alarming trends in the destruction of the natural environment to the increasing importance of space for military and commercial uses, also transcend national boundaries. Many emerging threats will not be resolvable by traditional military solutions; and they will require international cooperation. U.S. decisionmakers may refer nostalgically to the past four decades for having provided a relatively simple East-West framework for action. Now the demise of bipolar power and of the relatively clear division between industrial and nonindustrial states has left a conceptual vacuum. As one author noted in reference to the dramatic changes in Eastern Europe in late 1989, the confused reactions of some statesmen suggest they would prefer "the comforts of permanent aggression to the hardship of new choices and alignments."[3] But the United States must not only adapt to the transformation of Europe; it must also make its way in an increasingly interconnected global economic and security environment that will require collaborative management among many more countries and much more diverse cultures and political systems.

The proliferation of ballistic missiles, quite apart from its own serious ramifications, is a symptom of this interconnection. Thus efforts to control the spread of missile technology should be seen as steps toward developing an international infrastructure for understanding the dynamics of technology diffusion. But because controlling missile proliferation cuts across traditional boundaries of economic, diplomatic, and military policy, domestic jurisdictional frictions and international tensions are inevitable in attempts to define appropriate responses. Nevertheless, the endeavor will provide lessons for more comprehensive coordination of technology policies in the future.

In the longer term, an export cartel like the Missile Technology Control Regime is only one of several instruments that will have to be brought to bear on the broader problem of limiting the diffusion of technologies and weapons. In addition to efforts to encourage accommodations among combatant states and to contain the frequency and scope of regional conflicts, managing the transition to a more complex international system will require more coherent statements of industrial countries' policies toward new power blocs in the third world, and closer coordination.

This chapter describes three sets of policy reforms that could help manage the challenges posed by the diffusion of advanced military technologies: a more integrated domestic approach to managing exports of sophisticated weapons and components; greater assistance to third world countries to help them develop defensively oriented military forces and resolve regional conflicts; and more concerted attempts to reach broad international agreements to ensure the security of sophisticated technology and to manage conflicts.

Managing Military Trade in the 1990s

The effectiveness of supplier cartels and protectionist measures to control the diffusion of technology has continued to be a subject of considerable U.S. domestic controversy. Disputes over the appropriateness and extent of restrictions on sales of advanced technology to Eastern Europe and the Soviet Union have pitted advocates of trade liberalization in industry, the scientific community, and parts of the executive branch against remaining protectionist interests in Congress and the Department of Defense, and have set the United States at odds with its industrial allies. Despite the significant policy reforms under way, the outcome of this debate has yet to be determined, and it is clear that these issues will remain important to the administration as it struggles to define an effective response to the transformations occurring in Eastern Europe.

As long as the United States believes it must retain technological superiority to ensure its security, it will try to protect its most advanced military technologies against unplanned dissemination. Export controls may have outlived their usefulness for those technologies that are already widely diffused, but some market restrictions are needed for innovations critical to national defense, as well as for less advanced technologies, such as nuclear weapons, that are believed to be inherently destabilizing.

The problem is how to select the technologies that warrant attention, especially as innovation in defense industries becomes increasingly dependent on foreign components and U.S. commercial products and as the pace of dissemination and obsolescence accelerates. Moreover, assessing the scope and potential effectiveness of export controls requires a better understanding of how America will restructure its overall trade and industrial policies.

Policymakers and analysts concerned about managing the U.S. high-technology sector typically do not consider the problem of diffusion to the third world a particularly urgent concern. Developing countries' access to superconductors, microelectronics, fiber optics, advanced information systems, and other technologies considered critical by the Department of Defense continues, after all, to be constrained. And any problems posed by emerging weapons producers are overshadowed by seemingly much more pressing challenges, such as removing the impediments to U.S. military preparedness caused by the deteriorating competitiveness of the defense industrial base.

The options currently being considered for reforming U.S. trade and industrial policy could, however, come into conflict with concurrent efforts to restrain developing countries' access to military technology.

Multinational technological cooperation among industrial countries, for instance, which could help make the most of scarce allied resources, assist in the economic and political revitalization of Eastern Europe, and reduce the costs of innovation, might accord more foreign participants the competitive stature to oppose or circumvent U.S. export policies. As has been repeatedly demonstrated, many industrial and industrializing countries do not agree with the United States about the types of technologies that should be subject to controls. A more pronounced reliance on cooperative ventures with countries that are technological peers will diminish the ability of the United States to influence their actions through coercive means. Indeed, a growing number of collaborative international defense programs exclude the United States. Although these trends do not guarantee that foreign producers would necessarily oppose or deliberately subvert an international technology security regime, the need to accommodate a larger number of sovereign interests will make designing such a mechanism more challenging.

Greater U.S. dependence on foreign defense industries has been evident for some time, notwithstanding the protectionist propensities it provokes in Congress and U.S. industry. Until recently, America acquired more than 90 percent of its military goods from U.S. companies and dominated transatlantic defense trade as well. But in the past decade, collaborative weapon programs that grant foreign access to the U.S. market, offset agreements that require the United States to purchase foreign technology or commodities, increasing U.S. purchases of defense-related goods produced more efficiently overseas, and less stringent controls on the reexport of equipment containing American components have gradually whittled away at U.S. dominance. After years of rhetorical commitment to equalizing transatlantic trade, American policymakers have found rhetoric overtaken by reality. According to one estimate, the U.S. defense trade surplus with Europe plummeted from 7 to 1 in 1984 to 1.6 to 1 in 1989.[4]

Growing interdependence is not restricted to trade among NATO allies. A congressional push for cooperative arms production that was initiated by Senator Sam Nunn in 1987 has helped generate more than fifty multinational defense programs, with participation from Australia, Egypt, Israel, Japan, and Korea, as well as the NATO countries.[5] Similarly, the Department of Defense has pledged that 25 percent of the defense research and development budget will be based on international collaboration by the end of this decade; it was less than 3 percent in 1988.[6]

The progressive relaxation of East-West trade restrictions, including termination of the requirement for licenses among COCOM members for all but the most advanced technologies and the elimination of third-party retransfer prohibitions on equipment consisting of components that are less than 25 percent of U.S. origin, also reflect the accommodation of American policy to the demands of a more competitive market.[7] Underscoring this shift, the Department of Commerce has been given an unprecedentedly greater role in decisions about agreements to share military technology, a responsibility previously monopolized by the Department of Defense. As one administration official noted, "this is the first time there is a recognition that Commerce needs to play a role like MITI [Japan's Ministry of International Trade and Industry] to make sure we remain industrially competitive."[8] The statement reflects the degree to which industrial competitiveness has become a more prominent factor in weighing decisions about collaborative defense production ventures.

The trends toward multinational defense cooperation and liberalized trade between East and West have serious implications for developing countries' access to technology. Given most industrial countries' dependence on exports, the easing of trade barriers among them may raise the level and volume of defense technology available for purchase globally. In addition to Western exporters, former Soviet bloc states are likely to try to benefit from Western technology and diminished Soviet control of their military sectors by seeking military clients of their own.

With narrowing constraints on domestic investment in defense and increasing foreign penetration of the U.S. market, American industry may also seek a larger share of the global arms market. Many in industry believe that marketing weapons more aggressively is the only way expensive national research and development programs for futuristic technologies, such as stealth, can be made affordable. As an official of the Northrop Corporation argued in mid-1989, "The types of advanced weapons now under development in the U.S. . . . are not those which will easily be exported for some time. These weapons are highly sophisticated, contain technologies developed at enormous expense, and are highly classified. . . . Planning needs to begin immediately to develop products for future export."[9]

Without higher export revenues, rising weapon costs could require much larger government subsidies to companies involved in advanced research and development, funding that may be increasingly difficult to find as U.S. government budgets become tighter. How the United States decides to support its own high-technology sector could thus have consequences for global technology diffusion. Reduced federal financing for high-definition television, semiconductor manufacturing technologies, and other military research and development programs with commercial applications could force companies with an interest in such ventures to turn to the export market to stay economically viable.[10] Although developing states are still far from gaining access to these technologies, the structural linkage between other forms of technology diffusion and domestic defense industrial policy should not be overlooked.

A deepening dependency on exports of dual-use technologies thus could force the United States to liberalize arms and technology export policies in a manner that might not reflect its long-term foreign policy and military objectives. Controls on exports may seem an expendable luxury in a severely constricted economic environment, particularly if the restrictions seem to be cutting into U.S. military preparedness and economic competitiveness. Indeed, some Bush administration officials have begun informally to promote government incentives to further encourage U.S. arms exports. As one official said,

Defense exports provide an impetus to the continuation of the U.S. lead in developing high technology. They cannot and should not fully compensate for the decline in domestic defense procurements; however, they can and should provide the edge that enables our high technology industry to continue to invest in the future. It is both necessary and appropriate for the U.S. government to facilitate the export of defense articles where it does not conflict with U.S. national . . . interests.[11]

The economic penalties of export controls on high technology have been a source of political controversy for some time. A study by the National Academy of Sciences in 1988, for example, estimated that controls on high technology cost the U.S. economy $9 billion and close to 200,000 jobs in 1985.[12] As exports to developing countries involve more advanced and dual-use technologies, the trade-offs between economic and national security objectives could be subject to similar calculations, with commensurate political pressures to remove trade barriers.

A policy that sought to subsidize the costs of national security and sustain the nation's economic competitiveness by enhancing the capabilities of smaller states to wage war with advanced weapons would seem a paradox, but it is not out of the question. Even today, standard U.S. weapon systems such as the F-16, an aircraft touted by U.S. industry as a product America should market worldwide, are still very advanced by the standards of most developing countries. Because contracts with many of these countries are increasingly accompanied by a demand for access to manufacturing processes, end-use assurances and other such traditional means of control may become increasingly difficult for suppliers to enforce, further attenuating influence over the distribution and use of weapons technology. Third world consumers may augment their access to advanced military technology by using U.S. defense firms and even the U.S. military services to advocate more permissive technology-sharing agreements. This in fact occurred in recent controversies over the sales of aircraft to Japan and South Korea.

Other industrial sectors that contribute to technology diffusion also experience conflict between commercial pressures and policy restraints. Under current conditions, for example, the space industry may be the least able to adjust to interference in its commercial activities without substantial restructuring.[13] The high costs of space-launch activities already cause NASA, the European Space Agency, and the Soviet space program to seek foreign participation. Although cost considerations do not necessarily mean that companies will have to accelerate sales of equipment prohibited by the Missile Technology Control Regime, space-launch vehicles and other restricted technologies are important components of the prospective global demand of space industries. It cannot simply be assumed that recipients will permit advanced countries to dictate the content of this trade indefinitely. Although only a handful of nations can produce and launch satellites, additional states, including Brazil, China, India, and Israel, are beginning to manufacture them and may in time be able to undercut the current market hierarchy and compel industrial countries to share their technologies more freely.

Despite these trends, it is not yet the case that a free market is the only realistic arbiter of technology transactions. Supplier cartels may seem outmoded and transitory in light of the rapid transformations under way in the international system but, however imperfectly, they still constitute one of the few mechanisms by which advanced countries can influence the pace of developments.

The states that retain some control over sensitive technologies can influence demand by raising the financial and political costs of acquiring them. Technology will eventually be diffused to countries determined to achieve certain military capabilities. Trade restrictions, however, can buy time to devise ways to contain the instabilities posed by global militarization and to address the causes of international conflicts. The added time could also be used to help states develop force postures and doctrines oriented toward deterrence and stability and to devise international norms for managing the potential risks posed by the diffusion of advanced technologies.

Controlling Transfers of Advanced Technology

Strategic trade controls still enjoy multinational support, even if the geopolitical framework for their implementation is breaking down. The military self-interests of the major powers coincide on the necessity for protectionist measures to ensure the security of advanced technologies. The United States, in particular, has a strong interest in devising a more equitable distribution of the costs of defending the NATO alliance and in making sure that its own security is not being compromised by others' quests for commercial gains.

The first priority of a regime to control transfers of sensitive technologies must be to develop simpler guidelines that can win wide support. The guidelines would have to shorten the list of targeted technologies and provide more flexible decision rules that could accommodate rapid changes in the international technology market. As one official put it, a new regime would need "higher fences around fewer goods."[14]

Many experts have suggested that developed countries could increase their influence by focusing on a few so-called enabling technologies, those that make significant contributions to military capability. The diffusion of these technologies is still sufficiently contained that denial of a sale would have a real impact. As John Steinbruner has argued,

The prohibition of exports should be directed only to direct weapon products and to items so closely related to weapons applications that such an application predominates over all other applications. For militarily sensitive technologies that cannot meet this criterion, strictly applied, export licensing should require explicit, accurate, and complete end-use disclosure. For especially sensitive technologies, cooperative verification agreements should be made a condition of export.[15]

An export regime would thus rely less on prohibiting technology exports and more on strict requirements for disclosure about the uses of a given technology.

To assess the desirability of alternative controls, the United States will have to be more sensitive to the trade-off between the possibility that a technology will be compromised and the costs of failing to provide technology to allies and clients. With the exception of a few categories of items that could be restricted a priori, such as biological and chemical agents, decisions about what constitutes sensitive technologies will increasingly have to take into account the specific conditions in recipient states, including their industrial capabilities, local or regional enmities, the sophistication of their military forces, and the overall foreign policy objectives of suppliers and clients. In turn, to understand these conditions will require more emphasis on shared intelligence.

As William Webster, director of the Central Intelligence Agency, noted in a speech in 1989, economic developments in foreign countries are becoming a more important element of U.S. intelligence gathering relative to military activities per se because "along with the globalization of international finance has come the greater use of the financial system by governments and groups whose objectives threaten our national security interests.''[16] He included terrorist activities, illegal arms purchases, technology transfer, and nuclear proliferation. Although the CIA's focus still tends to be on East European nations, recognizing the importance of international economic and political trends for U.S. security could also increase the effectiveness of domestic efforts to monitor international technology flows.

To reform the export control system, building on existing institutions established for coordinating exports would probably work better than attempting to establish a wholly new apparatus. For all its imperfections, COCOM has experience in identifying and tracking technologies and— although this is its weakest activity—enforcing restraints. With fewer restricted goods, efforts to monitor technology flows with shared intelligence, to impose strict penalties for noncompliance, and to participate in joint efforts to pressure non-COCOM members to abide by the organization's guidelines could become more effective. Although there may never be full agreement about the scope and desirability of some safeguards, even general norms could provide a foundation for adjudicating disagreements.

The basic rationale for and structure of a new control structure will obviously have to be broad enough to take into account the changing patterns of military antagonisms, but this requirement was recognized well before the recent dramatic changes in Eastern Europe. The bipolar concept that underscored COCOM at its genesis is already recognized as an atavism of the cold war. Now as East European and industrializing countries look to the advanced countries for technology, they may be able to be brought into a new regime, sharing a collective interest in international stability and ensuring their continued access to Western assistance. As one American official said, "After all, if the Soviets can have an ambassador accredited to NATO, there is no reason for not having a Soviet observer accredited to COCOM.''[17] Indeed, it is past time to examine ways in which liberalized access to Western technology could be linked more explicitly to other Western diplomatic objectives, such as discouraging some kinds of weapons sales to countries in unstable regions.

A revised control apparatus could have several regional subgroupings, reflecting changes in power alignments in the international system. Although the basic structure could remain, with most power still in the hands of advanced industrial countries, additional consultative mechanisms could be established for areas such as East Asia, South Asia, and the Middle East. These regional groups could deepen international understanding about the emerging technology environment, an understanding that has for too long remained oblivious to developments outside the East-West context.

Given the growing complexities of reforming trade guidelines, advanced nations should consider elevating a regime to control military trade to the status of an international agency, even if membership remains strictly consensual. Such an apparatus could provide the expertise to anticipate transfers of precision-strike systems, biotechnologies, antisatellite systems, and other futuristic technologies that could threaten global stability and could help manage their dissemination in a more structured way.

Of course, no single agency could realistically accommodate the diverse interests of dozens of nations and remain effective. Like the nuclear nonproliferation regime, however, an international regime for controlling dual-use conventional technology could complement national policies and bilateral or regional diplomacy. Establishing such a mechanism will have to be an evolutionary process, based on developing flexible institutions that can adapt to the rapid changes in the international system.

With careful management and clear objectives, economic integration among industrial countries could bolster coordination of technology security policy. Inevitably, economic and military cooperation between East and West would be accompanied by closer consultation on political and diplomatic issues. At a minimum, by providing more routine interaction among participating governments, the working groups and other consultative mechanisms established to implement collaborative economic ventures could help consolidate interests in broader areas of policy.

Recent developments in the twelve-member European Commission suggest such consolidation is already occurring, albeit on a modest scale. Although the Treaty of Rome, which established the commission in 1957, prohibited it from regulating defense policy, an agreement reached in 1987 and known as the Single Market Act permits EC nations to coordinate economic policies that have a bearing on security. The policymaking apparatus of the commission has since become far more involved in defense and foreign policy matters.[18] Following the death threats by Iran against the author Salman Rushdie, for instance, members acting through the EC's adjunct European Political Cooperation (EPC) group exchanged proposals about responses, reviewed options, and agreed to a joint plan, including the recall of the countries' ambassadors to Tehran, all of which was accomplished in three days. Similarly, following a meeting of EC commissioners on chemical weapons controls, the EPC agreed to regulate the export of materials pertinent to producing chemical weapons.[19]

The success of these initiatives might not have been possible without the secure telex network connecting all EC members, the augmented staff assigned to monitor international developments of common interest, and other mechanisms put in place to aid economic integration. Though seemingly mundane, these innovations have given the concept of international collaboration actuality. According to one diplomat, "the most important development within the European Community is not any specific treaty, nor any organizational mechanism, but rather the habit of cooperation."[20] Although they will not be panaceas for resolving differences among allies, such multinational structures should be encouraged by the United States and could include U.S. participation where appropriate.

Additional reforms will be needed for even an informal export regime to be workable. One of the most basic problems is the absence of a comprehensive data base for monitoring the technology embodied in civilian and military products or for identifying its sources. Devising a U.S. export-control policy has long been hampered by this deficiency. In 1989, for instance, the General Accounting Office charged there was no coordination among U.S. agencies that were supposed to track dual-use technologies available internationally.[21] Without comprehensive information, national and international agencies cannot adjust controls to the realities of the market and cannot consider the effectiveness of alternative policies.

Far greater cooperation between industry and government may also be necessary to identify, let alone monitor, technologies deemed vital to security. As the European countries move to rationalize their high-technology industries by melding commercial and defense activities, for instance, companies will have to do more to ensure the security of their defense-related innovations. The sheer complexity of the international technology market, with its networks of legal and illegal suppliers, is already overwhelming the modest resources available to governments to track technological developments and create effective policy instruments. This kind of cooperation may be especially important in the case of Japan. As the world's leading source of sophisticated information technology, Japanese industry dominates what has become a crucial component for a wide range of advanced military missions, including command and control, intelligence, targeting, and guidance.[22] Without support from Japanese industry and government, any control regime could be readily subverted by Japanese exploitation of market opportunities if it is undertaken without adequate consideration of the collective security interests of other industrialized states.

A more ambitious international apparatus for industry-government cooperation, one that includes high-level official participation, will have to be established. A practical model for such cooperation might be found in efforts to control the spread of chemical weapons. The Chemical Manufacturers Association, whose members account for almost 90 percent of all chemical production in the United States, has actively helped devise the terms and mechanisms of a treaty to ban chemical weapons. According to one analyst, this "unprecedented industry-government relationship has given the diplomatic community access to technical expertise critical to understanding and resolving key outstanding treaty issues."[23] Without industry's assistance, the government could not have identified the thousands of items relevant to making chemical weapons or where they are produced, nor could it have evaluated the risks and benefits of alternative treaty limitations and their verification. And the chemical industry also benefited. The loss of sales that a treaty prohibiting military production creates is far surpassed by the necessity to preserve the industry's ability to make sure that any agreement does not impinge on its legitimate commercial activities.

As the developed countries move toward greater integration of their defense industries, they will have to agree about the disposition and security of their shared technologies. Defense companies will have a direct interest in these agreements. As is true of the chemical industry, participation and support for such arrangements may be necessary both to help compile information about sources of technology and to help design and implement workable safeguards that do not interfere unduly with legitimate activities of private enterprise.

The model of the chemical manufacturers may be particularly apt for the space industry. Commercial interests involved in promoting peaceful space cooperation have the most to lose from international opprobrium for the diversion of space technology for ballistic missiles or other offensive military uses. The immediate self-interest of such companies suggests that they could help governments restrain missile programs in unstable countries by identifying technologies needed for missile development and devising safeguards that can discourage the adaptation of civilian equipment for military programs. Although some might consider this undue encroachment on national sovereignty, this is one technology for which a few suppliers still have the leverage to influence the pace and content of production programs.

Subscribing to an international agreement limiting clients' military activities could also actually improve the competitiveness of companies in the space technology market. The future of space cooperation is extremely vulnerable to political sensitivities about "the militarization of space," and Congress has already threatened punitive measures against companies engaged in such military ventures. In the long term the belief that space companies are not cooperating in missile nonproliferation efforts could create hostility toward peaceful space ventures and impose costs that would exceed the revenues earned by accepting dubious foreign contracts.

The extent to which international economic imperatives could overwhelm foreign policy objectives, including restraints on technology exports, will depend on the nature and scope of the controls and the extent of cooperation that can be elicited to prevent countries from exploiting a restraint regime for unilateral advantage. If industrial countries' efforts to foster their competitiveness depend on increased arms and technology exports, even modest controls may be difficult to sustain domestically let alone internationally.

In trying to devise options for a more effective technology security policy, the United States and its allies could begin to redress the structural inefficiencies that account for the export dependency in their defense industries. The Groupe de Reserche et d'Information sur la Paix has calculated that arms exports accounted for one-third of total weapon production in Europe between 1980 and 1988, with more than three quarters of the exports going to the third world.[24] At these levels of excess capacity, even the most liberal arms export policy would be only a short-term palliative for the systemic problems faced by Western defense firms. As multinational cooperation becomes the dominant strategy for alliance planning, eliminating duplication of effort and other diseconomies could become more feasible, and could in turn temper export pressures that test prudent foreign policy.

Strengthening the Missile Technology Control Regime

The linkage between exports of advanced technology in the industrial world and technology diffusion to the third world is not formally recognized in the U.S. policy apparatus. Despite the obvious interrelationships, the prevailing view has been that although security concerns were addressed by restricting East-West technology transfers, promoting exports to friendly states in the developing world, or at least a fairly free market approach, would advance U.S. objectives. Similarly, liberalized access to Western technology among industrialized states has never been linked systematically with agreements to discourage destabilizing military exports to the third world.

But officials have now recognized a connection at the political level between trade policies for industrialized countries and those for developing countries. In 1989, for example, Secretary of State James Baker argued that liberalized trade and Soviet access to Western technology would depend in part on Moscow's assistance in limiting chemical and missile proliferation in the Middle East.[25] Similarly, attempts to restore exchanges of technology with China following the moratorium imposed after the massacre of students in Tiananmen Square has had as one justification efforts to get the Chinese to stop selling missiles to developing countries.[26]

More formal consolidation of trade and security policies is inevitable. As developing countries mature, the lists of restricted technologies pertinent to them and to industrial countries will increasingly overlap. Restrictions under COCOM guidelines need to be coordinated with nonproliferation objectives. But the existing foundations for consolidation are weak. Before the MTCR was initiated in 1987, there was no formal international apparatus to guide transfers of conventional technologies to developing countries. There is still very little interest in a regime that would curtail exports of weapons or dual-use technologies. Governments, including those that adhere to the MTCR and the Nuclear Non-Proliferation Treaty, have vigorously resisted controls on transfers of advanced aircraft and nonballistic missiles, despite their pertinence for the delivery of nuclear weapons and potentially for ballistic missile development.[27]

Thus, given the history of failed efforts to create even modest agreements to control transfers of conventional technology, the MTCR is a significant achievement. In light of the attempts to develop "trigger lists" for restricted equipment in nuclear nonproliferation efforts, which have always proved highly contentious, the MTCR also should be seen as a triumph of unusual technical consensus.

Those who devised the regime have gone a long way in identifying technologies that can contribute to missile development and securing agreement from eight countries about guidelines to control dissemination. The MTCR has also helped pinpoint the most difficult aspects of missile design, such as guidance technology, and target these for special scrutiny. The director of the Central Intelligence Agency acknowledged the importance of controls on these technologies in late 1989, arguing that "cutting off the supply of guidance technology can cripple a third world defense program."[28]

The MTCR has led to the development of a new bureaucratic infrastructure for monitoring one aspect of missile technology flows to developing countries and understanding the synergism among particular dual-use technologies that, added together, could augment missile production capabilities. In principle, the lists of controlled items compiled for the MTCR could become the basis for a more comprehensive approach to controlling technology diffusion, were there political support for such an objective. The guidelines are sufficiently flexible to accommodate new kinds of high-risk technologies that may become more widely available, including equipment pertinent to warhead design, improvements in missile accuracy and range, and antisatellite operations.

The MTCR has had some success in impeding missile programs. It is credited with helping stop the Argentinean-Egyptian-Iraqi Condor II program, discouraging Chinese sales of the M-9 missile, and forcing the West German government to crack down on private firms engaged in missile development efforts in Libya and Iraq. Partly as a result of pressure from Congress and the threat of legislated sanctions, countries are paying more attention to export violations, and some such as Germany may have emplaced entirely new procedures to ensure closer government scrutiny of technology exports.[29] And now that some Soviet industrial production is moving out of state-run enterprises, Moscow is finding that it too must develop domestic guidelines and enforcement mechanisms to monitor export activities.[30] At a December 1989 U.S.-Soviet meeting on missile proliferation, Soviet representatives are reported to have asked numerous questions about how to establish controls on industrial exports. The MTCR also has helped stem illegal transactions by drawing attention to proliferation: the United States successfully intercepted a shipment of chemicals from India to Iraq in July 1989, for instance, based on reports from intelligence sources.[31]

The MTCR, however, has no international agency to monitor compliance, no enforcement mechanism, and no institutionalized arrangements for regular meetings. Only two formal meetings of MTCR adherents have occurred since 1988, the most recent in December 1989, although bilateral meetings have taken place on an ad hoc basis.

Governments do not consider nonproliferation to be among their highest foreign policy priorities. In the United States the interagency apparatus responsible for the MTCR has lacked bureaucratic clout. And at least until recently, it was left to mid-level bureaucrats to adjudicate disputes about adherence to guidelines. The recent changes in the jurisdictional structure discussed in chapter 5 may help redress some of these problems.

Even with the MTCR's modest scope, implementing it has involved some serious international controversies. In late 1989, over strenuous objections from the United States, France proceeded with negotiations to sell Brazil liquid-fuel rocket engine technology, which could be useful for ballistic missile production, in return for a $60 million contract to launch two Brazilian communications satellites. Continued West German involvement in developing guidance technology for the Indian Agni missile has also been reported.[32]

Aside from controversies caused by differences among countries about their foreign policy objectives, tensions have been created by ambiguities in the text of the MTCR. These ambiguities need to be clarified to strengthen the regime.

First, it is unclear whether the MTCR is solely an adjunct of the Nuclear Non-Proliferation Treaty. Some would contend that its restrictions apply only to exports to states that have nuclear programs but are not treaty signatories, an argument used to justify China's sale of the CSS-2 to Saudi Arabia. The United States and Britain have declared that such sales of missile technology are not permissible, even to states that are signatories, but this position is still a source of potential controversy that could complicate efforts to gather additional support for the regime.

Second, the MTCR guidelines are unclear about what forms of cooperative space ventures are and are not permissible. Although the text states specifically that the regime is not designed to interfere with legitimate space programs, it also states that such efforts cannot be associated with the development of systems for delivering nuclear weapons. Because the technologies for space-launch vehicles and ballistic missiles are virtually indistinguishable, cooperation would seem to be precluded. But France has obviously taken a different view, and other countries may follow. The United States has been trying to forge a common position on this issue. Some individuals in the Arms Control and Disarmament Agency have argued that a blanket prohibition on exports of space-launch vehicles is not realistic and that devising safeguards on the uses of space technology is preferable. Officials with responsibility for the MTCR in the Department of Defense, however, oppose any loosening of the interpretation that the MTCR prohibits exports of these vehicles. This dispute continues and is confusing to countries that may be subject to competing views of U.S. policy.

A third ambiguity is the nature of national obligations that result from signing the MTCR. The regime has always been consensual, with participating governments interpreting and adapting the guidelines in their national export codes. It is not intended to override national policy, and individual states are supposed to be responsible for end-use assurances. Nevertheless, France's claim that it has the sovereign right to sell engine technology to Brazil and its assertion that it will prevent diversion to military uses by imposing its own safeguards has caused international concern.

Given developing countries' political sensitivity to a supplier cartel, some ambiguity may be a virtue. No supplier wants to state outright that third world space ventures are inherently illegitimate, and some flexibility in the application of guidelines is needed to accommodate differences among sovereign countries. Enforcement, however, is politically very volatile, and publicized disputes over apparent violations of the letter or spirit of the MTCR have damaged the credibility of the regime. The lack of binding enforcement authority already has prompted legislation in Congress that would impose punitive measures on countries and companies engaged in MTCR-restricted trade. Although there are differing views in Congress about the scope and nature of the sanctions that should be invoked, there is majority support for imposing formal penalties on violators, in some cases regardless of whether the exports in question originate in a country that has signed the agreement (see chapter 5).

Still, discussions of sanctions in Congress have prompted criticism from foreign governments and from the Bush administration. The executive branch considers the imposition of broad trade sanctions on foreign nationals, including denying violators access to U.S. government contracts and licenses, an excessive intrusion upon its authority, circumscribing the ability of the United States to use noncoercive means to persuade states to comply with the MTCR and, it is argued, to elicit the support of nonsignatory countries.[33]

Supporters of sanctions counter that trade restrictions are meaningless if they can be readily circumvented by renegade companies or countries and that the United States has the leverage to enforce compliance by threatening penalties that would exceed the benefits of violations. Senator Jeff Bingaman, a leading supporter of sanctions, argues that legislation to stem missile proliferation is no different from legislation on behalf of preventing the proliferation of nuclear technology, including the 1978 Nuclear Non-Proliferation Act.[34]

Regardless of one's view about the legitimacy or desirability of legislated sanctions, if MTCR adherants circumvent guidelines for their own advantage, other countries will see little point in joining the regime. Strengthening enforcement is thus an urgent priority if the MTCR is to survive and its membership expand. With stronger enforcement, for example, Eastern European countries looking to the West for much needed technological assistance would probably hesitate to export missile-related equipment, even if they had the means to do so.

Enduring support for the MTCR, however, is hindered by the absence of a common perception of the risks posed by proliferation. Leaving aside opposition from states that consider it discriminatory, the regime lacks a publicly compelling rationale. As Joseph Nye has argued, it has inherently limited legitimacy because ballistic missiles, unlike nuclear or chemical weapons, are not widely perceived to carry a "moral stigma."[35]

But wider support might be achieved by a clearer articulation of the MTCR's costs and benefits, a pragmatic calculus that would show that restraint of trade in missile and space technology is a prudent course of action for the industrial nations. Aside from disparate perceptions of the military importance of ballistic missiles, governments seem to have exaggerated estimates of the value of contracts that would be lost by adhering to the guidelines. Although the costs of the political antagonisms that sometimes result from denying access to technology cannot be assigned, the relatively modest impact on revenues and profits from forgoing missile sales could be demonstrated with reasonable precision. Emerging missile producers like Brazil may have ambitious plans to capture export revenues through missile sales, but more objective assessments suggest that the sales would represent a small fraction of such countries' total arms export revenues in the next decade.

This kind of economic analysis, if conducted jointly by the allies, might help demonstrate the advantages and disadvantages of restraint more realistically, and, perhaps, bolster the case for the MTCR. Similarly, developing a mechanism by which allied defense planners could estimate the effects of missile proliferation on their own force requirements should be considered. If, as one analyst has argued, "the costs of failing to control exports [to the third world] are likely to be higher than the costs of the additional military capabilities required to make up for a free market in weapons-related technology," the case for a supplier cartel could be made more persuasively on national security and budgetary grounds.[36]

Assessments of long-term threat should be incorporated into routine military planning, becoming an integral part of priorities for modernizing defenses. If the diffusion of missiles is taken seriously as a military risk, it should inform requirements for overseas basing, interventionary capabilities, and ways to help clients counter military instabilities in regions of high tension.

The risks associated with the diffusion of space technology should also be stated more clearly. Satellite reconnaissance images commercially available today can help nations plan attacks against adversaries and contribute to the accuracy of their missile forces. U.S. Landsat and French Spot images are believed to have been used by military planners in the Iran-Iraq war, for example.[37] In time, accurate satellite images may be available from a greater number of commercial sources. Space technologies may also help states conduct more effective military operations by improving command, control, and communications. Although some analysts would argue that greater openness among countries is a welcome, or at least inevitable, international trend, there is not much evidence that U.S. policy has kept pace with the military challenges that may also be posed.[38]

The diffusion of satellite and missile technology may mean that more nations will be able to conduct offensive operations in space. Some analysts in the Arab world have accused Israel of introducing a regional space race through its participation in collaborative research on lasers, high-energy particles, and other ventures related to the U.S. strategic defense initiative. Although Tel Aviv denies it, Arabs increasingly believe that Israel plans to use satellite programs for offensive military space operations.[39]

In the future, states that have missile programs might begin to consider antisatellite systems. Following the Israeli test of the *Ofek* satellite, Iraqi president Saddam Hussein announced that Iraq wanted to develop an antisatellite system and had recently tested a space-launch vehicle. Although any claim to incipient antisatellite capabilities is obviously fatuous, it suggests that efforts to acquire such capabilities, however quixotic, may be on the rise.[40]

As Paul Stares has commented, "Any ballistic missile capable of delivering a nuclear warhead within sufficient range of a space object to inflict damage or otherwise interfere with its normal functioning is technically an antisatellite weapon. This would include . . . any nuclear-armed missile system with the requisite reach." Although it would be far more challenging technically, conventionally armed space-launch vehicles could in principle be adapted to an ASAT role. As Stares goes on to comment, "States in possession of long-range ballistic missiles and sufficiently powerful radio transmitters will always have the inherent capacity to destroy and interfere with the functioning of objects in space."[41]

The acquisition of even rudimentary antisatellite capabilities among a wider number of countries could certainly complicate, if not vitiate, any agreement among the great powers to develop a space operations regime or to limit space weapons. And given its disproportionate reliance on satellites for a variety of security objectives, the United States has every reason to pay close attention to the global diffusion of space technology.

One other trend in military technology is worthy of attention. As the industrial countries reduce their nuclear arsenals, accurate non-nuclear weapons with strategic range may begin to replace nuclear forces. The implications of such a counterforce has been a subject of discussion in U.S. strategy for years. As one analyst has argued, "while such technologies will not come to possess the psychological or status value of nuclear arms, the lower stigma attached to their acquisition is likely to lead to their widespread proliferation."[42] Such systems could destabilize a region if they gave states the ability to launch preemptive strikes and encouraged aggressive military operations that would seem too risky with nuclear or chemical warheads.

In the final analysis, the MTCR has been plagued by its image as an idealistic arms control initiative designed to save the third world from itself, rather than a prudent gesture on the part of Western countries to stem the deterioration of military environments in which they may have to protect their own interests. Industrialized countries have abided by export restraints in the past because of an interest in containing military developments in areas in which their own forces might be placed at risk. This may not be an argument that wins supporters in developing countries, but it does have the virtue of reflecting the self-interest of industrial states that is embodied in the MTCR.

For now, the most significant impediments to missile proliferation are constraints within the developing countries themselves. The expense of missile programs, made worse by suppliers' restraints, have often stymied development. After all, as Jeffrey Richelson has commented with regard to satellite reconnaissance, ''An investment of several billion dollars is required to establish a launch site, build the launch vehicles, develop the satellite, construct a ground control station or network, purchase the necessary computers and imagery enhancement software, and maintain a staff of photointerpreters.''[43] Such ambitious undertakings are likely to be beyond the resources of all but a handful of nations for the foreseeable future.

As such, reducing global demand for missile technology by raising the economic and political costs of acquisition is still workable if suppliers agree that the resulting political frictions are worth it. To reduce demand, the MTCR could be strengthened by an agreement among developed nations for more formal guidelines, along the lines of the London Suppliers' Group controlling nuclear exports. The MTCR also needs to establish routine procedures for consultation among participants, to share intelligence, and to develop durable international norms for controlling broader areas of technology diffusion. To be credible, however, such a regime must be adhered to by a larger group of developing as well as developed states.

Although the Soviet Union is not a signatory to the MTCR, it shares common concerns about third world ballistic missile proliferation and has expressed continued interest in supporting the agreement. Disagreements between the superpowers, however, could complicate a formal expansion of the regime. These disagreements are particularly likely to concern how to treat the missile programs of close U.S. security partners such as Israel. There were indications in late 1989 that the Soviet Union might press for lower range and payload ceilings on the systems covered by the MTCR: the ceilings would include systems exceeding a range of 100 kilometers and a payload of 200 kilograms, and would include aircraft.[44] (The matter has not surfaced recently, however.) Such proposals clearly test the U.S. commitment to missile nonproliferation, potentially impinging on other sensitive areas of foreign policy.

Such differences must be discussed through quiet diplomatic channels, not in the court of international opinion. Any sign of joint U.S.-Soviet initiatives invariably raises hackles among third world recipients, who fear the emergence of a superpower condominium, as well as among allies in Europe and East Asia.

These concerns notwithstanding, the Soviet Union has given numerous signals that it will join the United States and other nations in containing regional conflicts. It has denounced Iranian terrorism, distanced itself from Libya and North Korea, told the Syrian government in 1987 that there could be no military solution to the Arab-Israeli struggle, and supported the multilateral defensive force confronting Iraq's invasion of Kuwait. These signs bode well for cooperation in missile restraint.

U.S. initiatives to control missile nonproliferation require more clearly stated objectives that can be supported by sustained bureaucratic attention. At a minimum, there must be sufficient consensus at the highest levels of government that the security threats posed by the diffusion of missile technology are worth the political costs that may be incurred in encouraging restraint. Leadership is vital to ensure that multilateral diplomatic efforts are consonant with overall foreign policy goals and to resolve the bureaucratic disputes that inevitably arise as restraint impinges on traditional international relationships.

The fundamental question is how stringently the United States wants to pursue missile export restraint and how much pressure it will put on missile suppliers and recipients on behalf of this goal. Although the Bush administration has been reluctant to support sanctions, Congress may demand an even more activist approach to international enforcement of the MTCR in the wake of the Iraqi crisis.

The United States has already demonstrated its leadership in assisting states to enforce export codes. Even such prosaic efforts as enforcing customs, automating data collection, and monitoring exports can improve the prospects for an effective export regime. Still, enforcement requires careful political management to defuse domestic disagreements and avoid giving the United States an exaggerated international profile as enforcer.

Enforcing the MTCR may require better intelligence gathering than is currently dedicated to this objective. As in the context of COCOM, improved intelligence could help enforcement by emphasizing the prevention of proliferation instead of trying to inflict punishment after the fact. To this end, procedures need to be established for pooling intelligence among allies. The economic and defensive integration of Europe, along with the diminished military threat from the Soviet Union, may make this kind of collaboration easier.

Whether the United States is prepared to offer client states incentives to limit their missile acquisition programs, and if so, what kind of incentives, is another unresolved question. The absence of effective coordination among agencies with jurisdiction over trade policy, security assistance, economic assistance, sensitive technology transfers, space policy, and arms control makes it difficult to consider mechanisms from which Washington could gain leverage.

In particular, devising criteria for space-related exports to the third world will require difficult choices about desirable and undesirable types of proliferation, so that technologies useful for development activities could be separated from their military applications. Aside from achieving greater consensus about the scope of permitted space activities, the United States and its allies should begin now to try to bring emerging space powers into an international regime and to present ways to manage military space operations together.

The President's Space Council could be encouraged to devise space-related incentives for countries that agree to abjure missile development and to develop concepts for an international space regime. It could, for instance, examine whether an international space-launch agency would work as an alternative to selling space-launch capabilities. The Space Council could also coordinate the development of the domestic space sector with America's foreign policy objectives. Coordination might, for instance, dampen unrealistic assumptions about the degree to which federal financing can support an expedition to Mars or other high-cost ventures that could lead to inefficient programs and perhaps create unexpected and intensified commercial pressures on companies that face declining levels of federal assistance.[45] Recessionary trends in the space sector that threaten vital programs could create insurmountable conflicts between commercial and security interests.

Agencies with responsibilities for international debt management and other concessionary transactions also need to be brought into the policy process to see if there may be ways to link financial incentives and military restraints. At a minimum, the policies of the World Bank, the International Development Agency, and other international lending agencies should be reviewed to ensure that assessments of a country's eligibility for credits and loans take into account the influence of its military, including the nature and relative burden of weapon development and production programs. Consideration should be given to a proposal by a House Foreign Affairs Committee task force to establish an International Development Cooperation Council in the White House, with jurisdiction over all international assistance mechanisms.[46] This is one way to encourage coordinated attention by senior officials and connect development assistance activities with other foreign policy objectives.

Finally, will the administration give national and international regulatory mechanisms for stemming missile proliferation priority over such countermilitary responses as promoting antitactical ballistic missile programs for key allies or even deploying strategic defenses in the United States? Although these instruments are not necessarily mutually exclusive, they represent wholly different approaches to the problem and may not ultimately be politically or bureaucratically compatible.

Promoting Regional Security

Efforts to restrain missile programs are more likely to be effective if they are part of broader initiatives to build a genuinely interdependent international system with codified and reliable means of resolving regional disputes peacefully. But governments have paid very little attention to policy instruments other than export controls that could be used to manage the transition to a world that has a greater diffusion of military power. The means by which third world countries might be encouraged to take up nonaggressive and defensively oriented postures even as they acquire more advanced weapons are not well understood. Although the United States has always made it an explicit policy to cooperate with foreign governments to promote stability, its efforts have been impeded by the competing idea that they could be construed as implicitly legitimating existing military ambitions.

Technical Arms Control Measures

Traditional forms of arms control, which derive from efforts to reduce the nuclear forces of the superpowers, may not pertain to attempts to control global missile proliferation. First, the relatively abstract nature of the East-West military competition has been quite different from the diffuse and highly volatile political-military conditions that exist in the third world and that defy uniform technical approaches.

The United States and the Soviet Union have had decades to develop the enabling agreements and technical foundations for reaching accommodations on nuclear and, more recently, conventional forces. Even so, the difficulties associated with defining the conventional balance in the European theater suggest the formidable challenges that would be posed in defining limitations in areas without so much as a rudimentary framework for common agreement. Negotiated limitations on third world arsenals will thus depend on a measure of political accommodation among adversaries that does not exist in the regions where missile proliferation is most dangerous. NATO and Warsaw Pact nations, for example, understand that the main purpose of nuclear weapons is that they never be used. This contrasts starkly with the incentives of regional adversaries to acquire ballistic missiles and other advanced military capabilities, many of whom are often intent on improving their arsenals specifically to prosecute ongoing military rivalries.

In light of these complexities, negotiated numerical ceilings on the numbers of missiles and warheads, limitations on the ranges of missiles, flight test bans, restrictions on deployment areas, and other technical limitations seem unpromising instruments for containing the threat of ballistic missiles. Examining the reasons why these technical approaches may not be feasible helps illuminate the variables that will have to be considered in developing more workable restraint policies.

NUMERICAL CEILINGS. Agreed ceilings on the numbers of particular types of weapons in nuclear inventories are a mainstay of strategic arms control agreements among the developed nations. Trying to achieve ceilings presupposes that governments can calculate, at least roughly, equivalencies among types of weapons and agree that fewer weapons would improve international stability. It also presupposes the acceptance of asymmetries among national arsenals in certain categories of weapons in return for offsetting limitations in other categories. Thus the definition of desirable limits derives from a common understanding of what is needed to achieve overall military parity and stability, the conditions for which must be reasonably within reach. Such assumptions, however, cannot be expected readily in the third world.

The task of defining balances is extremely difficult in regions where conflicts are occurring. For instance, Israel considers the inventories of the Arab and Persian Gulf states a collective threat to its security. Therefore it seeks qualitative superiority to offset those states' collective and overwhelming numerical strength in conventional weaponry and troops, as well as the advantages accorded them by geography. The Arab states believe Israel's nuclear and missile arsenals vastly outweigh their superiority in numbers and thus seek comparable qualitative capabilities to ensure security against the Israeli threat. Agreeing on parity is further complicated by political animosity among the Arab states. Antagonisms between Syria and Jordan, Egypt and Libya, and between all the moderate Arab states and Iraq preclude any agreement that would require the forces of the Arab nations to be counted collectively. Nor are enmities within a region limited to adjacent countries. Saudi Arabia considers Iran, Iraq, and Israel regional threats. India considers China as important in defining its military requirements as its more proximate adversary, Pakistan. In other words, political-military realities preclude definitions of coherent regions, let alone common concepts of parity or stability.

Even if balances could be outlined, the importance of numerical ceilings on missiles in these volatile regions is questionable. As was demonstrated in the War of the Cities between Iran and Iraq, small numbers of missiles can devastate civilian targets, and they could be even more lethal if armed with nonconventional weapons.

The possibility for negotiated numerical limits on a regional basis might seem more promising in Latin America, where antagonism stems from the military and economic rivalry between Brazil and Argentina. The problem posed by the two nations' missile programs, however, is less the result of military tensions between them than of their export programs. As such, curtailing missiles is more aptly a matter of providing economic or trade incentives to encourage deceleration of missile production and exports rather than arms control.

RANGE LIMITATIONS. Negotiating equitable and militarily meaningful range limitations in the Middle East and South Asia would be as difficult as determining ceilings. Israel, India, and even Saudi Arabia already possess missiles with ranges far greater than what could be considered an acceptable standard for restraint, exceeding the limits imposed by the United States and the Soviet Union in the Intermediate-range Nuclear Forces Treaty and far exceeding the limits of the MTCR. And because adversarial states in the Middle East, the Persian Gulf, and South Asia lie so close to one another, it would be difficult to achieve range limitations low enough to matter. The Syrian SS-21, for instance, is not considered a long-range missile, but it can fly fifty miles in less than five minutes, posing a very serious threat to Israeli military installations. Range limitations also are difficult to verify. They can be extended by reducing payloads or improving rocket engine efficiency; and restraints on such conversions would be hard to enforce.

Negotiated limits on new long-range missiles in North and South Korea could help reduce the uncertainties that arise from continued proliferation, especially the possibility of a disarming preemptive attack. But again, given the short distances between the two antagonists, no realistic range limitation could ease the dangers very much.

DEPLOYMENT LIMITATIONS. Agreements to delimit missile deployment areas—moving forces away from borders, for instance, and declaring fixed deployment sites that could be monitored continuously—could reduce perceived threats of surprise attacks and, in principle, be stabilizing. But as with other technical limitations, geographic and political conditions would mitigate the relevance of such agreements in many regions unless they were part of a broader security arrangement. Mobile missiles like the Syrian SS-21 could quickly violate any deployment limitation. In addition, the greater ranges of newer missile systems, and in most regions the short distances from launch sites to targets, renders any arrangement for restricted deployment areas meaningless.

The delineation of deployment zones is, however, not without successful precedent and could be an important element of more comprehensive bilateral or regional security pacts. The Sinai Demilitarization Agreement, for instance, which provides for peacekeeping forces and other enforcement mechanisms to watch for proscribed military activities in the area, has strengthened stability and reduced tensions between Israel and Egypt for many years.

Achieving this kind of agreement in other contexts, however, presupposes a level of political and military stability that has so far eluded diplomatic efforts, particularly in the Middle East. The Sinai agreement was possible only after Egypt and Israel achieved a political understanding in the Camp David accords. For now, no other military rivals seem promising candidates for such arrangements.

FLIGHT TEST BANS. Some analysts have suggested that the United States and other developed nations could press for a global ban on testing ballistic missiles. New missiles, they argue, cannot be deployed if they have not been tested. But such reasoning is politically faulty. It is not at all clear that the United States and the Soviet Union, let alone the European nuclear states, would ever agree to forgo missile testing, a proposal that has been raised informally for years but has never been negotiated seriously. To expect them to abandon testing in the hopes of persuading third world countries to follow suit is far-fetched. And even if they were willing to do so, most third world countries would not find the demonstration of industrial nations' restraint all that compelling, given the disparities between developed and developing nations in the size and sophistication of existing arsenals.

Building Confidence and Security

The limited applicability of technical measures for arms control suggests that constraining missile proliferation should be part of broader diplomatic efforts to end regional conflicts. In support of such efforts, nations might wish to explore confidence- and security-building measures, including exchanges of information and intelligence, on-site inspections of defense production and space-launch facilities, and prior notification of missile tests. These and other means to promote consultation among regional rivals could ease unwarranted suspicions about missile production efforts, limit the political and military consequences of these efforts, and, possibly, reduce some of the incentives now propelling the expansion of the programs. According to Barry Blechman, "A particular value of [confidence-building measures] is that their negotiation can by-pass questions of relative military capabilities, where problems of quantification, verification, and asymmetrical perceptions of the threat can bog down discussions. [The measures] aim directly at assessments of intent, regardless of actual capabilities."[47]

Confidence- and security-building measures can dispel some of the mystery about rivals' military activities, provide channels for routine interaction, and demonstrate adversaries' interests in reassuring other states about their military goals. Although such instruments are only valuable as indicators of political will and can be violated at any time, they can provide the foundations of a diplomatic infrastructure needed for broader accommodation.

Existing regional measures include a proposed agreement between India and Pakistan not to attack one another's nuclear facilities and to begin negotiations of a nuclear test ban. Argentina and Brazil have increased mutual reassurance through on-site visits to each others' nuclear facilities and declarations of nonhostile intent. And informal U.S. proposals have encouraged Middle Eastern countries to abjure first use of ballistic missiles and to notify one another of upcoming missile launches.[48]

Pledges not to use ballistic missiles preemptively and other declarations of intent would obviously not endure in a crisis, but they are nevertheless signs of political conciliation and should not be dismissed out of hand. Similarly, agreements to allow on-site visits and provide prior notification of test launches do nothing to stop dedicated missile programs, but they can reduce the climate of suspicion among adversaries that fuels efforts to advance missile programs despite their high economic and political costs.

Other confidence- and security-building measures that could be considered for missile restraint regimes include the application of international safeguards and on-site verification at space-launch facilities to ensure they are not being used to develop missiles; maintaining missile forces unarmed and unfueled during peacetime, subject to monitoring; and, in addition to prior notification of test launches, agreements to orient tested systems away from adversaries' territory. Further measures could include regional export controls, such as agreements not to sell missiles to terrorist states, and routine bilateral military exchanges between rival states to document the extent and pace of missile development plans and to discuss common security concerns.[49]

Achieving more significant curbs on the demand for missiles will depend on reducing overall regional tensions, but individual states can pursue incremental measures to improve confidence. The United States and the Soviet Union can provide encouragement for these activities, although the choice of initiatives must ultimately come from the states themselves and must reflect local realities.

As a first step, the United States can help countries develop routine mechanisms to exchange information about military programs, discuss mutual security concerns, and ultimately consider more ambitious arms control measures. America is a source of leadership and expertise on implementing such mechanisms, which are often genuinely unfamiliar to third world countries.

The United States could also provide technologies for more effective command and control, survivable basing modes, permissive action links, and other such systems that have long been vital to superpower military stability. This proposal is controversial, however. Some argue that emerging missile (and nuclear) powers should be discouraged from gaining confidence in their forces so that they will be less likely to contemplate using them. Others argue that unreliable command and control procedures or unsafe weapons help no one, and that the likelihood of using new missiles would be reduced if nations had greater confidence in their ability to use them when they were actually needed.

The decades of efforts by the superpowers to manage their nuclear rivalry could provide lessons for the third world and shorten the difficult transition from provocative to deterrent postures. Although judgments about the desirability of technological assistance for command and control would have to be made case by case, to assume that countries should be discouraged from developing modern force structures may not only be unrealistic but could unduly prolong the risks posed by force vulnerabilities and unconventional doctrines.[50]

Resolving Regional Conflicts

Perhaps the most important way the United States could work to increase regional security would be to cooperate with the Soviet Union to stem conflict between the nations they support. Given the current U.S.-Soviet reconciliation, such agreements seem possible.

The mutual interest in stopping global proliferation of missiles and weapons of mass destruction was summarized by Soviet Foreign Minister Edvard Shevardnadze in a speech on March 7, 1989:

"In the Near and Middle East . . . powerful weapons arsenals are being created. . . . Missiles have already appeared with an operational range of 2,500 km; that is, of precisely the same class that is being eliminated from Europe. . . . The conclusion is obvious: the process of disarmament in Europe and settlement in the Middle East have to be synchronized."[51]

In June 1989 the chairman of the Joint Chiefs of Staff and the chief of the Soviet General Staff signed an agreement to prevent and resolve crises arising from provocative activities by their respective armed forces. Although the Agreement on the Prevention of Dangerous Military Activities is a technical one and not a regional security accord, it was inspired in part by the experience of the Iran-Iraq war when, according to one analyst, "American and Soviet forces sometimes operated in proximity to each other, leading both sides to recognize the need for a mechanism to coordinate their activities."[52] The cooperation between the United States and the Soviet Union during the crisis over Kuwait highlights the degree to which superpower efforts to stem unstable military developments in the third world could become an integral element of international diplomacy.

As the superpowers' influence in the third world attenuates, agreements between them may be a necessary, if not sufficient, condition to contain the international consequences of wars—the arrangements that kept the world in a fragile peace for four decades may seem comparatively simple compared with the challenges of defining stability in a multipolar nuclear system. But regardless of progress in achieving formal regional security agreements, the superpowers' development of common understandings to guide crisis management and crisis resolution will become increasingly important as third world power alignments become more diffuse and clients more militarily dangerous, as the challenges of the Iraqi invasion of Kuwait demonstrated quite clearly. Although conflicts will occur in countries and regions over which neither superpower has decisive influence, without clearer codes of conduct, tacit or otherwise, as well as improved mechanisms for communicating during crises, they may find their ability to remain neutral during third world conflicts increasingly difficult. As a positive by-product of such understandings, moreover, recipients may have more difficulty demanding weapons from one or the other by playing on exaggerated perceptions of threats to security. And a client's threat to turn to the rival superpower if demands are denied could be limited.

Bilateral U.S.-Soviet talks on regional security, which have been pursued sporadically in the past, could also lead to diplomatic understandings tailored to specific areas. These should be conducted quietly to avoid otherwise inevitable third world fears of a superpower cartel or condominium. But because the volatility of the world is creating both new dangers and new opportunities for the superpowers, such talks should be an element of future U.S.-Soviet diplomacy.

Reaching for Global Agreements

In considering international agreements to limit the proliferation of missiles and other military technologies, one can draw lessons from the relative successes of supplier cartels formed for other purposes. The nuclear nonproliferation regime, however imperfectly, has clearly slowed the global diffusion of nuclear weapons. Similarly, the 1925 Geneva Protocol on chemical weapons and the 1975 Biological Weapons Convention have dissuaded states from acquiring or using these weapons, at least until recently.

There are, however, important distinctions to be made. The nuclear nonproliferation regime owes its genesis to the monopoly on nuclear weapons that the superpowers maintained for many years. The regime is held together by a widespread consensus about the unique dangers of these weapons, and it has operated with the clear objective of retaining a permanent hierarchy between nuclear and non-nuclear states. Multinational agreements to ban chemical and biological weapons were possible in large measure because of the less-than-compelling military utility of these weapons and the grave threat they pose to noncombatants. The proliferation of missile technologies shares few of these attributes: the monopoly is already shattered, the dangers are often disputed, the possibility of a hierarchy has been manifestly rejected, and perceptions of their utility overwhelm moral opprobrium.

In the current international political environment, an effort to transform the Missile Technology Control Regime into an international treaty seems at best quixotic. Developing countries would charge discrimination. And the argument that ballistic missiles need universal controls even though other delivery vehicles, including nonballistic missiles and aircraft, do not, is at least on the surface inconsistent. To the extent that the MTCR has been successful, in fact, its success has derived from its modest and consensual nature, and from the fact that it was negotiated outside the glare of the international spotlight.

More ambitious agreements have been proposed, including the universalization of the Intermediate-range Nuclear Forces Treaty banning missiles with ranges between 500 and 5,500 kilometers, or the creation of a regime similar to the one the Nuclear Non-Proliferation Treaty set up for missiles. But attempts to broaden the INF treaty would encounter difficulties in negotiating meaningful limits on missile ranges, difficulties that would be exacerbated because countries could still deploy missiles of intercontinental range and relatively short range. The logic is obscure, and less developed states would be certain to point out the great powers' hypocrisy in holding on to strategic and tactical missile inventories. The political friction such an initiative would generate would probably doom prospects for a successful international agreement.

A space-cooperation regime for stemming missile diffusion could, however, resemble the nuclear nonproliferation regime, making the possibility of such an agreement, however remote, worth further examination. For both missiles and nuclear weapons the consensus is that relevant technologies should be controlled but that peaceful uses should be encouraged. If countries could be persuaded that involvement in an international space regime would guarantee that they would receive needed technology, and thus the potential for greater security, they might join. Some observers have therefore advocated establishing an international space organization to provide launch services for countries that do not have their own space programs or for those willing to abjure diversion of their space investment to military uses. This idea is apparently supported by the Soviet Union.

The difficulties of distinguishing between military and nonmilitary space technologies would remain. Similar challenges have confronted the implementation of provisions in The Nuclear Non-Proliferation Treaty for years, because nuclear reactors and related processes, including enrichment technology and chemical separation facilities, have both civilian and military applications. But through the monitoring activities of the International Atomic Energy Administration the nonproliferation regime has institutionalized safeguards against transfers of targeted technologies and protected against diversions from civilian to military purposes. Although the safeguards have not been completely successful, the IAEA is generally considered an effective international institution.

A system of international safeguards could also be developed as part of a space cooperation regime. An agency made up of multinational inspectors, like the IAEA, or operating out of a revised COCOM structure could serve as the umbrella organization to conduct international inspections and verify compliance with the agreement. States would permit these on-site inspections of space facilities in return for satellite data and launch services.

There would, however, be some potentially intractable problems. The extent to which countries would be willing to forgo efforts to acquire independent space-launch capabilities would depend in part on how much concessionary assistance would be offered by advanced countries. Given the problems faced by space industries in the developed nations, sizable subsidies are difficult to envision. More important, all developing countries that have space programs also have missile programs; they might not want to abandon their programs, because it would seem to mean abandoning their ambitions to be free of control by the great powers. An agreement on space activities, moreover, would not address other, equally vital channels of missile-related technology diffusion.

Prospects of international agreement might be more promising in the regulation of antisatellite weapons. Acquiring operational antisatellite capabilities is a distant prospect for advanced countries, and certainly for any developing state. But as Donald Hafner has argued, "By continuing to offer open and generous access to their own space services, the superpowers can reduce the incentives of third states to go off on their own and acquire independent capabilities that could be turned to ASAT purposes."[53] The price, however, could be that the superpowers would have to impose ASAT restraints on themselves, a price that might be more willingly paid if the threat of international ASAT proliferation were taken seriously.

All current proposals for international agreements tend to reflect a bias in favor of the great powers, often with little sensitivity for the ambitions of developing states to become more equal partners in the international system. Too little is known about what kinds of incentives might draw an India or a Brazil into a system of international cooperation. To this end, a first step might be to convene an International Missile Conference under neutral auspices similar to the January 1989 conference on chemical weapons. Such a conference would be intended to permit a full airing of all countries' views on these matters and to set a framework for possible international cooperation. Some modest agreements along the lines of the confidence- and security-building measures discussed above might be achievable in the near term and might build momentum for more ambitious efforts. More far-reaching cooperation may be impeded by the smaller states' perception that the great powers are discriminating against them. Defining norms that can elicit genuine international support will require taking the objectives of developing countries seriously, and recognizing that those interests are as enduring as they are diverse.

Conclusion

The industrial powers may profess they no longer believe in warfare as a means of resolving their own disputes among themselves, but they have yet to renounce it as an extension of policy in third world regions where their economic and military interests may be at risk. If nothing else, their actions against Iraq in January 1991 reminded the world of this reality. They have yet to take seriously their need to alter significantly the premises and assumptions that guide their defense planning. Above all, belief in technological panaceas to counter emerging threats to security remains almost dogma among industrial countries.

But the quest for technological fixes may be quixotic, and it certainly distracts from the greater challenge of devising more effective ways to address the causes of military antagonisms and to help emerging powers develop militarily without increasing regional and international tensions. The historical experience of industrial countries suggests that the period of transition from fledgling military power to modern statehood holds the greatest potential for military instability. Yet the frameworks for promoting deterrence are so oriented toward a bipolar international system that the means for achieving a peaceful transition to a multipolar deterrent system are not well understood. No longer can the problem be ignored. The perception of the developing world as a collection of compliant client states is dangerously atavistic. Indeed, the concept of the "third world," if such a world ever existed, must be replaced by the recognition that competing regional powers have distinct ambitions and the ability to fulfill those ambitions with or without the sanction of the great powers.

Although the Missile Technology Control Regime is limited, although it sidesteps the problem of enforcement and does not cover delivery systems other than missiles that can threaten global stability, it could provide a framework for new instruments to control the diffusion of sensitive technology. Putting together a more ambitious regime, however, has to begin with more coherent policies among the advanced countries. Multinational efforts to share advanced technology among industrial countries may provide an avenue for greater coordination of arms export guidelines internationally.

In the third world the risks of missile proliferation, especially in the Persian Gulf, coupled with the fragility of the economic and technical infrastructures in these states, might constitute a reason for creating a selective supplier cartel to stem dangerous military developments. Indeed, the international concerns that have been raised about destabilizing alliances among such countries as Libya, Iran, and North Korea—and the international agreement since August 1990 to isolate Iraq—could spur the creation of a selective multinational regime that could, perhaps, become the basis for more comprehensive cooperation. This suggestion may lead to the conclusion that the MTCR and other such formal arrangements exist largely to penalize countries with whom adherents have minimal relations in any case, but such an intention is not unreasonable. It emphasizes the essentially political character of diplomatic instruments and the need for formal, technical controls to be calibrated against the realities of international politics.

Export cartels, however, are not a solution for removing the forces that impel countries to acquire advanced weapons. And any attempt to form a cartel should not be allowed to detract from the more urgent and difficult challenge of devising instruments to promote global stability and help nations achieve security. As the industrial countries move toward greater accommodation among themselves, they must not dismiss the efforts of other states to achieve similar accommodation and equilibrium. It is one thing to cast away strategies that have outlived their usefulness, but quite another to assume that the rest of the world can be induced to avoid the Faustian bargains that made the strategies necessary in the first place. The paradoxical concept that states must develop sophisticated weapons so they may never be used has been accepted as creed by the advanced countries for decades and is now being adapted by developing states. For advanced industrial countries to believe that developing states' objects will be susceptible to change through international example or coercion could prove self-defeating. The great powers' influence over developing countries may have been progressively attenuated, but the challenges involved in containing adverse developments posed by a global redistribution of military power are as urgent as they are complex.

Notes

Chapter One: The Challenge of Technology Diffusion

1. The two-stage Agni was launched from a temporary site at Chandipur, 750 miles southeast of New Delhi, following two failed attempts to test the system earlier in the year. See Barbara Crossette, "India Reports Successful Test of Mid-Range Missile," *New York Times,* May 23, 1989, p. A9; Richard M. Weintraub, "India Tests Mid-Range 'Agni' Missile," *Washington Post,* May 23, 1989, p. A1; and "Indian IRBM Details Revealed," *International Defense Review,* no. 3, 1989, p. 247.

2. A working definition of a ballistic missile is provided in a Congressional Research Service study: "a self-propelled weapon-delivery system that is guided during a portion of its ascent, then follows a ballistic (unpowered and unguided) trajectory over the remainder of its flight." This definition covers most unmanned, guided delivery vehicles that operate in surface-to-surface mode, but it distinguishes them from cruise missiles, which have air-breathing engines and are guided throughout their flight, and unguided short-range rockets. See Robert D. Shuey and others, *Missile Proliferation: Survey of Emerging Missile Forces* (Congressional Research Service, October 3, 1988), p. 1, note 1. Although U.S. policy on missile nonproliferation restricts the transfer of cruise missile technologies as well, the focus has until recently been on ballistic systems. This analysis discusses cruise missiles as being of potential interest to emerging missile powers but treats them as functionally distinct from ballistic missiles. For further discussion of cruise missiles, see chap. 2; and W. Seth Carus, *Ballistic Missiles in the Third World: Threat and Response* (Washington: Center for Strategic and International Studies; and New York: Praeger, 1990).

3. White House spokesman Roman Popadiuk, quoted in "U.S. Is Dismayed," *New York Times,* May 23, 1989, p. A9.

4. Letter to President George Bush, May 22, 1989. Principal sponsors were Senators John McCain and Jeff Bingaman, and Representatives Gerald Solomon and Howard Berman.

5. Krishna Chandra Pant, Minister of State for Defense, quoted in Crossette, "India Reports Successful Test," p. A9.

6. The defense minister indicated India would proceed with its missile programs and refuse to accede to "pressure" from the United States. See "India Won't Yield to U.S. on Missile," *Washington Times,* July 25, 1989, p. A2. See also "India's Missile Technology Development Program," unpublished memorandum from the Embassy of India, April 21, 1989. Although the Agni is said to be a "technology demonstrator" and decisions about production were still pending at the end of 1990, the system is part of India's Integrated Missile Development program begun in 1983, which aims to achieve total self-reliance in missile development and production. Interviews with Dr. K. Subrahmanyam, former director of the Indian Institute for Defence Studies and Analysis, Washington, D.C., September 1989; and Indian Air Commodore Jasjit Singh, Bellagio, Italy, October 1989.

7. David B. Ottaway, "Bush Administration Debates Sale of Missile-Testing Device to India," *Washington Post*, May 28, 1989, p. A8.

8. John J. Fialka, "Space Research Fuels Arms Proliferation: Indian Missile Suggests U.S., West German Parenthood," *Wall Street Journal*, July 6, 1989, p. 8; and Ottaway, "Bush Administration Debates Sale," p. A8. The transfer of CAVCTS to India was denied in August 1989: David B. Ottaway, "U.S. To Bar India's Buying Missile Device," *Washington Post*, August 17, 1989, p. A12. The Indian government responded by announcing plans to develop missile-testing devices indigenously: "India To Make Own Missile-Testing Device," Reuters, August 14, 1989.

9. "U.S. Is Dismayed," p. A9.

10. In April 1987 the Reagan administration announced the Missile Technology Control Regime, an agreement among seven industrial countries to abide by restraints on exports of missile-related technology. The details of the agreement appear in "Missile Technology Control Regime: Fact Sheet To Accompany Public Announcement," Department of Defense, April 16, 1987.

11. For a variety of views on the FS-X controversy, see Democratic Study Group, "The FSX Deal," report 101-7, House of Representatives, May 10, 1989; James Fallows, "Japan: Let Them Defend Themselves," *Atlantic*, April 1989; John Heinz, "The FSX Deal with Japan Is a Fire Sale," *Washington Post*, March 30, 1989, p. A23; Congressman Richard A. Gephardt, remarks to the Telocator Spring International Convention, Orlando, Florida, May 5, 1989; and Statement of Secretary of Defense Richard B. Cheney, *United States–Japanese Security Cooperation and the FSX Agreement*, Hearings before the Subcommittee on Arms Control, International Security and Science; on Asia and Pacific Affairs; and on International Economic Policy and Trade of the House Committee on Foreign Affairs, 101 Cong. 1 sess. (Government Printing Office, 1989), pp. 55–68.

12. "The FSX: Done Deal at Last," *Economist*, May 30, 1989, p. 32. A congressional amendment to impose additional restrictions on Japanese access to U.S. technology in the FSX contract was vetoed by President Bush in July 1989; Stuart Auerbach, "Bush Vetoes Effort to Curb FSX Project," *Washington Post*, August 1, 1989, p. C9.

13. For further discussion of these trends, see John D. Steinbruner, ed., *Restructuring American Foreign Policy* (Brookings, 1989), especially pp. 1–48 and 119–57; and Charles H. Ferguson, "America's High-Tech Decline," *Foreign Policy*, no. 74 (Spring 1989), pp. 123–33.

14. The terms *third world, developing countries,* and *industrializing countries* are used interchangeably in this analysis to encompass states outside of NATO, the Soviet Union, Eastern Europe, Australia, New Zealand, and Japan. The concept of the third world has always been a geopolitical artifice and is extremely imprecise. One analyst claims it is derived from the French concept of the third estate to refer to "developing countries that seek to avoid domination by the superpowers and to preserve their freedom of maneuver between East and West." As a political concept, this is as good a definition as any, but it ignores the diversity of countries covered under this broad rubric. See Michael H. Armacost, "U.S. Policy toward the Third World," *Department of State Bulletin*, vol. 87 (January 1987), pp. 56–60.

15. See for instance Stephanie G. Neuman, *Military Assistance in Recent Wars: The Dominance of the Superpowers* (Washington: Center for Strategic and International Studies; and New York: Praeger, 1986).

16. For a broader discussion of the trends in the arms export market, see Paul L. Ferrari and others, *U.S. Arms Exports: Policies and Contractors* (Cambridge, Mass.: Ballinger, 1988); Michael T. Klare, *American Arms Supermarket* (University of Texas

Press, 1984); and Richard F. Grimmett, *Trends in Conventional Arms Transfers to the Third World by Major Supplier, 1982–1989* (Congressional Research Service, June 1990).

17. For additional discussion of export dependency in the industrial countries, see Ferrari and others, *U.S. Arms Exports,* pp. 87–90; Marvin Leibstone, "U.S. Defence Exports: An Industry at the Crossroads," *Military Technology,* vol. 13 (July 1989), pp. 17–19; and chap. 5.

18. For further discussion of the proliferation of defense production technology in the developing world, see Michael Brzoska and Thomas Ohlson, eds., *Arms Production in the Third World* (London: Taylor and Francis, 1986); Michael T. Klare, "The Unnoticed Arms Trade: Exports of Conventional Arms-Making Technology," *International Security,* vol. 8 (Fall 1983), pp. 72–87; Janne E. Nolan, *Military Industry in Taiwan and South Korea* (St. Martin's Press, 1986); and chap. 2.

19. Aaron Karp discusses the blurring of distinctions between commercial and military space technology in "Space Technology in the Third World: Commercialization and the Spread of Ballistic Missiles," *Space Policy,* vol. 2 (May 1986), pp. 157–68. For discussion of this phenomenon with respect to other technologies, see Benjamin N. Schiff, "Conventional Lessons from Nuclear Export Policy Experience," paper prepared for the 1984 annual meeting of the International Studies Association; James R. Golden, "A Domestic Perspective: Technology Transfers, U.S. Interests, and Policy," in Asa A. Clark IV and John F. Lilley, eds., *Defense Technology* (New York: Westport; and London: Praeger, 1989), pp. 64–81; and chap. 6.

20. The political and military implications of the global spread of reconnaissance satellite technology is discussed in Michael Krepon, "Peacemakers or Rent-A-Spies?" *Bulletin of the Atomic Scientists,* vol. 45 (September 1989), pp. 12–15; and Peter D. Zimmerman, "From the SPOT Files: Evidence of Spying," *Bulletin of the Atomic Scientists,* vol. 45 (September 1989), pp. 24–25.

21. The linkage between the proliferation of nuclear weapons and missiles is discussed in Leonard S. Spector, *The Undeclared Bomb* (Cambridge, Mass.: Ballinger, 1988), chap. 2; and Maurice Eisenstein, "Third World Missiles and Nuclear Proliferation," *Washington Quarterly,* vol. 5 (Summer 1982), pp. 112–15. For Israel and South Africa, the connection is perhaps unusually direct: South Africa is alleged to be providing Israel with uranium in return for assistance in developing a long-range missile. See R. Jeffrey Smith, "Israel Said To Help S. Africa on Missile," *Washington Post,* October 26, 1989, p. A36.

22. For further discussion, see, for instance, Office of Technology Assessment, *Holding the Edge: Maintaining the Defense Technology Base,* OTA-ISC-420 (April 1989).

23. Ashton B. Carter, "Analyzing the Dual-Use Technologies Question," paper presented to the Workshop on Military and Civilian Technologies: A Changing Relationship, Harvard University, November 1989, p. 15.

24. Concern about the proliferation of ballistic missiles in regional arsenals was noted by Soviet General Secretary Mikhail Gorbachev and President Ronald Reagan in the joint statement issued at the Moscow summit in 1988. See "Joint Statement on the Moscow Summit," May 29–June 2, 1988, p. 7.

25. For additional discussion of the "War of the Cities," see Shahram Chubin, "Iran and the War: From Stalemate to Ceasefire," in Efraim Karsh, ed., *The Iran-Iraq War: Impact and Implications* (St. Martin's Press, 1989); and W. Seth Carus, "Missiles in the Middle East: A New Threat to Stability," *Policy Focus,* research memorandum 6, Washington Institute for Near East Policy, June 1988. On the sale of the Chinese CSS-2 to Saudi Arabia, see John M. Goshko and Don Oberdorfer, "Chinese Sell Saudis Missiles Capable of Covering Mideast," *Washington Post,* March 18, 1988, p. A1; and

Hannaford Company, "Facts about the Proposed Sale of Support Services for Saudi Arabia's AWACs," report prepared for the Saudi Arabian government, May 1988. For details of the South African, Iraqi, Israeli, and Libyan missile programs, see Shuey and others, *Missile Proliferation,* pp. 51–55 (Iraq), 56–61 (Israel), 61–63 (Libya), and 66–67 (South Africa).

26. Arms Control and Disarmament Agency, "Ballistic Missile Proliferation in the Developing World," *World Military Expenditures and Arms Transfers 1988,* publication 131 (1989), pp. 18–19.

27. The military significance of ballistic missiles is discussed in Shuey and others, *Missile Proliferation,* pp. 7–11; Aaron Karp, "Ballistic Missiles in the Third World," *International Security,* vol. 9 (Winter 1984–85), pp. 168–75; and chap. 4.

28. A. U.S. installation has already been the target of a missile attack. In 1986 Libya fired two Scud-Bs against bases on the Italian island of Lampedusa. Although they missed by a wide margin, the attack prompted tighter security measures at U.S. embassies and bases around the world: Richard Halloran, "U.S. on World Alert," *New York Times,* April 16, 1986, p. A18. U.S. planners have also been concerned about the threat of Syrian SS-21s or even Scuds against American forces in Lebanon. For additional discussion, see W. Seth Carus, "Testimony," *Missile Proliferation: The Need for Controls (Missile Technology Control Regime),* Hearings before the Subcommittees on Arms Control, International Security, and on Science and International Economic Policy and Trade of the House Committee on Foreign Affairs, 101 Cong. 1 sess. (GPO 1989), pp. 102–03; Shuey and others, *Missile Proliferation,* pp. 11–12; Gerald M. Steinberg, "The Middle East in the Missile Age," *Issues in Science and Technology,* vol. 5 (Summer 1989), pp. 35–36; and Karp, "Ballistic Missiles in the Third World," pp. 168–69.

29. Senator John McCain has argued that Iraq's use of chemical weapons in its war with Iran "has already accelerated the efforts of other nations to create major stockpiles of such weapons." See "Gas Warfare and the Proliferation of Weapons of Mass Destruction: The Need for American Action," draft paper, November 1988, p. 1. For more precise discussion of the incentives for countries to acquire chemical weapons, see Elisa D. Harris, "Chemical Weapons Proliferation: Current Capabilities and Prospects for Control," in *New Threats: Responding to the Proliferation of Nuclear, Chemical, and Delivery Capabilities in the Third World* (Aspen Strategy Group and University Press of America, 1990), pp. 67–87.

30. "Third World Missiles: Look What I Found in My Backyard," *Economist,* May 27, 1989, pp. 44–45.

31. C. Raja Mohan and K. Subrahmanyam, "High–Technology Weapons in the Developing World," in Eric H. Arnett, ed., *New Technologies for Security and Arms Control: Threats and Promise* (Washington: American Association for the Advancement of Science, 1989), pp. 229–30.

Chapter Two: The Context of Third World Defense Investment

1. For example, a United Nations document produced for the 1987 International Conference on Disarmament for Development lists nineteen national proposals put forward in the UN since 1973 linking development and disarmament, most of them

initiated by France and the Soviet Union, two leading arms suppliers. See "Preparatory Committee for the International Conference on the Relationship between Disarmament and Development, Document," cited in Jacques Fontanel and Jean-François Guilhaudis, "Arms Transfer Control and Proposals To Link Disarmament to Development," in Thomas Ohlson, ed., *Arms Transfer Limitations and Third World Security* (Oxford University Press, 1988), p. 215, note 1.

2. For a discussion of the international migration of technology, see Joseph Grunwald and Kenneth Flamm, *The Global Factory: Foreign Assembly in International Trade* (Brookings, 1985).

3. The manufacture of major weapon systems by third world countries is concentrated in India, Israel, South Africa, Taiwan, Brazil, Argentina, Pakistan, South Korea, and North Korea, which together account for more than three-quarters of this market. Less significant producers include Egypt, members of the Association of South East Asian Nations (ASEAN), Iran, and Iraq. Countries with very limited production capabilities include Burma, Chile, Colombia, the Dominican Republic, Gabon, Libya, Madagascar, Mexico, Peru, Senegal, and Sri Lanka. For a comprehensive overview of the major third world producers, see Michael Brzoska and Thomas Ohlson, eds., *Arms Production in the Third World* (London: Taylor and Francis, 1986); and James Everett Katz, ed., *Arms Production in Developing Countries: An Analysis of Decision Making* (Lexington, Mass.: Lexington Books, 1984).

4. For various opinions on the effects of military expenditures on economic development, see Nicole Ball, "Defense and Development: A Critique of the Benoit Study," in Helena Tuomi and Raimo Vayrynen, eds., *Militarization and Arms Production* (St. Martin's, 1983), chap. 3; Mary Kaldor, *The Baroque Arsenal* (Hill and Wang, 1981); Steve Chan, "The Impact of Defense Spending on Economic Performance: A Survey of Evidence and Problems," *Orbis*, vol. 29 (Summer 1985), pp. 403–34; Wayne Joerding, "Economic Growth and Defense Spending," *Journal of Development Economics*, vol. 21 (April 1986), pp. 35–40; and Emile Benoit, "Growth and Defense in Developing Countries," *Economic Development and Cultural Change*, vol. 26 (January 1978), pp. 271–80.

5. On the connection between U.S. defense spending and technological innovation, see Kenneth Flamm and Thomas L. McNaugher, "Rationalizing Technology Investments," in John D. Steinbruner, ed., *Restructuring American Foreign Policy* (Brookings, 1989), pp. 119–57; and Office of Technology Assessment, *Holding the Edge: Maintaining the Defense Technology Base*, OTA-ISC-420 (April 1989).

6. Indigenous development of advanced weapons in the third world is almost always more expensive than importing finished systems. The more sophisticated the weapon system and the more limited the producer's industrial capacity, the higher the production costs. Axiomatically, countries that have less experience with complex technologies must spend more to create the necessary conditions for building defense industries. Although licensed production of weapons should in theory lower costs by obviating the need to spend money on research and development, such ventures have proved relatively more expensive compared with importing finished systems because production runs in many third world countries are limited by modest demand and severe scarcities of capital and scientific expertise. For further discussion, see Michael Brzoska, "The Impact of Arms Production in the Third World," working paper 8, Centre for the Study of Wars, Armaments, and Development, University of Hamburg, February 1987. On the costs of missile production specifically, see Mark Balaschak and others, *Assessing the Comparability of Dual-Use Technologies for Ballistic Missile Development*, report prepared for the Arms Control and Disarmament Agency, ACOWC 113 (MIT, June 1981).

7. For further discussion of these countries' defense production sectors, see Brzoska and Ohlson, eds., *Arms Production in the Third World*, chaps. 3, 9, 11.

8. Cited in *Missiles, Space, and Other Defense Matters*, Hearings before the Preparedness Investigating Subcommittee of the Senate Committee on Armed Services in conjunction with the Committee on Aeronautical and Space Sciences, 86 Cong. 2 sess. (Government Printing Office, 1960), p. 5.

9. For further discussion of the economic and industrial benefits sought through defense investment, see Stephanie G. Neuman, *Military Assistance in Recent Wars: The Dominance of the Superpowers* (Washington: Center for Strategic and International Studies; and New York: Praeger, 1986); Janne E. Nolan, *Military Industry in Taiwan and South Korea* (St. Martin's Press, 1986), chap. 1; and K. Subrahmanyam, "Problems of Defense Industrialization in India," *Institute for Defense Studies and Analysis Journal* (New Delhi, India), vol. 13 (1981), pp. 363–77.

10. Aaron Karp, "Space Technology in the Third World: Commercialization and the Spread of Ballistic Missiles," *Space Policy*, vol. 2 (May 1986), pp. 157–59. For additional discussion of development benefits, see Y. S. Rajan, "Benefits from Space Technology: A View from a Developing Country," *Space Policy*, vol. 4 (August 1988), pp. 221–28; and Juan G. Roederer, "The Participation of Developing Countries in Space Research," *Space Policy*, vol. 1 (August 1985), pp. 311–17.

11. For discussion of dual-use technologies and missile development, see Balaschak and others, *Assessing the Comparability*.

12. Stephanie G. Neuman, "Third World Arms Production and The Global Arms Transfer System," in Katz, ed., *Arms Production in Developing Countries*, p. 27.

13. For further discussion of South Korea's missile program, see Janne Nolan, "South Korea: An Ambitious Client of the United States," in Brzoska and Ohlson, eds., *Arms Production in the Third World*, pp. 223–24; and chap. 3 in this volume.

14. The cooperative effort among Iraq, Egypt, and Argentina appears to have ground to a halt after Egypt announced its withdrawal in late 1989; see "Missile Proliferation in the Third World," *Strategic Survey 1988–1989* (London: Brassey's for International Institute for Strategic Studies, 1989), pp. 20–21; and David B. Ottaway, "Egypt Drops out of Missile Project," *Washington Post*, September 20, 1989, p. A32. For the North Korean Scud program, see W. Seth Carus and Joseph S. Bermudez, Jr., "Iran's Growing Missile Forces," *Jane's Defence Weekly*, July 23, 1988, p. 130.

15. For Israel's assistance and exports to Taiwan and South Africa, see *DMS Market Intelligence Report: Missiles/Israel* (Defense Marketing Services: Greenwich, Conn., 1988), p. 17; and "Israel-South Africa Connection Suspicious," *Atlanta Constitution*, November 1, 1989, p. A16. On cooperation between Israel and China, see Jim Mann, "Israeli Arms Technology Aids China," *Los Angeles Times*, June 13, 1990, p. A1. On China and Arab states, see "Arms Transfer Tables," *Defense and Foreign Affairs*, vol. 17 (August 7, 1989), pp. 42–43. Elaine Sciolino, "Chinese Missiles Sold in Mideast Worrying Shultz," *New York Times*, July 16, 1988, p. A1; and Ihsan A. Hijazi, "Arab Lands Said To Be Turning to China for Arms," *New York Times*, June 24, 1988, p. A3.

16. Edward H. Kolcum, "Brazil, China Form Space Launch Venture," *Aviation Week and Space Technology*, vol. 130 (May 29, 1989), p. 35; and Clarence A. Robinson, Jr., "French Missile Technology May Land in Libya," *Washington Times*, July 18, 1989, p. A1.

17. Edward J. Laurence, "The New Gunrunning," *Orbis*, vol. 33 (Spring 1989), p. 229. See also "Missile Proliferation in the Third World," *Strategic Survey 1988–1989*, pp. 20–21.

18. Although precise statistics on the size of the international arms trade are not available, limited data on illegal sales of American arms suggest significant growth in

recent years. See Laurance, "The New Gunrunning," pp. 225–34. On Iraq, see Janne E. Nolan, "How To Stymie Iraq—For a While," *New York Times,* April 3, 1990, p. A23.

19. K. C. Pant, "Philosophy of Indian Defence International Transformation," *Strategic Analysis* (New Delhi: Institute for Defence Studies and Analysis), vol. 12 (August 1989), p. 480.

20. Jerome Paolini, "French Military Space Policy and European Cooperation," *Space Policy,* vol. 4 (August 1988), p. 209.

21. For a summary of the evolution of U.S. and Soviet missile development, see Browne and Shaw Research Corporation, *The Diffusion of Combat Aircraft, Missiles, and Their Supporting Technologies,* report prepared for the Office of the Assistant Secretary of Defense, International Security Affairs, DA-49-083 (Waltham, Mass.: October 1966).

22. Despite official prohibitions on transfers of missile-related technology, both the United States and West Germany provided support to France at various times, including, in the case of the United States, information pertinent to its own nuclear program. Browne and Shaw Research Corp., *Diffusion of Combat Aircraft,* p. 12; Richard H. Ullman, "The Covert French Connection," *Foreign Policy,* no. 75 (Fall 1989), pp. 3–33; and Ullman, "U.S. Confirms Giving Arms Secrets to France," *Washington Post,* May 29, 1989, p. A21.

23. According to Browne and Shaw Research Corp., *Diffusion of Combat Aircraft,* "Embargoes may occasionally force the establishment of partial or complete domestic substitution efforts which, although slower and more costly, will result in the creation of a supply source which is unencumbered by agreements barring retransfer. U.S. refusals to grant missile production licenses to France . . . resulted in the EBB (Basic Ballistic Studies) program, one step of which was the development of the Topaze solid-fuel missile. The Topaze . . . provides the basis for current French missile development assistance to Israel" (p. 13). For additional discussion of French arms export policy, see Edward A. Kolodziej, *Making and Marketing Arms: The French Experience and Its Implications for the International System* (Princeton University Press, 1987).

24. West Germany played a key role in helping Egypt establish a rocket and missile industry in the 1950s, including the Sakr factory for developed industries, which was engaged in a variety of missile projects by the early 1960s. See Kolodziej, *Making and Marketing Arms,* p. 20; and R. Väyrynen and Thomas Ohlson, "Egypt: Arms Production in the Transnational Context," in Brzoska and Ohlson, eds., *Arms Production in the Third World,* pp. 117–18.

25. The contribution of European companies to third world missile and nuclear programs received wide publicity after the disclosure in 1988 of extensive West German exports of nuclear and other materials to India and Pakistan and the participation of West German firms in building a chemical plant in Libya. See, for instance, Gary Milhollin, "Let Bonn Atone for Its Nuclear Sins," *International Herald Tribune,* June 16–17, 1990, p. 4; Milhollin, "German Nuclear Presents for South Asia," *International Herald Tribune,* June 15, 1990, p. 6; Leonard S. Spector, "Alleged Sensitive Nuclear, Missile, and Chemical Weapons Exports Involving West German Firms and Nationals since 1981," summary of recent press reports (Washington: Carnegie Endowment for International Peace, May 11, 1989); Robert J. McCartney, "Bonn Acts To Tighten Export Control: Fines To Double for Violators of Chemical, Nuclear Strictures," *Washington Post,* January 11, 1989, p. A16; and Stephens Broening, "U.S. Expects Aid Cutoff to Libya Plant," *Sun* (Baltimore), January 17, 1989, p. A1. On the general role of European suppliers in third world missile development, see Gary Milhollin, "India's Missiles—With a Little Help from Our Friends," *Bulletin of the Atomic Scientists,* vol.

45 (November 1989), pp. 31–35; Statement of W. Seth Carus, *Ballistic and Cruise Missile Proliferation in the Third World*, Hearings before the Subcommittee on Defense Industry and Technology of the Senate Committee on Armed Services, 101 Cong. 1 sess. (Government Printing Office, 1989), pp. 48–49. Robinson, "French Missile Technology May Land in Libya," p. A1; and Robinson, "U.S. Says France Trading Sensitive Technology to Brazil," *Philadelphia Inquirer*, October 6, 1989, p. A10.

26. The United States supplied ballistic missiles directly to only three countries in the developing world: Israel, Taiwan, and South Korea. For discussion of arms export policies during the Nixon administration, see Nolan, *Military Industry*, pp. 24–29. For information on U.S. exports of missiles to Asian countries, see Bruce A. Smith, "Koreans Seek New Military Air Capacity," *Aviation Week and Space Technology*, vol. 111 (October 22, 1979), pp. 62–63; Robert Karniol, "Home-Made Missiles: Local Development Aims at Self-Sufficiency," *Far Eastern Economic Review*, vol. 137 (July 30, 1987), p. 16; and Leonard Spector, *The Undeclared Bomb* (Cambridge, Mass.: Ballinger, 1990), chap. 2.

27. "Missile Proliferation in the Third World," *Strategic Survey, 1988–1989*, pp. 14–25; and Steven Zaloga, "Ballistic Missiles in the Third World: SCUD and Beyond," *International Defense Review*, vol. 21 (November 1988), pp. 1423–27.

28. "Missile Proliferation in the Third World," *Strategic Survey, 1988–1989*, p. 16.

29. For further discussion of Soviet commercial space activities, see *Soviet Space Programs: 1981–1987: Piloted Space Activities, Launch Vehicles, Launch Sites, and Tracking Support*, Committee Print, Senate Committee on Commerce, Science, and Transportation, 100 Cong. 2 sess. (GPO, May 1988), pt. 1, pp. 253–56.

30. For trends in Soviet arms exports, see Richard F. Grimmet, *Trends in Conventional Arms Transfers to the Third World by Major Supplier, 1982–1989* (Congressional Research Service, June 1990), p. 4; Cynthia Roberts, "Soviet Arms Transfer Policy," unpublished, 1982; and William C. Potter and Adam N. Stulberg, "The Soviet Union and Ballistic Missile Proliferation," Monterey Institute of International Studies, April 1990.

31. Andrei V. Shoumikhin, "Soviet Policy toward Arms Transfers to the Middle East," paper prepared for the Carnegie Conference on Arms Control and the Proliferation of High Technology Weapons in the Near East and South Asia, Bellagio, Italy, October 1989.

32. Japan has undertaken a major program to expand its missile production, a development some observers believe is inevitably directed toward achieving export capabilities. Eduardo Lachica and Masayoshi Kanabayashi, "Growing Arsenal: Japan's Arms Builders Vie for Orders after Long Hesitancy," *Wall Street Journal*, August 19, 1987, p. A1; and Ralph Vartabedian, "Missile Launch," *Los Angeles Times*, June 11, 1989, p. IV-2.

33. Raymond Vernon, "International Investment and International Trade in the Product Cycle," *Quarterly Journal of Economics*, vol. 80 (May 1966), pp. 190–207. The characterization by Karp is in "Space Technology," p. 159.

34. The combination of maturing defense industries in developing countries and fiscal constraints in the industrial countries may lead to more significant agreements for overseas production of Western defense products. Israel, for instance, already has sold electronic systems, remotely piloted vehicles, and missile decoy systems to the United States and is developing the Arrow antitactical ballistic missile under contract. Gerald M. Steinberg, "Indigenous Arms Industries and Dependence: The Case of Israel," *Defense Analysis*, vol. 2 (November 1986), p. 304. See also "Egypt Wins U.S. Fighter Parts Orders," *London Financial Times*, May 31, 1989, p. 7.

35. Bernard Weintraub, *New York Times*, March 6, 1985, cited in Neuman, *Military Assistance*, p. 118.

36. Andrew L. Ross, "Do-It-Yourself Weaponry," *Bulletin of the Atomic Scientists*, vol. 46 (May 1990), p. 20, based on data in Brzoska and Ohlson, eds., *Arms Production in the Third World*, pp. 8, 10, 30; and Arms Control and Disarmament Agency, *World Military Expenditures and Arms Transfers, 1988* (1989), p. 69.

37. See for instance Daniel Southerland, "China Assures Carlucci on Mideast Arms Sales: Peking Seen Curbing Missile Supply Role," *Washington Post*, September 8, 1988, p. A31.

38. Discussing the evolution of strategic trade controls from 1948 to 1951, Secretary of State Averill Harriman stated that the informal committee established to coordinate exports among Western countries had made great progress in agreeing on export restraints. He emphasized that the progress made in this committee was "all the more striking in view of the fact that many countries had to reorient their export control systems in the light of security objectives . . . [and] had to deal with domestic, economic, and political problems raised by their control policies." See *Mutual Defense Assistance Control Act of 1951: First Report to Congress*, P.L. 213, 82 Cong. (GPO, October 15, 1952), p. 9.

39. Philip A. Trezise, "What's Next with Export Controls?" in *Critical Choices* (Brookings, 1989), p. 171.

40. Michael T. Klare, *American Arms Supermarket* (University of Texas Press, 1984), p. 45. Among other important exceptions to policy, in mid-1978 the Carter administration, which was trying to temper political tensions with Seoul following an abortive initiative to reduce American troops on South Korean soil, approved $800 million worth of military transfers to South Korea, including significant coproduction contracts, despite the official prohibition on such contracts under the new restraint policy. See Nolan, *Military Industry*, pp. 29–34; and chap. 3 in this volume.

41. David Schoenbaum, "Regional Arms Control and Proliferation: the Persian Gulf," paper prepared for the 1976 International Institute for Strategic Studies Annual Conference on Proliferation of Force and the Diffusion of Power, pp. 2–3.

42. Janne E. Nolan, "U.S.-Soviet Conventional Arms Transfer Negotiations," in Alexander L. George, Philip J. Farley, and Alexander Dallin, eds., *U.S.-Soviet Security Cooperation: Achievements, Failures, Lessons* (Oxford University Press, 1988), pp. 510–23.

43. On Israel and Saudi Arabia, see W. Seth Carus, *Ballistic Missiles in the Third World: Threat and Response* (Washington: Center for Strategic and International Studies; and New York: Praeger, 1990), chap. 2.

44. According to Gary Milhollin, "India's Missiles," p. 32, the director of the Indian Atomic Energy Commission asked NASA about the possibility of building an Indian version of the Scout. NASA responded that the transfer of Scout technology potentially could be approved for scientific research but would have to go through the State Department's Office of Munitions Control. NASA did provide unclassified technical reports about the Scout, and there is speculation that India's first satellite launcher, the SLV-3, was based on the Scout design.

45. Carus, *Ballistic Missiles*, chap. 2 and note 17.

46. On Soviet policy toward weapon coproduction, see Neuman, *Military Assistance*, pp. 116–18. On missile transfers, see W. Seth Carus, "Missiles in the Middle East: A New Threat to Stability," *Policy Focus*, research memorandum 6, Washington Institute for Near East Policy (June 1988), pp. 2–3; and Zaloga, "Ballistic Missiles," p. 1423.

47. Spector, *Undeclared Bomb*, p. 40.

48. See Spector, "Alleged Sensitive Nuclear, Chemical and Missile Weapons

Exports"; and A. F. Mullins, Jr., *Born Arming: Development and Military Power in New States* (Stanford University Press, 1987).

49. "Missile Technology Control Regime: Fact Sheet To Accompany Public Announcement," Department of Defense, April 16, 1987.

50. Department of Defense officials have recently emphasized the growing importance of cruise missile proliferation, noting that countries may be able to use satellite data from the U.S. Global Positioning System or the Soviet GLONASS to target such systems more accurately. Barbara Starr, "Ballistic Missile Proliferation: A Basis for Control," *International Defense Review*, vol. 23 (March 1990), p. 267; and Carus, *Ballistic Missiles*, p. 39.

51. On February 10, 1990, after a meeting between Secretary of State James Baker and Foreign Minister Eduard A. Shevardnadze in preparation for the June summit, the United States and the Soviet Union issued a joint statement: "The sides conducted a discussion of the problem of nonproliferation of missiles and missile technology. They noted that they both adhere to the export guidelines of the existing regime relating to missiles, which applies to missiles capable of delivering at least 500 kilograms of payload to a range of at least 300 kilometers." According to a Bush administration official, the United States and the Soviet Union had also discussed restraints in a bilateral meeting in Paris in December 1989. Informal discussions with regional partners, especially in the Middle East, have been in progress since mid-1988. See, for instance, Michael W. Gordon, "U.S. Urges Talks on Missiles in Mideast," *New York Times*, December 27, 1988, p. A3; and "U.S. Presses Mideast Missile Talks: Separate Meetings with 2 Allies Eyed," *Washington Post*, December 28, 1988.

52. Statement of Reginald Bartholomew, *Nuclear and Missile Proliferation*, Hearings before the Senate Committee on Government Affairs, 101 Cong. 1 sess. (GPO 1989), p. 69.

53. During the May 1990 summit in Washington, the United States and the Soviet Union agreed to "affirm their support for the objectives of the Missile Technology Control Regime, covering missiles, and certain equipment and technology relating to missiles capable of delivering at least 500 kg of payload to a range of at least 300 km and they call on all nations that have not done so to observe the spirit and the guidelines of the regime." See "Joint Statement on Non-Proliferation," U.S.-Soviet Summit, Washington, May 30–June 3, 1990.

Chapter Three: The Producers

1. A 1966 study for the Department of Defense estimated that developing and producing even a "relatively simple" missile required "an annual GNP of $3 billion or higher, industrial work force of 200,000 or larger, a military budget of $350 million or larger, and at least some current aviation or rocket activity." In addition, a country would need extensive support from an industrial supplier, be willing to sustain high program costs for at least ten years, and would have to concentrate on a single modest program in which the first test vehicle differed little from the final production model. See Browne and Shaw Research Corporation, *The Diffusion of Combat Aircraft, Missiles, and Their Supporting Technologies*, report prepared for the Office of the Assistant Secretary of Defense, International Security Affairs, DA-49-083 (Waltham, Mass., October 1966), p. 9.

2. The relative difficulty of achieving different stages of missile development is

discussed in Mark Balaschak and others, *Assessing the Comparability of Dual-Use Technologies for Ballistic Missile Development,* report prepared for the Arms Control and Disarmament Agency, ACOWC 113 (MIT, June 1981), pp. 24–55. For additional discussion of the applicability of dual-use technologies for missile development, see Science Applications International, *Technology List for Observing Possible Indigenous Development/Production of a Surface-to-Surface Missile by a Less Developed Country (LDC),* AC8WC122 (McLean, Va.: Arms Control and Disarmament Agency, April 1979). Cruise missiles, which are essentially unmanned aircraft and are relatively less difficult to produce, are not discussed in detail.

3. The range of a missile is defined as the distance between its launch point and a target. Ranges of missiles used by third world countries can be as little as 20 miles for the Iranian Oghab to as much as 2,000 miles for the Chinese CSS-2 sold to Saudi Arabia. Israel and India may be able to achieve far longer ranges through their programs to convert space-launch vehicles.

Missile accuracy is commonly measured by a system's circular error probable (CEP), the radius of a circle within which 50 percent of a missile's projectiles are expected to land. CEPs of current third world missiles are estimated to range from more than 2 miles for the Iraqi al-Abbas to a few hundred yards for the Soviet-supplied Syrian SS-21. By contrast, recently developed U.S. missiles, such as the Pershing II, have accuracies of a few feet.

The payload of a missile refers to the warheads, reentry vehicles, or associated cargo that can be carried by a particular system, and varies according to whether the munition carried is nuclear, chemical, or conventional. The Scud-B system found in the inventories of at least seven developing countries has an estimated payload of 1,100 pounds, but the Saudi Arabian CSS-2 can carry up to a 4,500 pound high-explosive warhead. For further discussion on all of these performance characteristics, see chap. 4, especially tables 4-1 and 4-2; Arms Control and Disarmament Agency, *World Military Expenditures and Arms Transfers 1988,* publication 131 (1989), p. 18; International Institute for Strategic Studies, *The Military Balance 1988–1989* (London, 1988), pp. 210–19; and Robert D. Shuey and others, *Missile Proliferation: Survey of Emerging Missile Forces,* 88-642F (Congressional Research Service, October 1988), pp. 7–9.

4. Shuey and others, *Missile Proliferation,* pp. 16–21; and Gerald M. Steinberg, "Two Missiles in Every Garage," *Bulletin of the Atomic Scientists,* vol. 39 (October 1983), p. 45.

5. Arms Control and Disarmament Agency, *World Military Expenditures and Arms Transfers 1987,* p. 26.

6. Balaschak and others, *Assessing the Comparability,* p. 24.

7. Shuey and others, *Missile Proliferation,* p. 20.

8. Shuey and others, *Missile Proliferation,* p. 20.

9. For a full discussion of the availability of commercial inertial guidance systems, see Balaschak and others, *Assessing the Comparability,* pp. 25–26. According to the criteria controlling guidance technology under the Missile Technology Control Regime, guidance systems that can provide accuracy of 6 miles or less at a range of 180 miles are subject to the most restrictive category I restraints; systems for shorter-range missiles are exempted. As noted by an official Arms Control and Disarmament Agency publication, this measure is "very imprecise, but it is precise enough to be of concern when nuclear weapons are considered." *World Military Expenditures and Arms Transfers 1987,* p. 26.

10. Analysts traditionally believed that ballistic missiles required high accuracy or highly destructive payloads to be effective. As such, inaccurate systems of the kind being developed in the third world were at first considered threatening largely because they implied nuclear aspirations. Moderately accurate systems carrying chemical or

high-explosive weapons, however, could be effective against certain military targets. See Janne Nolan and Albert Wheelon, "Ballistic Missiles in the Third World," in *New Threats: Responding to the Proliferation of Nuclear, Chemical,and Delivery Capabilities in the Third World* (Aspen Strategy Group and University Press of America, 1990), pp. 104–05, and note 10. Still, the performance of these systems cannot be compared with advanced missiles produced by industrial countries. Such ballistic missiles as the U.S. Pershing IA and the Soviet SS-20 have CEPs of 40 meters, far lower than any system currently under development in the third world. Emerging technology, moreover, is making it possible to destroy fixed targets at long ranges with accuracies of 1 to 3 meters using conventional munitions. See, for instance, Commission on Integrated Long-Term Strategy, *Discriminate Deterrence* (Washington, January 1988).

11. See Balaschak and others, *Assessing the Comparability*, p. 26.

12. Shuey and others, *Missile Proliferation*, p. 21. Gerald Steinberg argues that the Titan II ballistic missile navigation system is derived from the Delco Carousel Aircraft Inertial Navigation system, used in many commercial aircraft; "Two Missiles in Every Garage," p. 46.

13. For analysis of the convertibility of commercial INS systems, see Shuey and others, *Missile Proliferation*, p. 21; Balaschak and others, *Assessing the Comparability*, pp. 26–27; and Nolan and Wheelon, "Ballistic Missiles in the Third World," appendix 3. Aaron Karp has argued that the difficulty of converting commercial aircraft INS to missile use is underestimated in the analysis by Balaschak and his colleagues (telephone interview, December 1989).

14. W. Seth Carus, *Ballistic Missiles in the Third World: Threat and Response* (Washington: Center for Strategic and International Studies; and New York: Praeger, 1990), p. 39. Cruise missiles designed in the United States have very sophisticated internal guidance systems, including terrain-contour matching sensors (TERCOM) that enable the system to correct the flight path automatically in response to changes in terrain. This technology is not available to third world missile producers. For further discussion of the cruise missile issue, see Arms Control and Disarmament Agency, *World Military Expenditures and Arms Transfers 1987*, p. 26; and Richard Speier, "Proliferation of Ballistic Missiles and Other High-Technology Weapons: Implications for Regional Stability and Possible Controls," in Eric H. Arnett, Elisabeth J. Kirk, and N. Thomas Wander, eds., *Science and Security: Technology Advances and the Arms Control Agenda* (Washington: American Association for the Advancement of Science, 1990), p. 256.

15. Patrick M. Cronin and Jonathan T. Dworken, "Weapons Proliferation and U.S. National Security," Center for Naval Analyses symposia series, July 1990, p. 9.

16. Shuey and others, *Missile Proliferation*, p. 22.

17. See Missile Technology Control Regime, "Fact Sheet To Accompany Public Announcement," Department of Defense, April 16, 1987; and Arms Control and Disarmament Agency, *World Military Expenditures and Arms Transfers 1987*, p. 26.

18. Balaschak and others, *Assessing the Comparability*, pp. 45–46; and Steinberg, "Two Missiles in Every Garage," p. 44.

19. Balaschak and others, *Assessing the Comparability*, p. 46.

20. Browne and Shaw Research Corp., *Diffusion of Combat Aircraft*, p. 14.

21. Balaschak and others, *Assessing the Comparability*, pp. 46–47. For additional discussion of the techniques of converting rockets to ballistic missiles, see also pp. 48–55.

22. Balaschak and others, *Assessing the Comparability*, pp. 48–55.

23. See, for instance, Elisa D. Harris, "Chemical Weapons Proliferation: Current Capabilities and Prospects for Control," in *New Threats*, pp. 67–87.

24. Remarks of William H. Webster, cited in Carus, *Ballistic Missiles in the Third World*, p. 7.

25. Shuey and others, *Missile Proliferation*, pp. 23–26.

26. Leonard S. Spector, *The Undeclared Bomb* (Ballinger, 1988), pp. 80–153.

27. For additional discussion, see Carl H. Builder, "The Prospects and Implications of Non-Nuclear Means for Strategic Conflict," Adelphi Papers 200 (International Institute for Strategic Studies, Summer 1985); and C. Raja Mohan and K. Subrahmanyam, "High-Technology Weapons in the Developing World," in Eric H. Arnett, ed., *New Technologies for Security and Arms Control: Threats and Promise* (Washington: American Association for the Advancement of Science, 1989), pp. 229–31.

28. Balaschak and others, *Assessing the Comparability*, p. 66.

29. Thomas G. Mahnken and Timothy D. Hoyt, "Missile Proliferation and American Interests," *SAIS Review*, vol. 10 (Winter–Spring 1990), p. 112.

30. Browne and Shaw Research Corp., *Diffusion of Combat Aircraft*, pp. 8–9.

31. Joe D. Pumphrey, "Status of Third World Ballistic Missile Technology," Defense Intelligence Agency, September 1986, p. 2. See also Browne and Shaw Research Corp., *Diffusion of Combat Aircraft*, pp. 9–10.

32. Pumphrey, "Status of Third World Military Technology," p. 1.

33. Arms Control and Disarmament Agency, *World Military Expenditures and Arms Transfers 1987*, p. 26.

34. Congressional Research Service, *Soviet Space Programs, 1966–1970*, staff report prepared for the Senate Committee on Aeronautical and Space Sciences (1971), p. 131, cited in Steinberg, "Two Missiles in Every Garage," p. 44.

35. According to one estimate, 350 U.S., French, and Soviet sounding rockets were launched in India between 1963 and 1975. Gary Milhollin, "India's Missiles—With a Little Help from Our Friends," *Bulletin of the Atomic Scientists*, vol. 45 (November 1989), p. 32. For details on India's space-launch program, see "Step by Step towards Eventual Self-Reliance," *Far Eastern Economic Review*, vol. 137 (August 1987), pp. 51–53; and H. P. Mama, "India's Space Program: Across the Board on a Shoestring," *Interavia* (January 1980), pp. 60–62. See also Shuey and others, *Missile Proliferation*, pp. 72–76. On the role of German engineers in the Agni program, see Milhollin, "India's Missiles," pp. 31–35. On the U.S. contribution to India's missile program, see Milhollin, "India's Missiles," pp. 31, 32, 35; James A. Russell, "U.S. Firms To Aid Indian Jet Effort, *Defense Week*, May 4, 1987, p. 7; and Thalif Deen, "India's Light Combat Aircraft May Use U.S. Technology," *Jane's Defence Weekly*, July 15, 1989, pp. 72–73.

36. Jerrold F. Elkin and Brian Fredericks, "Military Implications of India's Space Program," *Air University Review*, vol. 34 (May–June 1983), p. 57.

37. Congressional Research Service, *Soviet Space Programs 1976–1980*, Committee Print, Senate Committee on Commerce, Science, and Transportation, 97 Cong. 2 sess. (December 1982), pt. 1, p. 7.

38. Official Soviet accounts always emphasize the strictly peaceful nature of the space cooperation. When the Soviet Union congratulated India on the Agni missile test (it was the only country to do so), the Soviet ambassador to India, Victor Isakov, stressed that the program "would in no way contribute to a missile race in the Indian subcontinent." Quoted in S. Bilveer, "AGNI: India Fires into the Missile Age," *Asian Defense Journal* (September 1989), p. 73.

39. For further discussion of the Indian arms industry, see H. Wulf, "India: The Unfulfilled Quest for Self-Sufficiency," in Michael Brzoska and Thomas Ohlson, eds., *Arms Production in the Third World* (London: Taylor and Francis, 1986), pp. 125–45. On Soviet policy toward weapon coproduction with India, see Stephanie G. Neuman, *Military Assistance in Recent Wars: The Dominance of the Superpowers* (Washington:

Center for Strategic and International Studies; and New York: Praeger, 1986), p. 117.

40. See Congressional Research Service, *Soviet Space Programs: 1976–1980* (May 1985), pt. 3, p. 885.

41. Elkin and Fredericks, "Military Implications," p. 57.

42. Elkin and Fredericks, "Military Implications," p. 57; and Shuey and others, *Missile Proliferation,* p. 74. For additional details on India's space-launch program, see Mama, "India's Space Program," pp. 60–62; and "Step by Step towards Eventual Self-Reliance."

43. Elkin and Fredericks, "Military Implications," pp. 57–58.

44. R. R. Subramanian, "Military Potential of India's Space Program," *Strategic Analysis* (New Delhi, India: Institute for Defence Studies and Analysis), pp. 387–88.

45. Steven R. Weisman, "Launching of a Satellite Fails in India," *New York Times,* July 14, 1988, p. A5; and Amarnath K. Menon, "ASLV Damning Findings: Review Committees Raise Troubling Questions," *India Today,* January 15, 1989, p. 94.

46. "Polar Satellite Launch Vehicle's Test Successful," Delhi Domestic Service, October 21, 1989, in Foreign Broadcast Information Service, *Daily Report,* 89-203, October 23, 1989, p. 56.

47. Dr. A. E. Muthunayagam, director of the Liquid Propulsion Systems Centre of the Indian Space Research Organization, claimed in April 1990 that the second and fourth stages of the PSLV would be completed by the end of 1990. He added that all technologies of the PSLV were produced in India, except for a French-supplied Viking motor for the second stage. See "India Develops Rocket Engines," *Beijing Xinhua,* April 19, 1990.

48. Elkin and Fredericks, "Military Implications," p. 58.

49. Hubert Curien, French minister for research and technology, stated in October 1989 that France had two proposals under negotiation with India, one for the sale of cryogenic engines and one involving the transfer of engine technology. Asked about the Missile Technology Control Regime's limits on this technology, Curien replied, "We will respect the treaty we have signed, but also we have the right to judge on our own to whom we are giving the technology." "French Rocket Tech Transfer and India," *Press Trust of India,* October 30, 1989.

50. For full discussion of the role of Germany and France, see Milhollin, "India's Missiles."

51. Satish Dhawan, former chairman of the Indian Space Commission, stated in 1974 that India could build intermediate-range ballistic missiles. Cited in Subramanian, "Military Potential," p. 387.

52. Subramanian, "Military Potential," p. 388.

53. The program is budgeted to cost $1.3 billion over a ten-year period and will include development of five missile systems, including the Agni and Privthi surface-to-surface systems, the Akash and Trishul surface-to-air systems, and the Nag antitank system. Jasjit Singh, "The Strategic Deterrent Option," *Strategic Analysis,* vol. 12 (September 1989), pp. 585–87; Bilveer, "AGNI," p. 71; and "Paper Details Missile Production Plans," *Hindustan Times,* February 27, 1988, p. 1.

54. See, for instance, Carus, *Ballistic Missiles,* p. 20.

55. "Indian Missile 2nd Test," *Jane's Defense Weekly,* October 7, 1989, p. 701. According to Thomas Mahnken, the Privthi may be in part an outgrowth of an abortive effort in the 1970s to reverse-engineer the Soviet SA-2 surface-to-air missile. Interview with Thomas Mahnken, 1990.

56. For details on the Privthi, see Shuey and others, *Missile Proliferation,* pp. 71–72. India completed a second successful test of the Privthi on September 27, 1989;

"Surface-to-Surface Missile Prithvi Fired," *News India,* October 6, 1989; and "Advanced SSM Tests Planned," Hong Kong AFP, 1550 GMT, May 26, 1989.

57. On the capabilities of the Agni, see Bilveer, "AGNI," p. 71; Mahnken and Hoyt, "Missile Proliferation and American Interests," p. 109; and Singh, "Strategic Deterrent Option," pp. 586–87.

58. Singh, "Strategic Deterrent Option," pp. 586–87.

59. Milhollin, "India's Missiles," p. 34. Germany collaborated on a joint project in 1972 associated with the Autonomous Payload Control Rocket experiment, which was aimed at developing more effective inertial guidance systems and is believed to be the basis of the Agni guidance package.

60. In 1988, for instance, the United States approved Indian imports of ring-laser gyros and other advanced components designed for use in an Indian-designed plane but in theory also applicable for missile guidance systems; see Deen, "India's Light Combat Aircraft," p. 73. The United States is also helping build a test range at Balasore for testing Indian air-to-air and surface-to-surface missiles, for which it will provide range instrumentation radar; Russell, "U.S. Firms To Aid Indian Jet Effort"; and Richard W. Weintraub, "Carlucci Cites Deals with India, Pakistan: U.S. To Supply High-Tech Parts to New Delhi," *Washington Post,* April 7, 1988, p. A25.

61. K. Subrahmanyam, "U.S. at the Old Game," *Hindustan Times,* July 31, 1989, in *JPRS, Near East and South Asia,* August 29, 1989, p. 13; and "India To Go It Alone with Missile Device," *Journal of Commerce,* August 9, 1989, p. 10.

62. Elkin and Fredericks, "Military Implications," p. 60.

63. "Zero Option for India," *Vikrant* (November 1981), p. 2, cited in Elkin and Fredericks, "Military Implications," p. 59.

64. Quoted in Sheila Tefft, "India Steps up Arms Race," *Christian Science Monitor,* April 25, 1989, p. 1.

65. Browne and Shaw Research Corp., *Diffusion of Combat Aircraft,* p. 14.

66. Weintraub, "Carlucci Cites Deals," *Washington Post,* p. A25.

67. See, for instance, Tim Carrington and Robert S. Greenberger, "Bureaucratic Battle—Fight over India's Bid for Computer Shows Disarray of U.S. Policy," *Wall Street Journal,* February 24, 1987, p. 1.

68. Interview with analyst from the Soviet USA and Canada Institute, Moscow, October 1989.

69. Text of statement by Mikhail Gorbachev to a Joint Session of the Indian Parliament, November 17, 1986.

70. For additional discussion of U.S. policy and the evolution of South Korea's defense industrial base, see Janne E. Nolan, *Military Industry in Taiwan and South Korea* (St. Martin's Press, 1986); and Young-Sun Ha, "South Korea," in James Everett Katz, ed. *Arms Production in Developing Countries: An Analysis of Decision Making* (Lexington, Mass.: Lexington Books, 1984), pp. 225–33. On the range of products produced by South Korean defense companies, see John D. Morrocco, "South Korea Drives toward Greater Military Autonomy," *Aviation Week and Space Technology,* vol. 130 (June 12, 1989), pp. 176–79. The most significant venture South Korea is about to undertake is to produce under U.S. license a new fighter aircraft, the FX. Part of an overall program of force modernization, the fighter acquisition will be accompanied by major Korean investments in command and control, intelligence, and communications. See, for example, "The Next Battle: South Korea's F-X Fighter Program," *Estimate,* June 9–22, 1989, insert; and "FX Fighter Program To Set Stage for Air Force Modernization Plan," *Aviation Week and Space Technology,* vol. 130 (June 12, 1989), p. 191.

71. On the role of the Carter administration, see Nolan, *Military Industry,* p. 34; and

Malcolm H. Perkins and Wilhelm Bolles, "Security Assistance to South Korea: Assessment of Political, Economic and Military Issues from 1975–1979," Masters thesis, Air Force Institute of Technology, Air University, September 1979.

72. In the 1980s North Korea launched an extensive missile program based on modifications of the Soviet Scud-B and is apparently producing chemical weapons. Joseph S. Bermudez, Jr., "Meeting the Threat from the North," *Jane's Defense Weekly,* July 29, 1989, p. 161.

73. On Park's initiation of the South Korean missile program, see Nolan, *Military Industry,* pp. 73–74. On North Korean missile production, see Joseph Bermudez, Jr., and W. Seth Carus, "The North Korean Scud-B Programme," *Jane's Soviet Intelligence Review,* vol. 1 (April 1989), pp. 177–81.

74. On the Nike-Hercules maintenance program, see Nolan, *Military Industry,* p. 74. As a Pentagon study noted, "there are several indirect implications of SAM transfers for SSM diffusion. SAMs provide experience in the operation and maintenance of advanced electronic systems. In addition, familiarity with the guidance systems and components of these missiles may be of benefit to a nation which is attempting to acquire the competence to develop its own missiles." See Browne and Shaw Research Corp., *Diffusion of Combat Aircraft,* p. 15.

75. Shortly after diplomatic exchanges between the United States and South Korea about the latter's missile program, the United States approved delivery of equipment to improve the Honest John and Nike-Hercules missiles already in the South Korean inventory. See, for instance, *DMS Market Intelligence Report for China (Taiwan) and South Korea* (Greenwich, Conn.: Defense Marketing Services, 1981), p. 49. A recently declassified letter from Congressman Anthony C. Beilenson to Secretary of State Cyrus Vance in August 1979 contains details of U.S. missile-related equipment sold to South Korea in the mid-1970s, including nose cone materials, guidance systems, blueprints, and assembly equipment associated with the Atlas Centaur ICBM. See "Asia/Pacific Nonproliferation Notes," *Pacific Research,* Peace Research Center, Australian National University, vol. 2 (May 1989), p. 20.

76. These include the Sidewinder air-to-air missile, the Maverick air-to-surface missile, and the Harpoon antiship missile. South Korea has already adapted the Honest John short-range battlefield rocket to an indigenous design and is reportedly developing a short-range, laser-guided antiship missile, the Sea Dragon, with help from Texas Instruments and with rocket production equipment transferred by the Lockheed Corporation in the mid-1970s. Shuey and others, *Missile Proliferation,* p. 82.

77. For additional discussion of the South Korean missile program, see Nolan, *Military Industry,* pp. 73–75; and Shuey and others, *Missile Proliferation,* pp. 80–82. For additional discussion of the missiles' capabilities, see *Jane's Weapon Systems, 1984–1985* (London: Jane's Publishing, 1984); Bruce A. Smith, "Koreans Seek New Military Air Capacity," *Aviation Week and Space Technology,* October 22, 1979, pp. 62–63; and Shuey and others, *Missile Proliferation,* pp. 80–81.

78. Cited in "South Korea," *Asian Survey,* no. 1 (January 1979), p. 44.

79. A film on Korean defense production made by the Korean Institute for Defense Analysis and shown to the author in March 1981 presented the capabilities of the Nike-Hercules–Korea (NH-K) without any reference to the contribution of the United States. For additional discussion, see "South Korea's Arms Industry: Boom-Boom," *Economist,* December 2, 1978, p. 86.

80. Shuey and others, *Missile Proliferation,* pp. 80–81; and Doug Richardson, "World Missile Directory," *Flight International,* vol. 123 (February 5, 1983), p. 320.

81. "Korea To Launch Nation's First Research Satellite by 1996," *Korea Times,* May 21, 1987, p. 3.

82. On the South Korean nuclear program, see Spector, *Undeclared Bomb*, pp. 70–72.

83. Shuey and others, *Missile Proliferation*, p. 81.

84. For further discussion of the Condor program, see Pialvisa Bianco, "Men and Condor: The Definitive Story of Nine Italians Recruited by a Swiss Company To Supply Hussein with a New Weapon," *Europeo* (September 1989), pp. 21–23; William Safire, "Beware the Condor," *New York Times*, June 29, 1990, p. A25; and Simon Henderson, "West Blocks Advance of Condor II Missile," *London Financial Times*, August 31, 1989, p. 3.

85. Carus, *Ballistic Missiles*, pp. 18, 63–64. In 1990 the Argentinian government announced suspension of the Condor program, citing financial strains and excessive difficulty in acquiring needed technology because of actions by the Missile Technology Control Regime. See, for instance, "Argentina Ends CONDOR II; Cites Political, Financial Pressure," *Aerospace Daily*, April 24, 1990.

86. On the proliferation of Scud missiles during the Iran-Iraq war, see Steven Zaloga, "Ballistic Missiles in the Third World: SCUD and Beyond, " *International Defense Review*, vol. 21 (November 1988), pp. 1424–25.

87. On the Soviet denial of the sale of the SS-12s to Iran, see David C. Isby, "Arms for Baghdad," *Amphibious Warfare Review* (Winter 1989), p. 55. For additional discussion of the Iraqi arms inventory, see Aaron Karp, "Ballistic Missile Proliferation in the Third World," *World Armaments and Disarmament: SIPRI Yearbook 1989* (Oxford University Press, 1989), pp. 13–15.

88. For additional analysis of the Soviet-Iraqi arms relationship, see Isby, "Arms for Baghdad." The size of the Scud transfer was considered particularly significant in light of a Defense Intelligence Agency estimate that the Soviets only produce about 300 short-range missiles a year. Zaloga, "Ballistic Missiles," p. 1425.

89. On sources of arms to Iraq during this period, see Alan Friedman, Victor Mallet, and Richard Donkin, "Britain Says Iraqi 'Undercover Network' Taps West's Technology," *Financial Times*, September 13, 1989, p. 1. For discussion of the assistance received by Iraq to modify its Scud missiles, see W. Seth Carus and Joseph S. Bermudez, Jr., "Iraq's *Al-Husayn* Missile Programme," *Jane's Soviet Intelligence Review*, vol. 2 (May 1990), pt. 1, pp. 204–09; and Zaloga, "Ballistic Missiles," pp. 1423–25. On Soviet disapproval of Scud transfers, see "Moscow: Missiles Sent Iraq Were Short-Range," *Washington Post*, March 10, 1988, p. A41.

90. Karp, "Ballistic Missile Proliferation in Third World," p. 14.

91. Carus and Bermudez, "Iraq's *Al-Husayn* Missile Programme," pt. 1, p. 207, believe Iraq began to develop missiles in 1982, concentrating on simpler technologies such as artillery rockets. The impetus to produce the Al-Husayn may have come from Iran's acquisition of Scud-B missiles from Libya and their use against Baghdad in March 1986.

92. On the conversion of Scuds see Carus and Bermudez, "Iraq's *Al-Husayn* Missile Programme"; and Zaloga, "Ballistic Missiles," pt. 2, pp. 1423–25. On the use of ballistic missiles in the Iran-Iraq war, see W. Seth Carus, "Missiles in the Middle East: A New Threat to Stability," *Policy Focus*, Washington: Institute for Near East Policy research memorandum 6 (June 1988), pp. 5–6; Thomas L. McNaugher, "Ballistic Missiles and Chemical Weapons: The Legacy of the Iran-Iraq War," *International Security*, vol. 15 (Fall 1990); and Aharon Levran, "Threats Facing Israel from Surface-to-Surface Missiles," *IDF Journal* (Winter 1990), p. 37. On the testing of the two missiles, see Zaloga, "Ballistic Missiles," pp. 1423–25.

93. Carus and Bermudez conducted a detailed analysis of al-Husayn program in mid-1990, based in part on information about the system provided by Iran. Experts from the

Iranian Air Force and Islamic Revolutionary Guard were able to recover and examine complete warheads because some of the 190 missiles launched against Iran during the war did not detonate. Iran also reportedly found intact al-Husayn fuselages. See "Iraq's *Al-Husayn* Missile Programme," pt. 1, p. 205. Iranian officials claim that the al-Husayns fired at Tehran were three times less accurate than the Scud-B missile fired by Iran at Baghdad (p. 206). The authors estimate the actual CEP for the system as 1,500 to 2,000 meters.

94. Carus and Bermudez, "Iraq's *Al-Husayn* Missile Programme," pt. 2, p. 246, argue that the system could not carry a full-size warhead because if it did, the Iraqis would have had to extend the missile's range by one-third while quadrupling the weight of the payload.

95. Carus and Bermudez, "Iraq's *Al-Husayn* Missile Programme," pt. 1, p. 204.

96. See, for instance, David B. Ottaway, "Iraq Reports Successful Test of Antitactical Ballistic Missile," *Washington Post,* December 19, 1988, p. A4; and Hazim T. Mushtak, "Arms Control and the Proliferation of High Technology Weapons in the Near East and South Asia: An Iraqi View," paper prepared for the Carnegie Conference on Arms Control and the Proliferation of High Technology Weapons in the Near East and South Asia, Bellagio, Italy, October 1989. Refutations of Iraqi claims are from interviews with Department of Defense officials, January 1990.

97. "Brazilians Probe Links with Iraq," *Jane's Defense Weekly,* May 26, 1990, p. 989.

98. Michael R. Gordon reported the erroneous information in "U.S. Confirms Iraq Has Launched Rocket That Can Carry Satellites," *New York Times,* December 9, 1989, p. A7. Based on analysis of a videotape of the launch aired on Iraqi television, Carus and Bermudez, "Iraq's *Al-Husayn* Missile Programme," pt. 2, p. 46, conclude that the stages did not separate, that the second-stage engine was never ignited, and that the al-Abid probably reached an altitude of 12,000 meters.

99. In February 1990, Smir Hammudi al-Sa'di, an official of the Iraqi Ministry of Industry and Military Industrialization, announced that the al-Abid would be used to launch Iraqi satellites; "Official: Non-Military Purposes," *Paris AFP,* February 7, 1990. See also Alfonso Chardy, "Space Race in Mideast Shifts Power Balance," *Miami Herald,* May 2, 1990, p. 13; and Hugh Carnegy and Victor Mallet, "Launch of Iraqi Space Rocket Fuels Fears in Israel," *Financial Times,* December 20, 1989, p. 4.

100. *Mednews: Middle East Defense News,* May 8, 1989, p. 8, cited in Carus and Bermudez, "Iraq's *Al-Husayn* Missile Programme," pt. 2, pp. 244–45.

101. See, for instance, "Middle East Missile Production: A New Era," *Defense and Foreign Affairs Weekly,* May 8–14, 1989, p. 3; and Karp, "Ballistic Missile Proliferation in the Third World," p. 14.

102. Alan George, "Saddam's Secret Weapons," *Middle East,* no. 176 (June 1989), p. 21. For additional discussion, see "Missile Sites Approach Completion in Iraq," *Flight International,* vol. 135 (May 13, 1989), pp. 20–21; "New Missile Project Said Nearing Completion," *Al-Sharq Al-Aswat,* April 24, 1989, translated in *FBIS-NES,* 89-080, April 27, 1989, p. 21; and "Sa'ad 16: Iraq's Military 'Business Park,' " *Financial Times: Mid-East Markets,* May 1, 1989.

103. David B. Ottaway, "U.S. Firms Helped Iraq Gain Ability To Make Missiles, Officials Say," *Washington Post,* May 3, 1989, p. A19; and "U.S. Inadvertently Helps Iraq Boost Missile Capability," *Financial Times,* November 21, 1989, p. 1.

104. Carus and Bermudez, "Iraq's *Al-Husayn* Missile Programme," pt. 1, p. 204.

105. See Bill Gerty and Rowan Scarborough, "Saddam Close to Nuclear Weapon," *Washington Times,* November 28, 1990. Its ability to produce nuclear weapons, however, is still considered to be several years away.

106. Spector, *Undeclared Bomb*, pp. 207–10.

107. Leonard Spector, interview, April 1990.

108. Patrick E. Tyler, "Iraqi Warns of Using Poison Gas," *Washington Post*, April 3, 1990, p. A1; Alan Cowell, "Iraq Chief, Boasting of Poison Gas, Warns of Disaster if Israelis Strike," *New York Times*, April 3, 1990, p. A1; and Robert Pear, "Iraq Can Deliver, U.S. Chemical Arms Experts Say," *New York Times*, April 3, 1990, p. A8.

109. W. Seth Carus, "Chemical Weapons in the Middle East," *Policy Focus*, Washington Institute for Near East Policy research memorandum 9 (December 1988), pp. 3–4.

110. For instance, APV, a British company, sold vertical mixers for propellant compounds to the Italian company SNIA BpD, which resold them to Argentina. This technology was indirectly available to Iraq when it was participating in the Condor program; International Institute for Strategic Studies, *Strategic Survey, 1988–1989*, (London, 1989), p. 21. It is also alleged that a West German company, MBB, supplied Romania with missile technology by shipping it through Iraq and Egypt, adding an East-West dimension to the technology diffusion associated with third world missile proliferation; Karl Gunther Barth and Rudolph Lambrecht, "How German Scientists Developed a New Medium-Range Missile for Egypt and Argentina Which Can Carry Nuclear Warheads," *Stern Magazine* (English translation), August 25, 1988; and Alan George, "Flight of the Condor," *Middle East* (April 1989), p. 20.

111. For further discussion of Iran's defense production capabilities, see Shuey and others, *Missile Proliferation*, pp. 47–51; and A. T. Schultz, "Iran: An Enclave Arms Industry," in Brzoska and Ohlson, eds., *Arms Production in the Third World*, pp. 147–61.

112. Shuey and others, *Missile Proliferation*, p. 50.

113. For a discussion of Iran's acquisition of Scud missiles, see Zaloga, "Ballistic Missiles," pp. 1423–25. Bermudez and Carus assert that 90 to 100 Scud-Bs produced in North Korea were delivered to Iran between mid-1987 and early 1988 as part of a $500 million arms agreement signed in June 1987. Iran allegedly received these systems before the Korean army. See "North Korean Scud-B Programme," pp. 177–81.

114. Stephanie G. Neuman, *Military Assistance in Recent Wars: The Dominance of the Superpowers* (Washington: Center for Strategic and International Studies; and New York: Praeger, 1986), p. 117.

115. On the involvement of China in Iran's missile development, see "Middle East Missile Production: A New Era," *Defense and Foreign Affairs Weekly*, vol. 17 (May 8, 1989), p. 38; Mark Daly, "Iranian rockets head SECARM display," *Jane's Defense Weekly*, February 11, 1989, p. 219; " 'Sources' Say PRC Helping To Build Missile Plant," *Kyodo* (Tokyo), March 9, 1989, in *FBIS-NES*, 89-045, March 9, 1989, p. 48; "Missile Production with PRC Discussed," *Al-Ittihad* (Abu Dhabi), September 18, 1989, translated in *FBIS-NES*, 89-181, September 20, 1989, p. 56; and "Official: China Aids Iran with Factory," *Defense News*, March 13, 1989, p. 28.

116. Shuey and others, *Missile Proliferation*, p. 27; and "Middle East Missile Production," p. 38.

117. "Middle East Missile Production," p. 38.

118. Joseph Bermudez and W. Seth Carus, "Show Throws Light on Iran's Arms Industry," *Jane's Defense Weekly*, November 19, 1989, pp. 1252–53. Carus asserted in an interview with the author, June 1990, that the Iranian claim is "quite reasonable, given the large number of Oghabs launched during the war."

119. Carus, "Chemical Weapons in the Middle East," p. 4.

120. Israeli charge on Iraqi chemical weapons.

121. Spector, *Undeclared Bomb*, pp. 219–26.

122. Ed Blanche, "Iran Reported Set To Buy Arms from Soviet Union," *Philadelphia Inquirer*, May 2, 1989, p. 8.
123. Cecil Victor, "Agni as Strategic Currency," *Delhi Patriot*, June 2, 1989, p. 4.
124. K. Subrahmanyam, "U.S. at the Old Game," *Hindustan Times*, July 31, 1989, p. 13.

Chapter Four: The Military Significance of Ballistic Missiles

1. Robert D. Shuey and others, *Missile Proliferation: Survey of Emerging Missile Forces*, 88-642F (Congressional Research Service, October 1988), summary.
2. The MTCR originally was interpreted by U.S. officials and those of other adherents as an adjunct of efforts to discourage nuclear proliferation, and especially an effort to stem the spread of nuclear-capable delivery vehicles. Since 1988, the Department of Defense, in particular, has emphasized that the MTCR covers all classes of ballistic missiles, with nuclear or conventional armament, that can carry a 500 kilogram payload and travel 300 kilometers. This emphasis remains a source of debate and confusion among MTCR partners, however (see chap. 6).
3. Comparing the performance of aircraft and missiles, a study conducted at Stanford University's Center for International Security and Arms Control concludes that missiles do not necessarily accord states new combat capabilities. Many missions can be conducted as well or better with high-performance aircraft, which are not subject to the same policy restraints as missiles. Uzi Rubin, "Reappraising the Issue of Ballistic Missile Proliferation," draft, April 18, 1990. Thomas McNaugher, for instance, argues that "the crucial differences between chemical and nuclear weapons make it less likely that such a balance will be highly unstable"; "Ballistic Missiles and Chemical Weapons: The Legacy of the Iran-Iraq War," *International Security*, vol. 15 (Fall 1990), p. 33. For alternative views on the impact of advanced technology on regional stability, see Jasjit Singh, "The Strategic Deterrent Option," *Strategic Analysis*, New Delhi, India: Institute for Defense Studies and Analysis, vol. 12 (September 1989), pp. 600–02; C. Raja Mohan and K. Subrahmanyam, "High-Technology Weapons in the Developing World," in Eric H. Arnett, ed., *New Technologies for Security and Arms Control: Threats and Promise* (Washington: American Association for the Advancement of Science, 1989), pp. 229–37; George H. Quester, "Predicting the Impacts of Third World Weapons Spread," paper prepared for SAIC Conference on Changing Dimensions of the Third World Military Environment, McLean, Va., Science Applications International, June 1989; Janne E. Nolan, "An International Perspective: Technology, Arms Races, and the Distribution of Power," in Asa A. Clark IV and John F. Lilley, eds., *Defense Technology* (New York: Westport; and London: Praeger, 1989), pp. 49–63; and Guy J. Pauker, *Military Implications of a Possible World Order Crisis in the 1980s*, R-2003-AF (Santa Monica: Rand Corporation, November 1977).
4. In the last months of World War II Germany fired more than a thousand V-2 ballistic missiles, each carrying a ton of explosives. Egypt fired a few Scud missiles against Israel in 1983, Libya fired two against a U.S. Coast Guard station in Lampedusa in 1986 in retaliation for an American air raid against Tripoli, and the Soviet-supported Afghan army used them against the Mujaheddin in 1988. The most extensive use in recent history was by Iran and Iraq in the last phases of their war. Most Western analysts

have concluded that missile strikes were not decisive in any of these actions, either in securing clear military advantages or in hastening the end of the war. See, for instance, McNaugher, "Ballistic Missiles and Chemical Weapons." Others, however, including some analysts from the third world, have come to a different conclusion. As an Iraqi military specialist summarized his government's view, "the Iraq-Iran war, for the first time in modern history, has conclusively proved and operationally demonstrated that land-to-land missiles could be effective weapons in armed conflict or total war specifically, even if they are armed with conventional warheads." Hazim T. Mushtak, "Arms Control and the Proliferation of High Technology Weapons in the Near East and South Asia: An Iraqi View," paper prepared for the Carnegie Conference on the Proliferation of High Technology Weapons in the Near East and South Asia, Bellagio, Italy, October 1989, p. 5.

5. The consensus is expressed by McNaugher, "Ballistic Missiles and Chemical Weapons": "The effectiveness of [missiles] in 1988 rested largely on factors lying beyond their technical capabilities" (p. 6).

6. A definitional problem arises from differences in the ways analysts define the problem of missile proliferation. Some focus mainly on the spread of ballistic missiles per se. Others discuss proliferation as a problem because of linkage to the proliferation of nuclear and chemical weapons. The latter analysts often refer to missiles as "weapons of mass destruction," out of a belief that they are invariably associated with ambitions to acquire chemical or nuclear weapons. Several third world countries that have missiles may also have chemical or nuclear programs or both, but except for Israel's nuclear-armed Jericho II and Syria's reported production of chemical warheads for its Scud missile, reports have not been confirmed.

7. Under traditional definitions, short-range systems are defined as having ranges of less than 1,000 kilometers, intermediate-range less than 5,500 kilometers, and long-range as exceeding 5,500 kilometers.

8. Stephens Broening, "Israel Could Build Missiles To Hit Soviets, U.S. Thinks," *Sun* (Baltimore), November 11, 1988, p. A1. For additional discussion of missile ranges, see International Institute for Strategic Studies, *Strategic Survey 1988–1989* (London, 1989), pp. 15–19.

9. On the capabilities of artillery, see Christopher Chant, *Compendium of Armaments and Military Hardware* (London: Routledge and Kegan Paul, 1987), pp. 73–100.

10. Static comparisons of range capabilities among aircraft and missiles are not precise and depend on the kind of operations being carried out. As Seth Carus has pointed out, aircraft ranges vary considerably according to altitude and payload. "An airplane carrying a lot of ordnance and flying at low altitude will have a much shorter range than one flying at low altitudes with only a small payload. Performance is also affected by the need to carry defensive systems (chaff and flares and electronic jamming gear to counter enemy defenses). Aircraft also do not necessarily fly direct flight paths, often flying around areas heavily defended by enemy air defenses or attempting to attack a target from an unexpected direction to enhance surprise." Memo to author, May 1990.

11. Aaron Karp, "Assessing the Impact of Ballistic Missile Proliferation in East Asia and the Pacific," cited in Laura Lumpe, Federation of American Scientists, "Long-Range Delivery of Chemical Agent," (draft) p. 9, note 31.

12. For missile payload capabilities, see Shuey and others, *Missile Proliferation*, table 3.

13. Chant, *Compendium of Armaments*. On aircraft payload, see International Institute for Strategic Studies, *The Military Balance: 1989–1990* (London: Brassey's, 1989), pp. 216–25.

14. The bomb load capability of an aircraft accounts for the total weight of the

weapon systems carried. See W. Seth Carus, *Ballistic Missiles in the Third World: Threat and Response* (Washington: Center for Strategic and International Studies; and New York: Praeger, 1990), p. 35.

15. See Carus, "Missiles in the Middle East: A New Threat to Stability," *Policy Focus*, Washington Institute for Near East Policy research memorandum 6 (June 1989), p. 4.

16. Memorandum to author, May 1990.

17. McNaugher, "Ballistic Missiles and Chemical Weapons," p. 30.

18. Lumpe, "Long-Range Delivery," p. 17. As Thomas G. Mahnken and Timothy D. Hoyt argue, "The delivery of chemical weapons by ballistic missile also requires sophisticated technology such as a proximity fuse to detonate the warhead at the proper distance from the target, and a burster charge to disperse the chemical agent." It also requires a warhead capable of holding a large volume of the chemical agent. See "Missile Proliferation and American Interests," *SAIS Review* (Winter–Spring 1990), p. 102.

19. Rubin, "Reappraising the Issue," p. 6.

20. In 1989 William Webster, director of the Central Intelligence Agency, stated that Iran, Iraq, Syria, and Libya "are also quietly producing and amassing a variety of munitions that can be used as delivery systems for chemical agents. Bombs, artillery shells, artillery rockets and in some cases battlefield missiles have been filled with chemical agents." "Chemical Weapons Give the Poor Man's Answer to Nuclear Armaments," *Officer* (June 1989), p. 8. On nuclear capabilities, see Leonard S. Spector, *The Undeclared Bomb* (Cambridge, Mass.: Ballinger, 1988), pp. 27–47.

21. Rubin, "Reappraising the Issue," p. 7.

22. Most developing countries will not have access to the kinds of high-performance aircraft discussed in the preceding analysis, and those that do acquire systems like the Tornado may still experience difficulty in operating them effectively. In the case of Iran and Iraq, for instance, the use of high-performance aircraft was hindered by the lack of reconnaissance and intelligence to locate precise targets and the lack of trained personnel. The planes were thus used largely for indiscriminate attacks on cities, their precision strike capabilities notwithstanding. Steven Zaloga, "Ballistic Missiles in the Third World: Scud and Beyond," *International Defense Review*, vol. 21 (November 1988), p. 1423.

23. Memo to author, May 1990.

24. Carus, *Ballistic Missiles*, pp. 29–31.

25. Zaloga argues that the high attrition rate of aircraft carrying out deep strikes in the Iran-Iraq war, as well as the scarcity of modern fighters and trained pilots, made missiles a cost-effective alternative. See "Ballistic Missiles in Third World," p. 1425. Aircraft costs vary widely, ranging from from $20 million to $40 million each. See, for instance, Lumpe, "Long-Range Delivery," p. 12.

26. On the CEP of selected surface-to-surface missiles, see Chant, *Compendium of Armaments*, pp. 498–502. On the CEP of the Scud missile, see also Barton Wright, *World Weapons Database, vol. 1: Soviet Missiles* (Lexington, Mass.: Lexington Books, 1986), pp. 376–81.

27. Carus, *Ballistic Missiles*, p. 33.

28. Aaron Karp, "Ballistic Missiles in the Third World," *International Security*, vol. 9 (Winter 1984–85), p. 168. According to calculations of impact accuracies conducted by Albert Wheelon, third world ballistic missiles could achieve higher accuracies by adapting relatively crude inertial guidance systems that are available commercially. With such an upgrade in guidance, a Scud-B carrying 1,200 lbs. of high explosives or chemical agents to its full range of 180 miles could achieve a CEP of 40 yards (compared with its current CEP of 1,000 yards), at which point it would become effective against area targets such as airfields. See Janne Nolan and Albert Wheelon, "Ballistic Missiles in

the Third World," in *New Threats: Responding to the Proliferation of Nuclear, Chemical, and Delivery Capabilities in the Third World* (Aspen Strategy Group and University Press of America, 1990), p. 122, note 10.

29. Henry S. Rowen and Albert Wohlstetter, "Varying Response with Circumstance," in Johan J. Holst and Uwe Nerlich, eds., *Beyond Nuclear Deterrence: New Aims, New Arms* (Crane, Russak, 1977), p. 233.

30. Details of the ATCM can be found in Carus, *Ballistic Missiles*, p. 38. Carus also emphasizes the importance of cruise missiles combined with cluster munitions, intelligent submunitions, and fuel-air explosives (p. 14).

31. Cited in *Missiles, Space, and Other Major Defense Matters,* Hearings before the Preparedness Investigating Subcommittee of the Senate Committee on Armed Services in conjunction with the Senate Committee on Aeronautical and Space Sciences, 86 Cong. 2 sess. (GPO, 1960), p. 11.

32. For additional discussion, see Rubin, "Reappraising the Issue."

33. Carus, *Ballistic Missiles*, p. 31.

34. Browne and Shaw Research Corporation, *The Diffusion of Combat Aircraft, Missiles, and Their Supporting Technologies,* report prepared for the Office of the Assistant Secretary of Defense, International Security Affairs, DA-49-083 (October 1966), p. 11.

35. Counterforce refers to "the employment of strategic air and missile forces in an effort to destroy, or render impotent, selected military capabilities of an enemy force under any of the circumstances by which hostilities may be initiated." Joint Chiefs of Staff, *Department of Defense Dictionary of Military and Associated Terms,* JCS pub. 1 (Washington, January 1, 1986), p. 93.

36. Presentation by Uzi Rubin, Brookings Institution, July 1990. This excludes nuclear-armed missiles. Rubin argues that whereas missile acquisitions can contribute to regional arms races, their effect on regional tensions or in enhancing measurable military capability has been exaggerated. For further discussion, see Uzi Rubin, "Ballistic Missiles in the Middle East: An Evaluation," paper prepared for the Stanford Center for International Security and Arms Control, April 1990, p. 8.

37. Letter to author, June 1990. Part of the difference in assessments of the utility of missiles stems from disagreements about the missions that can be conducted with nonnuclear missiles of low accuracy. Seth Carus argues that third world ballistic missiles have two primary military missions: "They can be used to attack strategically important military targets distant from the front lines, such as air bases, equipment storage depots, command posts, air defense sites, or logistics facilities. Alternatively, missiles can be employed against hostile ground forces near the front lines, thus interdicting the movement of units approaching the front. Enemy force concentrations can be subjected to bombardment. In either situation, the missiles would be used in roles once the exclusive preserve of attack aircraft." In this case, missiles become "significant" because they purportedly can conduct operations as efficiently as aircraft or more efficiently. *Ballistic Missiles,* p. 10. Most analysts, however, do not subscribe to this broad definition of utility.

38. Aharon Levran, "Threats Facing Israel from Surface-to-Surface Missiles," *IDF Journal* (Winter 1990), p. 43.

39. Rubin, "Ballistic Missiles in the Middle East," p. 7.

40. Procurement decisions, in particular, seem to be driven as much by perceptions as any other factor. A state that believes an adversary has augmented its military capability with a missile force will likely take appropriate countermeasures. Indeed, the ongoing debate in the United States among proponents of strategic defenses, who argue

that America must protect itself against an unspecified third country missile threat, may be a good example.

41. Among Arab states, Saudi Arabia putatively has the most significant missile capability. But the CSS-2 surface-to-surface missile is extremely inaccurate, and Saudi Arabia does not now have chemical or biological weapons. After U.S. pressure following its purchase of the missiles, Saudi Arabia became a signatory to the Non-Proliferation Treaty. For additional discussion of the acquisition of the CSS-2 and its capabilities, and for information on the missile capabilities of the other surrounding Arab states, see Shuey and others, *Missile Proliferation*, pp. 63–65. On the Saudi decision to sign the treaty, see John M. Goshko, "Saudis To Cut Ties with Iran," *Washington Post*, April 26, 1988, p. A1.

42. The Syrian Golan Heights have been annexed as Israeli territory since the 1967 war. On July 31, 1988, King Hussein of Jordan renounced Jordan's claim to the Israeli-occupied West Bank in favor of the Palestine Liberation Organization. See Robert Pear and John Kifner, "Hussein Surrenders Claims on West Bank to the P.L.O.; U.S. Peace Plan in Jeopardy," *New York Times*, August 1, 1988, p. A1.

43. Arms Control and Disarmament Agency, *World Military Expenditures and Arms Transfers 1988* (1989), p. 18.

44. For additional discussion of Israel's missile capabilities, see Carus, "Missiles in the Middle East"; Shuey and others, *Missile Proliferation*, table 3; and David B. Ottaway, "Israel Reported To Test Controversial Missile," *Washington Post*, September 16, 1989, p. A17. Because of the performance of the Shavit, Steven Gray claims that Israel has the capability of building ballistic missiles with a range of 2,800 miles and a 2,200 pound payload. See "Israeli Missile Capabilities," Lawrence Livermore Laboratory, October 7, 1988. A similar estimate, using a different methodology, is presented in Nolan and Wheelon, "Ballistic Missiles in the Third World," p. 125, note 17.

45. Plans for the second test were cited in Anton La Guardia, "Israel Plans To Launch Second Spy Satellite," *Daily Telegraph* (London), September 7, 1989, p. 14.

46. For a detailed discussion of the military balance in the Middle East, see Aharon Levran, "The Military Balance in the Middle East," in Aharon Levran, ed., *The Middle East Military Balance: 1987–1988* (Boulder, Colo.: Westview Press, 1988), pp. 135–255.

47. On Israel's defense industry, see Gerald Steinberg, "Israel: High-Technology Roulette," in Michael Brzoska and Thomas Ohlson, eds., *Arms Production in the Third World* (London: Taylor and Francis, 1986), pp. 163–93. Israel's Arrow ATBM program is funded almost entirely by the United States under the Strategic Defense Initiative program; Elaine Sciolino, "U.S. and Israel To Build Defensive Missile," *New York Times*, June 30, 1988, p. A3; and David B. Ottaway, "U.S., Israel To Develop New Missile," *Washington Post*, June 29, 1988, p. A1. If Israel acquires the advanced Patriot air defense system from the United States, it could further augment its antimissile capability; interviews with official from the Defense Security Assistance Agency, March 1990.

48. In November 1989 the Department of Defense confirmed that Israel has nuclear and chemical warheads for the Jericho I missile; Norman Kempster, "Pentagon Discloses Israel Nuclear Missile," *Los Angeles Times*, November 5, 1989. For a comprehensive analysis of Israel's nuclear weapon program, see Spector, *Undeclared Bomb*, pp. 164–95.

49. Shuey and others, *Missile Proliferation*, p. 40; and Carus, "Missiles in the Middle East," p. 3.

50. Michael R. Gordon, "Syria Is Studying New Missile Deal," *New York Times*,

June 22, 1988, p. A6; David B. Ottaway, "China Missile Sale Report Concerns U.S.," *Washington Post*, June 23, 1988, p. A33; and Michael R. Gordon, "U.S. Fears That China May Again Sell Missiles," *New York Times*, November 9, 1989, p. A14.

51. W. Seth Carus, "Chemical Weapons in the Middle East," *Policy Focus*, no. 9 (December 1988), pp. 4–5; and statement of William H. Webster, *Global Spread of Chemical and Biological Weapons*, Hearings before the Permanent Subcommittee on Investigations and the Senate Committee on Governmental Affairs, 101 Cong. 1 sess. (GPO, 1990), pp. 10–28.

52. According to Aharon Levran, "the principal threat to Israel resides in Syria, which possesses accurate SS-21 missiles and is at an advanced stage of developing chemical warheads for its intermediate-range SCUD missiles. The Syrian arsenal also includes as many as 200 advanced attack aircraft. Moreover, Syria's declared readiness to inflict painful retaliation upon Israel for 'provocative' military actions against it would seem to be an allusion to SSMs." "Military Balance in the Middle East," p. 212.

53. Levran, "Military Balance in the Middle East," pp. 197–211.

54. For a detailed discussion of the threat posed to Israel by Syrian missiles and chemical weapons, see Levran, "Military Balance in the Middle East," pp. 222–29. On Israeli perceptions of the missile threat, see Carus, "Ballistic Missiles in the Middle East," p. 7.

55. For additional discussion of Israel's preemptive counterforce doctrine, see, for instance, Geoffrey Kemp, "Middle East Opportunities," *Foreign Affairs*, vol. 68 (1989), p. 139; and Shai Feldman, "Security and Arms Control in the Middle East: An Israeli Perspective," paper prepared for the Carnegie Conference on Arms Control and the Proliferation of High Technology Weapons in the Near East and South Asia, Bellagio, Italy, October 1989.

56. For a detailed account of this particular scenario, see Levran, "Military Balance in the Middle East," pp. 228–29.

57. See Carus, "Missiles in the Middle East," p. 7. For additional discussion, see Gerald M. Steinberg, "The Middle East in the Missile Age," *Issues in Science and Technology*, vol. 5 (Summer 1989), p. 22.

58. Carus, "Missiles in the Middle East," p. 7.

59. Levran, "Military Balance in the Middle East," p. 224.

60. Levran, "Military Balance in the Middle East," pp. 228–29. With respect to the capabilities of the SS-21, Uzi Rubin argues that the "shorter-range, higher accuracy missiles are apparently designed to interdict air bases, suppress air defenses, and destroy [command and control] sites behind the front lines. If indeed missiles of the SS-21 type can effectively perform such tasks, they may be strategically important. Any defence doctrine that is based on air superiority assumes the relative immunity of its rear assets from the effects of interdiction. If the SS-21 type missile can destroy such immunity, it may force the defender to renovate his doctrine and perhaps his force structure, thus shifting the balance of power for a period of time (which may be quite long)." "Ballistic Missiles in the Middle East," p. 8.

61. Feldman, "Security and Arms Control," p. 7.

62. Levran states that "the Arab side must take into account Israel's strong retaliation potential and, in the case of an Arab chemical weapons attack, the possibility of a devastating Israeli response using alternative means at its disposal—in other words, Israel's strong deterrent capability." One can only assume he is referring to nuclear weapons. "Military Balance in the Middle East," p. 226.

63. For additional discussion, see, for instance, Feldman, "Security and Arms Control," p. 7.

64. Steinberg, "Middle East in the Missile Age," p. 32.

65. See Geoffrey Kemp with Shelly Stahl, *Playing with Fire—Weapons Proliferation in the Middle East and South Asia: Arms Control and U.S. Policy* (Washington: Carnegie Endowment for International Peace, forthcoming).

66. Levran, "Military Balance in the Middle East," p. 227, argues that "chemical weapons are an important element in the Syrians' concept of overall 'strategic parity' with Israel—particularly parity with Israel's perceived nuclear capability."

67. For additional discussion of possible regional confidence-building measures, see Kemp with Stahl, *Playing with Fire*, chap. 7; and Steinberg, "Middle East in the Missile Age," pp. 39–40.

68. For a broader discussion of the Iran-Iraq war, see Majid Khadduri, *The Gulf War: The Origins and Implications of the Iraq-Iran Conflict* (Oxford University Press, 1988); Shahram Chubin and Charles Tripp, *Iran and Iraq at War* (Boulder, Colo.: Westview Press, 1988); and Efraim Karsh, ed., *The Iran-Iraq War: Impact and Implications* (St. Martin's Press, 1989).

69. See, for instance, Shahram Chubin, "Iran and the Lessons of the War with Iraq: Implications for Future Defense Policies," paper prepared for the Carnegie Conference on Arms Control and the Proliferation of High Technology Weapons in the Near East and South Asia, Bellagio, Italy, October 1988.

70. Zaloga, "Ballistic Missiles in the Third World," p. 1423.

71. International Institute for Strategic Studies, *Military Balance: 1988–89* (London: Brassey's, 1989), pp. 101–02; Kenneth R. Timmerman, "Iraqi Arms—From Russia, with Love," *Wall Street Journal*, March 31, 1988, p. 22; and Kemp with Stahl, *Playing with Fire*, chap. 3.

72. On the history of Iraq's chemical weapon program, see Gary Thatcher and Timothy Aeppel, "The Trail to Samarra: How Iraq Got the Materials To Make Chemical Weapons," *Christian Science Monitor*, December 13, 1988, p. B2; and Carus, "Chemical Weapons in the Middle East." On its development of biological weapons, see Stephen Engelberg, "Iraq Said To Study Biological Arms," *New York Times*, January 18, 1989, p. A7.

73. For further analysis of the performance of the Iraqi military during the opening days of Operation Desert Storm, see, for instance, Michael R. Gordon, "Iraq's Military Reported Hurt But Not Halted in 5 Days' Raids," *New York Times*, January 22, 1991, p. A1.

74. Memorandum to author from W. Seth Carus, May 1990.

75. Carus, "Chemical Weapons in the Middle East," p. 4.

76. Shuey and others, *Missile Proliferation*, pp. 47–49.

77. Chubin, "Iran and the Lesson of the War with Iraq," p. 19.

78. Spector, *Undeclared Bomb*, pp. 219–20.

79. See Chubin and Tripp, *Iran and Iraq at War*, pp. 42–49. For a detailed discussion of the effects of the war on the Iranian military, see Shahram Chubin, "Iran and the War: From Stalemate to Ceasefire," in Karsh, ed., *The Iran-Iraq War*, pp. 13–25.

80. Chubin, "Iran and the Lessons of the War with Iraq," p. 5.

81. In "Military Balance in the Middle East," p. 215, Aharon Levran has stated, "Iran's reaction to the missile attacks appears to have been generated less by the casualties it suffered than by strategic and psychological shock." For a discussion of the Iran-Iraq conflict and the lessons for future wars, see Philip A. G. Sabin, "Escalation in the Iran-Iraq War," in Karsh, ed., *The Iran-Iraq War*, pp. 280–95.

82. Chubin, "Iran and the Lessons of the War with Iraq," p. 12.

83. See for instance, Mushtak, "Arms Control and the Proliferation of High Technology Weapons"; and Carus, "Chemical Weapons in the Middle East."

84. Zaloga, "Ballistic Missiles in the Third World," p. 1425.

85. "Therefore, it behooves us to declare clearly that if Israel attacks and strikes, we will strike powerfully," Hussein said. "If [Israel] uses weapons of mass destruction against our nation, we will use against it the weapons of mass destruction in our possession." FBIS-NES, 90-103, May 29, 1990, p. 5.

86. Statement of Jasjit Singh, in Sadruddin Aga Khan, ed., *Non-Proliferation in a Disarming World: Prospects for the 1990s* (Geneva: Bellerive Foundation, 1990), p. 150. In 1990 Egyptian President Hosni Mubarak proposed a ban on "weapons of mass destruction" in the region, by which he meant chemical, biological, and nuclear weapons. See "Mubarak Proposal on Weapons Sent to UN," Cairo *MENA,* April 16, 1990, in FBIS-NES, 90-074, April 17, 1990, p. 3.

87. On the history of Indo-Pakistani relations, see S. M. Burke, *Mainsprings of Indian and Pakistani Foreign Policies* (University of Minnesota Press, 1974); and Sumit Ganguly, *The Origins of War in South Asia* (Boulder, Colo.: Westview Press, 1986).

88. Shiela Tefft, "India Steps up Arms Race," *Christian Science Monitor,* April 24, 1989, p. A2.

89. See, for instance, Ross Masood Husain, "Arms Control and the Proliferation of High Technology Weapons in South Asia and the Near East: A View from Pakistan," paper prepared for the Carnegie Conference on Arms Control and the Proliferation of High Technology Weapons in the Near East and South Asia, Bellagio, Italy, October 1988.

90. Despite efforts to diversify, 80 percent of India's military equipment is of Soviet origin. Amit Gupta, "India's Military Buildup: Modernization in Search of a Threat?" *Swords and Ploughshares,* vol. 3 (December 1988), p. 7.

91. Congress voted Pakistan a six-year, $3.2 billion economic and military aid package in the Foreign Assistance Act of 1981, section 670(b)(2). In December 1987 it again authorized aid to Pakistan, this time only two-and-a-half years of the administration's proposed six-year $4.02 billion package, in the Foreign Assistance Act of 1987, section 620E(d). For a more general discussion of the U.S.-Pakistani relationship, see Shirin Tahir-Kheli, *The United States and Pakistan* (Praeger, 1982).

92. Husain, "Arms Control and Proliferation."

93. See Spector, *Undeclared Bomb,* especially pp. 128–30.

94. "Army Chief: Surface to Surface Missiles Tested," Islamabad Domestic Service, February 5, 1989, in Foreign Broadcast Information Service, *Daily Report: Near East,* 89-023, February 6, 1989, p. 72; Barbara Crossette, "Pakistan Claims Major Gains in Developing Its Own Arms," *New York Times,* February 6, 1989, p. A6; and "Parade Day Debut for Pakistani Missiles," *Jane's Defence Weekly,* April 15, 1989, p. 635.

95. The Agni is included in the Integrated Missile Plan. Interview with Krishna Subramanyam, October 1989.

96. Chant, *Compendium of Armaments,* p. 444.

97. Chant, *Compendium of Armaments,* p. 392.

98. Sanjoy Hazarika, "India Plans To Increase Arms Imports and Exports," *New York Times,* February 5, 1989, p. A6; and Shuey and others, *Missile Proliferation,* p. 79.

99. Stephen P. Cohen, "Controlling Weapons of Mass Destruction in South Asia: An American Perspective," paper prepared for the Carnegie Conference on Arms Control and the Proliferation of High Technology Weapons in the Near East and South Asia, Bellagio, Italy, October 1988.

100. Hussain, "Pakistan Responding to Change."

101. Elisa D. Harris, "Chemical Weapons Proliferation in the Developing World,"

in Royal United Services Institute for Defence Studies, ed., *Rusi and Brassey's Defence Yearbook 1989* (London: Brassey's, 1989), p. 74.

102. For discussion of the risks and high cost of an Indo-Pakistani rivalry in high technology, see Husain, "Arms Control and Proliferation"; and Roger Frost, "Pakistan's New Defense Minister on Missiles, Self-Reliance and Afghanistan," *International Defense Review,* vol. 22 (April 1989), pp. 427–28.

103. Cohen, "Controlling Weapons," p. 19.

104. Cohen, "Controlling Weapons," p. 14.

105. Cohen, "Controlling Weapons," p. 14.

106. Jerrold F. Elkin and Brian Fredericks, "Military Implications of India's Space Program," *Air University Review,* vol. 34 (May–June 1983), p. 61.

107. Spector, *Undeclared Bomb,* p. 33. See also Gupta, "India's Military Buildup," p. 8.

108. See, for instance, Edward A. Olsen, "Republic of Korea: The Peninsular Overachiever," in Rodney Jones and Steve Hildreth, eds., *Emerging Powers: Defense and Security in the Third World* (Praeger 1986), pp. 66–92. For further analysis of the situation in the Korean Peninsula, see Arms Control and Disarmament Agency, *Japan's Contribution to Military Stability,* report prepared for the Senate Committee on Foreign Relations (1980); Steven A. Raho III, "Korea and American National Security," *Parameters* (September 1989), pp. 69–80; Pat Towell, "Issue of Troop Strength Being Revived on Hill," *Congressional Quarterly Weekly Report,* September 2, 1989, pp. 2259–63; and Paul Bracken, "Korea and Northeast Asia: The Changing Military Environment," unpublished, July 1989, p. 12.

109. See John Keegan and Andrew Wheatcroft, *Zones of Conflict: An Atlas of Future Wars* (Simon and Schuster, 1986), pp. 67–73.

110. Bracken, "Korea and Northeast Asia"; and Joseph S. Bermudez and W. Seth Carus, "The North Korean Scud-B Programme," *Jane's Soviet Intelligence Review,* vol. 2 (April 1989), p. 177.

111. See Bermudez and Carus, "North Korean Scud-B Programme."

112. On the military balance in the peninsula, see Towell, "Issue of Troop Strength," pp. 2260–61.

113. For a comprehensive discussion, see Bermudez and Carus, "North Korean Scud-B Programme."

114. Chant, *Compendium of Armaments,* pp. 404, 444.

115. On the North's chemical weapons, see Bermudez and Carus, "North Korean Scud-B Programme." On the South's efforts, see Harris, "Chemical Weapons Proliferation in the Developing World," p. 67.

116. Joseph A. Yager, *Nuclear Nonproliferation Strategy in Asia,* Center for National Security Negotiations paper, vol. 1, no. 3 (McLean, Va.: SAIC, July 1989), pp. 11–17.

117. Bermudez and Carus, "North Korean Scud-B Programme," p. 180, claim that 91 of South Korea's 109 military installations would be within range of the improved Scud.

118. Based on a study of U.S. nuclear weapons in South Korea by William M. Arkin cited in Towell, "Issue of Troop Strength," p. 2261.

119. Bracken, "Korea and Northeast Asia," p. 13. W. Seth Carus argues that a Frog missile could reach major industrial areas in two or three minutes, and a Scud could reach Seoul in eight minutes. Memorandum to author, May 1990.

120. Stephanie G. Neuman, *Military Assistance in Recent Wars: The Dominance of the Superpowers* (Washington: Center for Strategic and International Studies; and New York: Praeger, 1986), p. 117.

121. Bracken, "Korea and Northeast Asia," p. 15.

122. See for instance Michael Krepon, "Spying from Space," *Foreign Policy,* no. 75 (Summer 1989), p. 92; and Peter D. Zimmerman, "From the SPOT Files: Evidence of Spying," *Bulletin of the Atomic Scientists,* vol. 45 (September 1989), p. 24.

123. Mahnken and Hoyt, "Missile Proliferation and American Interests," p. 108. On emerging third world space capabilities, see Thomas G. Mahnken, "Third-Party Space Capabilities: Programs and Implications," paper prepared for SRS Technologies, Arlington, Va., 1989.

124. Testimony of William H. Webster, Director, Central Intelligence Agency, *Nuclear and Missile Proliferation,* Hearing before the Senate Committee on Governmental Affairs, 101 Cong. 1 sess. (GPO, 1990), pp. 12–14, 26–27.

125. From analysis presented by General Lloyd Leavitt to the United Nations Seminar on Multilateral Confidence-Building Measures and Prevention of War, Kiev, USSR, September 1989.

Chapter Five: The Proliferation of Conventional Technology

1. Robert S. Greenberger, "Control Data Corp Will Sell India Computers Valued at $500 Million," *Wall Street Journal,* February 10, 1986, p. A25. Because of concerns about India's nuclear program and New Delhi's close relations with Moscow, the computer approved for sale was a less advanced model than the one requested. David E. Sanger, "Computer Sale Seen to India: U.S. Approval Includes Limits," *New York Times,* March 27, 1987, p. D1. For discussion of more recent U.S.-Indian transactions, see Neel Patri, "India Seeks Closer Ties with U.S. in Technology," *Journal of Commerce,* December 28, 1989, p. A5.

2. Because supercomputers are produced only in the United States and Japan, many observers believe their diffusion to be controllable. Others, however, point to the diffusion of computer technology that can approximate the capabilities of U.S. and Japanese systems. See, for instance, John Markoff, "Export Restrictions Fail To Halt Spread of Supercomputers," *New York Times,* August 21, 1990, p. A1. Opposition to the sale of supercomputing technologies was summarized in 1989 by Senator John Glenn of Ohio: "Selling supercomputers to countries that may be pursuing nuclear weapons or long-range ballistic missiles would be an extremely ill-advised move." Quoted in "Pentagon Says Israel Is Working on Bomb," *Washington Times,* November 3, 1989, p. A6. For a different view, see Jack Worlton, "Some Myths about High-Performance Computers and Their Role in the Design of Nuclear Weapons," Worlton and Associates technical report 32, June 22, 1990. On Israel, see also David B. Ottaway and R. Jeffrey Smith, "U.S. Knew of 2 Nations' Missile Work: Israel Said to Rebuff American Protests," *Washington Post,* October 27, 1989, p. A1.

3. For additional discussion of technology trade controls, see James R. Golden, "A Domestic Perspective: Technology Transfers, U.S. Interests, and Policy," in Asa A. Clark IV and John F. Lilley, eds., *Defense Technology* (New York: Westport; and London: Praeger, 1989), pp. 73–79.

4. On the implications of changes in COCOM guidelines to limit proliferation, see Wolfgang H. Reinicke, *Political and Economic Changes in the Eastern Bloc and Their Implications for COCOM: West German and European Community Perspectives,* study

prepared for the Panel on the Future Design and Implementation of National Security Export Controls (Washington: National Academy of Sciences, May 29, 1990). On opposition to changes in COCOM regulations because of deleterious effects on controlling transfers of technology to the developing world, see Gary Milhollin, "Attention, Nuke-Mart Shoppers!" *Washington Post*, July 22, 1990, p. C2.

5. *Report of the Task Force on Foreign Assistance*, document 101-32, House Committee on Foreign Affairs, 101 Cong. 1 sess. (Government Printing Office, February 1989), p. 29. See also David Silverberg, "Task Force Says Revamp Foreign Military Aid Plan," *Defense News*, vol. 4 (February 13, 1989), p. 1.

6. Commission on Integrated Long-Term Strategy, *Discriminate Deterrence* (January 1988), p. 68.

7. For additional discussion of the evolution of U.S. arms transfer policy see, for instance, Paul Y. Hammond and others, *The Reluctant Supplier: U.S. Decisionmaking for Arms Sales* (Cambridge, Mass.: Oelgeschlager, Gunn, and Hain, 1983), chap. 3; Thomas Ohlson, ed., *Arms Transfer Limitations and Third World Security* (Oxford University Press, 1988), introduction; and Andrew J. Pierre, *The Global Politics of Arms Sales* (Princeton University Press, 1981).

8. Leopold Yehuda Laufer, "Changing Perspectives in the Distribution of U.S. Foreign Aid," paper presented at the International Annual Conference on Shifting Global Centers: Marginality and Centrality, Hebrew University of Jerusalem, June 1988, p. 1.

9. Policy innovations during the Kennedy administration also included establishing a Strike Command for deployment in regional wars. See *United States Defense Policies in 1961*, H. Rept. 502, 87 Cong. 2 sess. (GPO, 1961), pp. 79–80.

10. Discussed in Office of Intelligence and Research, "The Outlook for U.S. Interests in the Middle East," intelligence report 7074 (Department of State, November 14, 1955), p. ii.

11. Munitions Control Office, Office of the Under Secretary of Defense, *Policies, Procedures, and Criteria for Controlling the Transfer of Sensitive Weapons Technology* (Department of Defense, July 6, 1982), table 1.

12. "The OMC and Export Licensing," *Defense and Foreign Affairs*, vol. 14 (April 1986), p. 19. In response to congressional and industry complaints about delays in processing requests, the State Department reorganized the export licensing system in January 1990. The Office of Munitions Control (OMC) was replaced by the Center for Defense Trade (CDT), under the Office of the Assistant Secretary of State for Political-Military Affairs. The CDT now has two components, the Office of Defense Trade Controls, which is largely the former OMC, and the Office of Defense Trade Policy. The State Department allocated $1.5 million in additional funds, most of which the CDT was to spend on equipment to computerize license review procedures. So far, however, these reforms have done little to reduce the time it takes to process cases, in part because there were major problems in adapting the new computers. Interview with defense industry representatives, July 1990. See also "Industry Still Wary of Export Licensing," *Defense News*, March 5, 1990, p. 13. The number of congressional notifications, about eighty a year in 1986 and said to be declining, is cited in "Life History of a Foreign Military Sale," *Defense and Foreign Affairs*, vol. 14 (April 1986), p. 12.

13. *U.S. Military Sales and Assistance Programs: Laws, Regulations, and Procedures*, Committee Print, House Committee on Foreign Affairs, 99 Cong. 1 sess. (GPO, July 23, 1985), p. 13.

14. According to Philip Trezise, "Defense, unsurprisingly, has advocated tight controls on a wide range of goods. Commerce's ties to the business community have made it a supporter, sometimes a cautious one, of a shorter control list and fewer

burdensome rules for exports to Western destinations. For State, the controls have plagued relations with allies almost from their beginning. State officials believe the solution lies in a single set of controls agreed to and enforced multilaterally." These agency positions have endured in almost every dispute over export controls since the 1940s. "What's Next with Export Controls?" in *Critical Choices: What the President Should Know about the Economy and Foreign Policy* (Brookings, 1989), p. 172.

15. For further discussion of the formulation of arms sales policy, see Hammond and others, *Reluctant Supplier*, pp. 83–124; and Michael T. Klare, *American Arms Supermarket* (University of Texas Press, 1984), pp. 54–76.

16. The reorganization of the State Department apparatus for overseeing arms sales has made the Bureau of Political-Military Affairs more explicitly responsible for both export promotion, through the Office of Defense Trade Policy, and export control, through the Office of Defense Trade Controls.

17. The agencies with jurisdiction for security assistance are discussed in *U.S. Military Sales and Assistance Programs*.

18. Nuclear reactors, fuel, and major components are licensed by the Nuclear Regulatory Commission with advice from the executive branch. The Department of Energy authorizes the sale of technology, and Commerce oversees the sale of dual-use equipment. The State Department does not actually license sales, but takes the lead in advising all departments about policy.

19. FMS financing (credits) has almost entirely replaced concessionary military aid. The credits are sometimes forgiven for special security partners such as Egypt, in effect making this a grant instrument. See Commission on Long-Term Strategy Regional Conflict Working Group, *Commitment to Freedom: Security Assistance as a U.S. Policy Instrument in the Third World* (May 1988), p. 21. For further discussion of FMS agreements, see "Life History of a Foreign Military Sale," pp. 7–13.

20. Richard F. Grimmett, *Trends in Conventional Arms Transfers to the Third World by Major Supplier, 1982–1989*, Report 90-298F (Congressional Research Service, June 1990).

21. For discussion of the statutory foundations of U.S. arms export policy, see *U.S. Military Sales and Assistance Programs*, pp. 3–5.

22. See Munitions Control Office, *Policies, Procedures*, pp. 7–12; and "Industry Still Wary."

23. Interview with Simon Worden, White House Space Council, September 1989.

24. Statement of Senator Jeff Bingaman, *National Security Implications of Missile Proliferation*, Hearing before the Senate Committee on Foreign Relations, 101 Cong. 1 sess. (GPO, 1989), p. 40. See also Martha Brannigan, "Firm's Bid To Export Machine to Iraq under Italian Bank Credit Is Studied," *Wall Street Journal*, September 14, 1989, p. A4. As another example of how development assistance can help diffuse technology, the UN Development program funded the establishment of a North Korean factory for making integrated circuits that is now alleged to be part of Pyongyang's continuing efforts to attract technology for use in developing missiles. See Joseph S. Bermudez, Jr., and W. Seth Carus, "The North Korean Scud B Programme," *Jane's Soviet Intelligence Review*, vol. 1 (April 1989), p. 177.

25. Patricia Rickey, "Foreign Military Sales: Who Gets What and How?" *Rotor and Wing International* (July 1989), p. 52.

26. The importance of the Defense Security Assistance Agency in implementing security assistance is discussed in Commission on Long-Term Strategy Regional Conflict Working Group, *Commitment to Freedom*, p. 24.

27. For discussion of the Arms Transfer Management Group see "Life History of a Foreign Military Sale," p. 11. Information about the policy coordinating committees

was provided by State Department and Arms Control and Disarmament Agency officials in interviews.

28. "Life History of a Foreign Military Sale," p. 12.

29. For a detailed discussion of the role of Congress in arms sales, see Barry M. Blechman, *Congress and U.S. Defense Policy from Vietnam to the Persian Gulf* (Oxford University Press, forthcoming), chap. 5.

30. For a breakdown of security assistance shares by recipient, see Grimmett, *Trends in Conventional Arms Transfers*; and John T. Tyler, "U.S. Arms Sales and Security Assistance Programs: What Does the Future Hold?" paper prepared for Frost and Sullivan, Inc., Fourth Annual Conference, December 10, 1986, pp. 3-4.

31. For a critique of current security assistance policy, see Commission on Integrated Long-Term Strategy Regional Conflict Working Group, *Commitment to Freedom*.

32. Klare, *American Arms Supermarket*, pp. 172-73.

33. See, for instance, Gene D. Tracey, "U.S. Military Coproduction Programmes: A Case of Skewing the Americans?" *Asian Defense Journal* (August 1989), p. 51.

34. Office of the Director of Defense Research and Engineering, *An Analysis of Export Control of U.S. Technology—A DOD Perspective* (Department of Defense, February 4, 1976), p. iii.

35. Tracey, "U.S. Military Coproduction," pp. 50-56.

36. Klare, *American Arms Supermarket*, pp. 175-80.

37. Klare, *American Arms Supermarket*, p. 166.

38. Dong Joon Hwang, "ROK-U.S. Defense Industrial Cooperation: A New Step to Security Enhancement," paper prepared for the Conference on ROK-U.S. Security Relations: Past, Present, and Future, Seoul, Korea, September 1988, pp. 12-13.

39. General Accounting Office, *Military Coproduction: U.S. Management of Programs Worldwide*, NSIAD-89-117 (March 1989), p. 3; and Tracey, "U.S. Military Coproduction Programs," p. 53.

40. General Accounting Office report cited in Associated Press, "Nuclear Secrets Trickle Abroad," *Washington Times*, August 8, 1989, p. A5.

41. See "Missile Technology Control Regime: Fact Sheet To Accompany Public Announcement," Department of Defense, April 16, 1987.

42. According to one Defense Department official, however, there was disagreement in the U.S. bureaucracy about when the regime's strictures were to be implemented. The Commerce Department, for example, claimed it was not legally bound by the MTCR until six months after the regime was established.

43. The following section is based on information provided in the "Equipment and Technology Annex" in the "Missile Technology Control Regime: Fact Sheet." See chapter 2 for additional discussion.

44. Statement of Henry Sokolski, acting deputy for nonproliferation policy, Office of the Assistant Secretary of Defense, International Security Affairs, *Missile Proliferation: The Need for Controls (Missile Technology Control Regime),* Joint hearing before the Subcommittees on Arms Control, International Security, and Science and on International Economic Policy and Trade of the House Committee on Foreign Affairs, 101 Cong. 1 sess. (GPO, 1989), p. 164.

45. Statement of James M. LeMunyon, deputy assistant secretary of commerce for export administration, *Missile Proliferation*, pp. 173-75.

46. Statement of James M. LeMunyon, *Missile Proliferation*, pp. 173-75.

47. Statement of Richard A. Clarke, assistant secretary of state for political-military affairs, *Missile Proliferation*, p. 140.

48. Statement of Richard Clarke, *Missile Proliferation*, p. 140.

49. Statement of Henry Sokolski, *Missile Proliferation*, p. 161.

50. Statement of James M. LeMunyon, *National Security Implications*, p. 65.

51. Statement of Senator Jeff Bingaman, *National Security Implications*, p. 38. For further discussion of U.S. aid to Iraq's missile program, see chapter 3.

52. Statement of Senator Jeff Bingaman, *National Security Implications*, p. 38.

53. *National Defense Authorization Act for Fiscal Year 1991*, H. Rept. 101-923, 101 Cong. 2 sess. (GPO, 1990), pp. 633–38.

54. For additional discussion of the French sale of rocket technology, see chap. 6.

55. Statements of Senator Jeff Bingaman, *National Security Implications*, p. 38; and W. Seth Carus, *Ballistic and Cruise Missile Proliferation in the Third World*, Hearing before the Subcommittee on Defense Industry and Technology, Senate Committee on Armed Services, 101 Cong. 1 sess. (GPO, 1989), pp. 50–51.

56. Iraq, for instance, insisted in April 1990 that the Arrow program was "a threat to the region." See Barbara Amouyal, "Iraqis Insist Including U.S.-Israeli Arrow in Middle East Arms Ban," *Defense News*, April 30, 1990, p. 25.

57. As noted previously, the question of the role of supercomputers in aiding nuclear programs is controversial. While some argue that their contribution has been vastly exaggerated, others, including W. Seth Carus, claim that advanced computer simulations can shorten development times and lower the costs of missile programs in vitally important ways. For additional discussion of the links between supercomputers and missile programs, see note 2 of this chapter. See also John Markoff with Stephen Engelberg, "U.S. Debates Selling Supercomputers to Three Nations," *New York Times*, August 20, 1989, p. 14; "High Stakes in High Technology," *Cleveland Plain Dealer*, August 28, 1989, p. 6B; and "Israel, Brazil, India Want Supercomputers," *Insight*, vol. 4 (September 18, 1989), p. 36.

58. Statement of Richard A. Clarke, *Missile Proliferation*, p. 143.

59. Statement of Senator John McCain, *National Security Implications*, p. 7.

60. The story was told by McGeorge Bundy; see Deborah M. Levy, "Export Controls: Benefit or Bust for U.S. Business?" *USA Today* (Society for the Advancement of Education), vol. 117 (July 1988), p. 22.

61. For an overview of the control lists and procedures, see, for instance, Michael Moodie, *The Dreadful Fury: Advanced Military Technology and the Atlantic Alliance* (Washington: Center for Strategic and International Studies; and New York: Praeger, 1989), pp. 77–78; and Levy, "Export Controls," p. 24.

62. Levy, "Export Controls," p. 24.

63. *National Security Export Controls: A Report by the National Academy of Sciences*, Hearing before the Subcommittee on International Economic Policy and Trade of the House Committee on Foreign Affairs, 100 Cong. 1 sess. (GPO, 1988); and Levy, "Export Controls," p. 24.

64. Moodie, *Dreadful Fury*, pp. 77–78.

65. Shawn Tully, "Europe's Arms Exporters Challenge the Superpowers," *Fortune*, August 5, 1985, p. 93.

66. "The Polish journal *Gazeta Torgowa* is a computer buff's shopping paradise," said one report. "Advertisers offer laptops, 750-megabyte hard-disk drives, even the high speed Intel 80386 chip that runs IBM's top-of-the-line PS/2 personal computer. All are available via mail order from companies in the Far East, with no questions asked. All are also embargoed by the U.S. Commerce Department as "militarily critical" technology that must be kept out of the Soviet bloc lest America's security be imperiled." Stephen Budiansky, "Chips for the Soviet Bloc?" *U.S. News and World Report*, October 9, 1989, p. 28; see also Joel M. Snyder, "Pact Countries Clone U.S. Computers," *Signal*, vol. 42 (December 1988), pp. 55–62.

67. Committee on Science, Engineering, and Public Policy, *Balancing the National*

Interest: U.S. National Security Export Controls and Global Economic Competition (Washington: National Academy Press, 1987), p. 264. For additional discussion see Steve Hirsch, "Export Control Policy," *Multinational Monitor*, vol. 8 (November–December 1987), pp. 29–35; and Thomas H. Naylor, "The Ban That Boomeranged," *Nation*, December 19, 1987, p. 755.

68. "Cheney's Ark," *Washington Times*, October 2, 1989, p. F2; and "Trade Victory," *Economist*, August 19, 1989, p. 18.

69. See, for instance, Steven Greenhouse, "U.S. Divided from Allies on Easing Export Bans," *New York Times*, October 27, 1989, p. D3; and Giovanni de Briganti, "U.S. Denies Dispute with COCOM Nations on East Bloc Exports," *Defense News*, October 30, 1989, p. 5.

70. Quoted in Giovanni de Briganti, "Both Sides Bend at COCOM," *Defense News*, June 11, 1990, p. 4. This article discusses the revisions in COCOM.

71. Allan Wendt, head of the U.S. delegation at COCOM, quoted in de Briganti, "Both Sides Bend at COCOM," p. 26.

72. For additional discussion of the "family of weapons" and disputes over export agreements, see William Perry, "The Effective Use of Friends and Allies," and Janne E. Nolan and Phillip Farley, "Commentary and Discussion," in *The Role of Technology in Meeting the Defense Challenges of the 1980s*, a report of the Stanford Arms Control and Disarmament Program (Stanford University, November 1981), pp. 112–35.

73. See *Toward a Stronger Europe: A Report of the Independent Study Team of the Independent European Programme Group (IEPG)* (Brussels, December 1986); and Aviva Freudmann, "Europeanization of Weapons? EC Defense Ministers Push Joint Programs," *Atlantic Trade Report*, September 16, 1989, p. 1.

74. See for instance Steven K. Vogel, "Let's Make a Deal," *New Republic*, June 19, 1989, pp. 14–15. Japan, however, may increasingly turn to Europe for military technology. British Aerospace, for instance, sold Japan the BA-125 radar-testing aircraft in June 1990, the first non-U.S. aircraft bought by the Japanese self-defense forces. Michael Green, "Japan Looking to Europe To Fulfill Military Needs," *Defense News*, June 18, 1990, p. 1.

75. Debra Polsky, "Japan Defense Exports on Horizon, Experts Warn," *Defense News*, October 16, 1989, pp. 3–4; "Meet the New Arms Exporters," *Economist*, August 12, 1988, p. 54; and "Now, Japan Is up in Arms," *U.S. News and World Report*, August 8, 1988, p. 41.

76. For additional discussion of these broad themes, see John D. Steinbruner, ed., *Restructuring American Foreign Policy* (Brookings, 1989).

Chapter Six: Toward an International Technology Security Regime

1. Steven R. Weisman, "Japan Weary of Barbs on Trade, Tell Americans Why They Trail," *New York Times*, November 20, 1989, p. A1.

2. In May 1989 the Department of Defense issued a report identifying technologies vital to weapon development in which Japan was superior, including microelectronic circuitry, robotics, superconductivity, biotechnology materials, and some kinds of integrated optics. See Martin Tolchin, "Technology Report Finds U.S. Lagging," *New York Times*, May 16, 1989, p. D7.

3. Quoted in Craig R. Whitney, "Unease Fills Western Allies over Rapid Changes in the East," *New York Times*, December 1, 1989, p. A1.

4. Quoted in Michael Moodie, *The Dreadful Fury: Advanced Military Technology and the Atlantic Alliance* (Praeger, 1989), p. 90.

5. *Electronic Engineering Times*, November 7, 1989, p. 30.

6. Stephanie G. Neuman, "The Arms Market: Who's on Top," *Orbis*, vol. 33 (Fall 1989), p. 520.

7. David Silverberg, "New Omnibus Trade Bill Affects Work Environment for U.S. Trade Partners," *Defense News*, September 5, 1988, p. 10.

8. Stuart Auerbach, "Accord Set on Technology Transfers," *Washington Post*, March 13, 1989, p. A24.

9. Wesley B. Truitt, "America Needs an Effective Arms Transfer Policy," unpublished paper, July 18, 1989, p. 8.

10. John Markoff, "Need for Re-evaluation Is Seen on Cutting High-Tech Aid," *New York Times*, November 17, 1989, p. D3.

11. Interview with Defense Department official, May 1990.

12. Committee on Science, Engineering and Public Policy, *Balancing the National Interest: U.S. National Security Controls and Global Economic Competition* (Washington: National Academy Press, 1988), p. 264.

13. See, for instance, William J. Broad, "Some Fear U.S. Rocket Industry Will Fizzle Out," *New York Times*, September 17, 1988, p. A38.

14. Moodie, *Dreadful Fury*, p. 80.

15. John Steinbruner, memorandum to the Members of the Export Control Panel, National Academy of Sciences, May 7, 1990.

16. Cited in Bill Gertz, "World Economy New Focus of U.S. Intelligence," *Washington Times*, September 20, 1989, p. A3.

17. Quoted in Stuart Auerbach, "CoCom Considered as Arms Sales Curb," *Washington Post*, August 2, 1990, p. C11.

18. Theresa Hitchens, "EC Urged To Control Arms Exports," *Defense News*, June 26, 1989, p. 38; and Hitchens, "EC Warily Crosses into Defense Realm," *Defense News*, November 6, 1989, p. 1.

19. Christopher W. Murray, "1992: Europe Moves toward Foreign Policy Cooperation," *Foreign Service Journal* (July–August 1989), p. 40.

20. Murray, "1992," p. 42.

21. Cited in *Electronic Combat Report*, September 8, 1989.

22. See, for instance, Gregory P. Corning, "U.S.-Japan Security Cooperation in the 1990s: the Promise of High Tech Defense," *Asian Survey*, vol. 29 (March 1989), pp. 268–86.

23. Kyle B. Olson, "The U.S. Chemical Industry Can Live with a Chemical Weapons Convention," *Arms Control Today*, vol. 19 (November 1989), p. 21.

24. Hitchens, "EC Urged To Control Arms Exports," p. 38.

25. Robert S. Greenberger, "Baker Is Pressing 'Linkage' with Soviets, Even Though Policy Has Its Limits," *Wall Street Journal*, March 6, 1989, p. 1.

26. Don Oberdorfer and David Hoffman, "Scowcraft Warned China of New Hill Sanctions," *Washington Post*, December 15, 1989, p. A2.

27. For discussion of other nuclear delivery vehicles, see Leonard S. Spector, *The Undeclared Bomb* (Cambridge, Mass.: Ballinger, 1988), pp. 25–61.

28. Testimony of William Webster, Director, Central Intelligence Agency, *Nuclear and Missile Proliferation*, Hearings before the Senate Committee on Governmental Affairs, 101 Cong. 1 sess. (GPO, 1989), p. 13.

29. Robert J. McCartney, "Bonn Acts To Tighten Export Control," *Washington Post,* January 11, 1989, p. A16.

30. Bill Keller, "Soviet Leader's Burden," *New York Times,* August 1, 1988, p. A1.

31. Keller, "Soviet Leader's Burden," p. A1.

32. See Clarence A. Robinson, "French Missile Technology May Land in Libya," *Washington Times,* July 18, 1989, p. A1; and Eduardo Lachica, "Bush Seeks Control on Products Usable To Make Weapons," *Wall Street Journal,* October 6, 1989, p. A4.

33. Statements of Richard A. Clarke and James M. LeMunyon, *Missile Proliferation: The Need for Controls (Missile Technology Control Regime),* Hearings before the Subcommittees on Arms Control, International Security and Science and on International Economic Policy and Trade of the House Committee on Foreign Affairs, 101 Cong. 1 sess. (Government Printing Office, 1989), pp. 132–48, 165–78.

34. Statement of Senator Jeff Bingaman, *National Security Implications of Missile Proliferation,* Hearing before the Senate Committee on Foreign Relations, 101 Cong. 1 sess. (GPO, 1989), pp. 34–35.

35. Joseph S. Nye, Jr., "Arms Control after the Cold War," *Foreign Affairs,* vol. 68 (Winter 1989–90), p. 60.

36. Benjamin N. Schiff, "Conventional Lessons from Nuclear Export Policy Experience," paper prepared for the 1984 annual meeting of the International Studies Association, p. 2.

37. Michael Krepon, "Spying from Space," *Foreign Policy,* no. 75 (Summer 1989), p. 100.

38. See, for instance, William J. Broad, "Non-Superpowers Are Developing Their Own Spy Satellite Systems," *New York Times,* September 3, 1989, p. A1; and Thomas G. Mankhen, "Third Party Space Capabilities: Programs and Implications," *SRS Technologies* (January 1989).

39. See Abdel Monem Said Aly, "Quality vs. Quantity: The Arab Perspective of the Arms Race in the Middle East," paper prepared for the Carnegie Conference on Arms Control and the Proliferation of High Technology Weapons in the Near East and South Asia, Bellagio, Italy, October 1989.

40. See American Association for the Advancement of Science, "Will Interest in ASAT Weapons Spread?" draft report.

41. Paul B. Stares, "The Problem of Non-Dedicated Space Weapon Systems," paper prepared for UNIDIR Expert Group on Problems of Definitions and Demarcation in the Prevention of an Arms Race in Outer Space, November 1989, p. 3.

42. Carl H. Builder, "The Prospects and Implications of Non-Nuclear Means for Strategic Conflict," Adelphi Papers 200 (International Institute for Strategic Studies, Summer 1985), p. 30.

43. Jeffrey Richelson, "Military Intelligence: SPOT Is Not Enough," *Bulletin of the Atomic Scientists,* vol. 45 (September 1989), p. 26.

44. According to Alexander Zhgutov, Embassy of the USSR, January 18, 1990.

45. "Industrial Policy in Space?" *Washington Times,* August 3, 1989, p. 53.

46. *Report of the Task Force on Foreign Assistance,* document 101-32, House Committee on Foreign Affairs, 101 Cong. 1 sess. (GPO, February 1989).

47. Barry Blechman, "Confidence Building in the North Pacific: A Pragmatic Approach to Naval Arms Control," Peace Research Centre working paper 29, Australian National University, Canberra, February 1988, p. 14.

48. For additional discussion of confidence- and security-building measures, see Spector, *Undeclared Bomb,* pp. 309–26; and Steinberg, "Middle East in the Missile Age," pp. 39–40.

49. Steinberg, "Middle East in the Missile Age," pp. 35–36.

50. See, for instance, Shai Feldman, "Security and Arms Control in the Middle East: An Israeli Perspective," paper prepared for the Carnegie Conference on Arms Control and the Proliferation of High Technology Weapons in the Near East and South Asia, Bellagio, Italy, October 1989; and Paul Bracken, "Korea and Northeast Asia: The Changing Military Environment," Yale University, 1989.

51. *Pravda,* March 7, 1989, in Foreign Broadcast Information Service, *Daily Report, Soviet Union,* 89–43, p. 4.

52. Burrus M. Carnahan, "Decreasing the Danger in Military Activities: The Meaning of the New U.S.-Soviet Agreement," *Arms Control Today* (August 1989), p. 13.

53. Donald I. Hafner, "For the Benefit and in the Interests of All: Superpower Space Programmes and the Interests of Third States," in Walter Stutzle, Bhupendra Jasani, and Regina Cowen, eds., *The ABM Treaty: To Defend or Not To Defend* (Oxford University Press, 1987), p. 201.

Index

HICs, NICs, & LICs — A NEW INTERNATIONAL DIVISION OF LABOR

① Pre-War
  * the old international order
    North – industrialized, manufactured products exporter
    South – raw-material exporters

② * World War II   │ 1950-70s
    – internationalization of capital
    – internationalization of production
  * export-led growth / import substitution industrialization
  * the new protectionism (third world agenda)   │ 1980s
  * graduation issue (HICs agenda)

③ * trade blocs (1990s)
    – Western Hemisphere (carrying the Latin American NICs)
    – European Community (carrying the African LICs) Eastern European NICs?
    – Asia community (carrying the Asian NICs)

*disclaimer: this is not a policy-oriented study

① 1. thesis statement: paradox of national insecurity

2. laying out the issues (dispelling myths)

②   a) the diffusion of technology (production networks)

   b) developed countries' attempt to control diffusion

     – critique: why only great power has "national security" concerns?

3-4
     – the status question: isn't status an important component in national-security policy-making because if confers prestige – "reputation for power"

     – patronizing quality to the argument that scarce resources should be better spent on development (isn't the same argument used against Reagan military build-up)

     – if neorealists are right – the structure forces them to behave in this way (system-maintaining role)

   c) developing country's dilemma (Third World)

     – taking advantage of diffusion

     – the myth of development and security (military industrialization leading to security)

5-10
     * the need to export

     * the only security that military industrialization has brought in many cases is "regime security" (counterinsurgency weapons)

     – threat perception and technological race

3. the move toward system-transformation

     * conventional technology and diffusion controls

11-18
     – against the dependency argument: internal causes as retarding development (little linkage between society and military industrialization)

     – bilateral relations among asymmetrical powers (U.S.-Brazilian case reconsidered)